THE
EVERYTHING®
Intermediate Spanish Book with CD

Dear Reader,

As an intermediate student of Spanish, you're already on your way to mastering the language. You've already studied the basics and are ready to refine what you know and learn even more.

Learning a new language is an important step in understanding the world from another point of view. Think of how many countries Spanish is spoken in, and you'll begin to realize how much bigger that world can be. Spanish can enrich your life wherever you choose to use it, giving you access to individuals, information, and ideas that would be out of reach otherwise.

Your knowledge of Spanish may already have created interesting opportunities for you at home, in your community, at work, or at play. If not, that's something else you have to look forward to as you continue your studies. The more you learn, and the more you practice your language skills, the likelier it is that Spanish will open more doors than you ever imagined. Enjoy the journey!

Sandie Rosenstiel

The EVERYTHING® Series

Editorial

Publisher	Gary M. Krebs
Director of Product Development	Paula Munier
Managing Editor	Laura M. Daly
Associate Copy Chief	Sheila Zwiebel
Acquisitions Editor	Brielle Kay
Development Editor	Katie McDonough
Associate Production Editor	Casey Ebert
Language Editor	Saskia Rombouts

Production

Director of Manufacturing	Susan Beale
Production Project Manager	Michelle Roy Kelly
Prepress	Erick DaCosta
	Matt LeBlanc
Interior Layout	Heather Barrett
	Brewster Brownville
	Colleen Cunningham
	Jennifer Oliveira
Cover Design	Erin Alexander
	Stephanie Chrusz
	Frank Rivera

THE
EVERYTHING®
INTERMEDIATE
SPANISH BOOK
WITH CD

Take your Spanish speaking, writing,
and reading skills to the next level

Sandra Rosenstiel, M.A.

Adams Media
Avon, Massachusetts

For my first two great teachers: my parents.
And, for my best friend and companion in life, my husband, Bruce.

An Everything® Series Book.
Everything® and everything.com® are registered trademarks of F+W Publications, Inc.

Published by Adams Media, an F+W Publications Company
57 Littlefield Street, Avon, MA 02322 U.S.A.
www.adamsmedia.com

ISBN 10: 1-59869-256-9
ISBN: 13: 978-1-59869-256-3

Printed in the United States of America.

J   I   H   G   F   E   D   C   B   A

Library of Congress Cataloging-in-Publication Data

Rosenstiel, Sandra.
The everything intermediate Spanish book with CD / Sandra Rosenstiel.
p. cm. – (Everything series)
Includes bibliographical references.
ISBN-13: 978-1-59869-256-3 (pbk.)
ISBN-10: 1-59869-256-9 (pbk.)
1. Spanish language–Textbooks for foreign speakers–English. I. Title.

PC4129.E5R66 2007
468.2'421–dc22

2007002037

This publication is designed to provide accurate and authoritative information with regard to the subject matter covered. It is sold with the understanding that the publisher is not engaged in rendering legal, accounting, or other professional advice. If legal advice or other expert assistance is required, the services of a competent professional person should be sought.

—From a *Declaration of Principles* jointly adopted by a Committee of the American Bar Association and a Committee of Publishers and Associations

Many of the designations used by manufacturers and sellers to distinguish their products are claimed as trademarks. Where those designations appear in this book and Adams Media was aware of a trademark claim, the designations have been printed with initial capital letters.

This book is available at quantity discounts for bulk purchases.
For information, please call 1-800-289-0963.

Contents

Acknowledgments

Many thanks to Brielle Kay and the entire team at Adams Media for all they have done to bring this project to press. *Un abrazo* to my friend and first great editor, Nancy Siddens. And to everyone else who directly or indirectly helped along the way, *¡mil gracias!*

Top Ten Reasons
for Learning Intermediate Spanish

1. You will be able to get your message across.

2. You'll finally take that trip to a Spanish-speaking country.

3. You'll gain confidence in communicating in Spanish.

4. You'll understand more movies in Spanish.

5. You can take those cooking classes in Oaxaca.

6. You can watch Mexican and Venezuelan soap operas.

7. You can finally go to that spa in Costa Rica.

8. You can work with your company's new Latin American business partners.

9. You can surf the Web in Spanish.

10. You can sing along with your favorite Spanish-language songs.

Introduction

▶ WELCOME TO THE NEXT PHASE of your Spanish-language learning journey! You already know some Spanish, and now you're ready to review and learn more. Whether you are brushing up on what you learned some time ago, polishing what you know, or preparing to meet new challenges in Spanish at home, work, your community, or abroad, *The Everything® Intermediate Spanish Book with CD* will help you achieve your goals.

Take a few minutes to think about your reasons for continuing to learn Spanish: personal enrichment, practical applications, career opportunities, or travel? By understanding your motivations, you'll find it easier to tailor your studies to your specific needs and help you focus your learning experience in a more meaningful way.

Keep in mind that, for most people, learning a language takes a significant amount of time, effort, and commitment. A sense of fun and adventure is also very helpful. Don't wait to know it all before you try out what you're learning! As you practice what you're studying in Spanish, make it a habit to play around with the possibilities. Then look around and seek out opportunities to practice Spanish with others in the real world, such as going to a Mexican restaurant and ordering in Spanish. If you're ready for a bit more of a challenge, you might seek out volunteer opportunities in your community where a basic knowledge of Spanish is valuable. Perhaps you have Spanish-speaking colleagues at work with whom you can practice or associates abroad with whom you can dialogue via e-mail. You'll soon discover that by interacting regularly with Spanish speakers, you can learn more than a book can possibly teach you!

Greater proficiency in Spanish also offers new opportunities to explore the diverse world of Spanish-speaking peoples and cultures first-hand. You'll be able to surf the Internet in Spanish, enjoy Spanish-language newspapers, magazines, films, and TV and radio programs. You might try reading some of the great literature written in Spanish, starting with any one of the ten Nobel Prize–winning authors from Spain and Latin America. And, hopefully, you'll be able to take your Spanish on the road and explore some of the twenty-one countries in the world where Spanish is spoken.

Be patient on your Spanish journey. It takes a great deal of time and loads of practice to become proficient in a new language. Progress may be slow, but your skills and knowledge will continue to improve if you study thoughtfully and practice diligently. Set realistic targets, and enjoy the process of reaching them.

How to Use This Book

You will need a few different tools as you use this book. First, you need a CD player so you can listen to the accompanying audio CD. (Keep in mind that some of the audio tracks have accompanying text in the book that you can read along with while you listen, while others are meant to be more challenging, purely auditory exercises.) You also need a notebook and a writing utensil in order to do the exercises given in the book. As you complete the exercises, this notebook will become a great study tool that you can refer back to again and again.

Chapter 1
Build on the Basics

As an intermediate Spanish student, you've already been introduced to the language and have a foundation to build upon. This is an exciting time—you're about to take your general knowledge of basic vocabulary and grammar to the next level. This chapter will help you evaluate and review what you have learned, build on that foundation, and overcome the barriers to effective communication that are common among intermediate speakers.

Review What You've Learned

If it's been a while since you last used your Spanish, the first step is to review carefully what you studied previously, and refresh your understanding and skills. There are many ways to do this, of course. A good starting point is to read through your elementary book and/or class notes again, taking the time to review practice activities and make sure that you still understand the concepts that were presented. If your book has an audio CD, listen to it again to get reacquainted with an authentic accent.

Schedule time for studying, and break up your review into manageable sessions. If you simply look over the book, plenty of the material will seem familiar, but you might make the mistake of assuming you really know the information when you don't.

Start Slowly

You didn't learn elementary Spanish in just a few days so don't expect to remember it all quickly either! Though much will seem familiar once you begin reviewing, it takes more time to internalize concepts and content so you use them comfortably and accurately. Begin slowly and simply. Break your review into manageable chunks. Once you are back in the swing of things, you can pick up the pace if you want. Here are a few suggestions for managing your review.

- **Remind yourself of what you already know.** For example, choose a category of content that you have studied and make a mental or written list of words and grammar points associated with it that you can remember.
- **Browse through your Spanish books.** Identify the chapters that you are most interested in reviewing. If you focus on specific themes, vocabulary, and grammar structures that you want to review, it will be easier to avoid being overwhelmed.

- **Practice vocabulary and verb conjugations with flash cards.** As you move through each chapter, make flash cards for the vocabulary and verb conjugations presented. If you organize vocabulary and verbs into specific contexts you'll find it easier to remember them.
- **Label your house in Spanish.** Surrounding yourself with contextualized vocabulary is one of the best ways to stop translating. Before long, you'll associate each item directly with its name in Spanish.
- **Write!** Another good review tactic is to try writing a few compositions, e-mails, or journal entries to practice Spanish in a less structured and more personalized way.
- **Listen!** To get your ear back in tune, watch some Spanish-language films. You can even turn on the subtitles in Spanish to read and listen at the same time. You can do something similar with music and sing along with the lyrics printed in the CD insert.
- **Practice speaking.** Get a study partner and hold regular conversation hours in Spanish. Go out to a Spanish or Latin American restaurant and place your order in Spanish. Name all the items on your table and make up sentences about them. Look around at the other diners and discreetly make up sentences to describe them and say what they are doing.

The reality is that the more you review, the easier it all becomes. In fact, this is the way you first learned language as a child—constant repetition and persistent experimentation. As an adult, you can speed up the process because you have a framework to hang new concepts on, but the only way a new language becomes second nature is through review and repetition.

You probably learn most new vocabulary by memorizing each word's meaning in English. To increase your skill, try to create definitions in Spanish for new words or associate them with visual images to help you remember them instead. Always thinking in English will slow you down and sometimes trip you up.

Outline Your Goals

Take some time to articulate your reasons for learning Spanish. Is it strictly for pleasure? Travel? For speaking with relatives or friends? Do you foresee using the language at work or do you hope to become more effective in a volunteer capacity? Your particular reasons for improving your Spanish are the key to outlining suitable goals and designing a program of study that will help you achieve them.

The most common response to the question, "Why do you want to learn Spanish?" is generally something like "I just want to be able to carry on a conversation." It sounds like a simple goal, but in fact, it's probably the most difficult one of all to reach. So-called "general conversation" can touch on any topic in any verb tense, and usually jumps from topic to topic and tense to tense in a pretty unpredictable way. The reality is that maintaining a "simple conversation" with someone requires a tremendous range of vocabulary and a very high level of grammatical proficiency.

Don't underestimate the complexity of "learning just enough Spanish to carry on a conversation"! If you set precise goals instead, and identify specific content areas to study, you will find it easier to manage your learning and track your progress.

Be realistic. Consider the specific ways that you hope to use Spanish and what level of proficiency you need to acquire to be effective in those contexts. For example, Spanish for travel primarily requires an understanding and application of the language for transportation, lodging, and restaurants. You will also want to be able to get and understand directions and recommendations as well as shop for souvenirs. These tasks rely much more on vocabulary than on grammar. In fact, effective communication for a traveler doesn't require much more grammar than the simple present tense, possibly the future with *ir a*, and some polite request phrases. Getting ready for a trip is a very manageable goal for a Spanish learner. Preparing to use Spanish in the business world, on the other hand, is a significantly larger task. So, your next step is to identify and evaluate the ways that you plan to use Spanish. Here are a few guidelines to help you:

- Articulate your specific needs for Spanish.
- Honestly evaluate your current language skills, and list your strengths and weaknesses.
- Outline how your current knowledge meets your needs, and identify gaps.
- Draw up a study plan tailored to your needs and goals.
- Keep it manageable. Re-evaluate and revise your study plan as necessary.
- Make it personal. Practice Spanish in the way you plan to use it.
- Make it unavoidable. Post your goals on your bathroom mirror, the refrigerator, at your desk, etc.

The only thing you need to do next is decide what kind of learning environments and what sorts of materials are suitable for your plan. How do you learn best—on your own or in a class? Do you prefer learning in a small group or with a private tutor? Do you live in an area where either of these is available? Of course, your budget and the availability of classes and tutors may make some of the decisions for you. If you are going to continue studying on your own, spend some time at the library and a bookstore to look over the materials available, and decide which books and other reference materials you need for what you want to learn.

Take the Next Step

Buying this book is an excellent next step. Your introductory studies of Spanish have established a base from which you can easily continue to learn; now it's time to build on that foundation.

All the techniques you learned when you began to study Spanish are equally important as you continue to learn. For example,

- Accept Spanish the way it is constructed rather expecting it to conform to English syntax.

- Focus on what you *can* understand first, then work on the rest. Get the gist, then the details.
- Break words down into identifiable prefixes and suffixes to help you understand their meaning. Learn to identify parts of speech so you recognize whether a word is a noun, verb, adjective, or adverb.
- Watch for cognates, words that are similar to the same word in English, such as *teléfono*, *dirección*, *computadora*, *presidente*. Look out for false cognates too.
- Schedule your study time carefully. Study when you are most receptive to learning. Schedule several short sessions rather than one long one.
- Practice each new concept in all four skill areas: reading, writing, speaking, and listening.
- Go beyond the book. Identify and use all the resources available to you—books, Internet, Spanish speakers, other Spanish learners, etc.

Most important, however, is to remember that *you* are your own worst enemy or your very best friend in this undertaking. If you believe you can learn Spanish and dedicate the time and energy necessary, you will succeed!

Expand Your Vocabulary

You won't get far without the right words! And there are so many words to learn, it seems a daunting task. This is where your specific goals come into play. Focus on what you need. You don't have to spend time learning business vocabulary if you plan to use Spanish to go mountain climbing in the Andes. But you certainly should learn every crucial word for mountaineering. And, that brings us to our first strategy: Learn vocabulary in context.

Let's say you're a sound-and-light technician in a theater in Miami that regularly books Hispanic performers from throughout the Spanish-speaking world. You probably won't need to talk to them about their favorite foods or movies, but you will have to talk about lighting and sound for their show. You'll want to learn all the vocabulary related to your profession, and practice it in the contexts in which you need to use it.

Related Words

Besides looking up words you need to know in a dictionary, spend a little time looking at the words that are related to the one you have looked up. For example, imagine you have just learned the verb *tener*. What other verbs can you associate with this one? How about *obtener* (obtain), *retener* (retain), *sostener* (sustain), and *detener* (detain)? Suddenly you have increased your vocabulary by four additional verbs that will be easy to remember because of their association. Do you suppose they are conjugated the same too? Of course they are. If one verb in a group has a stem change or an irregular preterite form, for example, all the verbs in that group will follow the same pattern.

While you're looking at the definition for *tener*, look at the idiomatic expressions that it is used in: *tener años* (to be . . . old), *tener hambre* (to be hungry), *tener frío* (to feel cold), *tener dolor de cabeza* (to have a headache), etc. If you study and practice new words and expressions in this way, your vocabulary will increase exponentially in a very short time.

Word Families

Another good vocabulary development strategy is to look at the whole word family. What is the noun form, the verb, the adjective, the adverb? Let's look at a few examples:

WORD FAMILIES

Noun	Verb	Adjective	Adverb
la alegría	*alegrar*	*alegre*	*alegremente*
happiness, joy	to make happy	happy, joyful	happily, joyfully
la determinación	*determinar*	*determinado*	*determinadamente*
determination	to determine	determined	determinably
el estudio	*estudiar*	*estudioso*	*estudiosamente*
study, studio	to study	studious	studiously
la expresión	*expresar*	*expresivo*	*expresivamente*
expression	express	expressive	expressively

This technique will not only expand your vocabulary; it will also help you become more familiar with the clues that identify different parts of speech, such as prefixes and suffixes. Keep in mind, however, that not all words have "full families." Notice that the last example has no adverb form; there is simply no single word related to "focused" to express the idea "in a focused manner." Additionally, plenty of words have only one or two forms rather than all four; and some have more than one word per form, like the two nouns *foco* and *enfoque*. The word *libro* (book), for example, only has another noun in its family: *la librería* (bookstore). And, don't be taken in by false family members! *Liberar* (to liberate) has nothing to do with *libros* unless you want to invent a philosophical quip like *Los libros liberan* (Books liberate) to link the two.

FACT

You will remember new words more readily if you learn and practice them in a logical context. Memorizing lists of unrelated words rarely increases your vocabulary effectively.

Say What You Mean: Using a Bilingual Dictionary

A bilingual dictionary is essential for a language learner. If you don't have one already, invest in one now. Each dictionary has its own personality, and it can be very interesting to look up the same word in several dictionaries to compare what they say about it. While perusing dictionaries may not be your idea of fun, any student of language needs to be aware of how a bilingual dictionary works and what its limitations are.

A bilingual dictionary can be your best friend or worst enemy. You have to use it carefully, or you may end up saying things you had no intention of saying. You should also learn about the features a good bilingual dictionary includes so you can take full advantage of the tools at your fingertips.

Features of a Bilingual Dictionary

Bilingual dictionaries generally offer more than an alphabetical listing of words in one language with their equivalents in another. In addition to the word entries, any bilingual dictionary worth your time and money will have a good number of the following helpful features:

- A pronunciation guide for one or both languages
- An explanation of how entries are arranged and marked
- A basic grammar
- A list of abbreviations used
- Verb conjugation charts, including regular and major irregular verbs
- Correspondence models, including formulaic expressions for a variety of written communications
- Alphabetic guide words at the top or bottom of the page
- A thumb index to quickly turn to each alphabetic section

Next, look over the word entries. Each entry should include a majority of the following elements:

- Pronunciation guide to the entry word
- Syllable division of the word
- Origin of the word
- Part(s) of speech of the word
- Gender of nouns
- Brief explanations to clarify specific usage of different equivalents
- Indication of fields in which particular equivalents are used: engineering, zoology, etc.
- Idiomatic uses of the word or phrases that include it
- Indications of regional uses or origin
- Indications of register: formal, informal, colloquial

So, a good bilingual dictionary has a lot more than lists of words and their translations.

Choosing a Bilingual Dictionary

All dictionaries are not created equal. Each has its strengths and weaknesses. Be aware that there are good dictionaries, bad ones, and those that are perfectly suited to certain applications but not to others. There are also plenty of dictionaries in between these extremes. You can find many specialized dictionaries: for business, for medical purposes, children's dictionaries, etc. Aside from the obvious monetary consideration, when you are buying a bilingual dictionary, think about how you plan to use it, and what you want it to do for you.

What about online and electronic dictionaries? Well, they have their uses, but keep in mind that they are typically programmed for simple word substitution, and do not normally offer you the expanded content of a dictionary entry. This can make it hard for you to decide which equivalent is the one you want. A pocket-sized translation computer can be very handy on a trip, but it probably won't be as useful for more complex applications.

So, there you are in the bookstore, looking at twenty or more dictionaries in your price range. How do you decide which one to choose? A good technique is to look up a word like "get," which has at least fifty definitions in English. Don't buy any bilingual dictionary that doesn't help you sift through the differences between "get" meaning "acquire" and "get" meaning "become," for example. A good bilingual dictionary should also include a fair number of the idiomatic phrases that include "get" like "get ahead, get off, get around."

Choosing the Right Word

Words acquire much of their meaning from the context in which they are used. For example, the word "run" can refer to a scoring play in baseball or a long hole in a stocking, or can be a warning to make a hasty departure! When looking words up in the dictionary, you must always consider what part of speech they are and what context they are being used in so you can choose the appropriate equivalent. Let's imagine you are shopping for some beautiful ceramics in Puebla, Mexico, but you can't remember how to say "plate." You look it up in your dictionary and find all sorts of options ranging from the nouns, *plato, platillo, bandeja, cubierto, placa, plancha,* and *lamina,* to the verbs, *recubrir, blindar,* and *acorazar.* First you determine that the "plate" you want is a noun rather than a verb. Next, you should review all the indicators in the word entry to help you choose the translation you want. To practice, look at the following excerpts from the dictionary* and decide which equivalent of "plate" is the one you need.

- **(prize)** *trofeo*
- **(Relig – collection ~)** *platillo, bandeja*
- **(Phot)** *placa*
- **dinner at $100 a ~:** *cubierto*
- **(dish)** *plato*

If you chose *plato*, it's likely that you'll come home with a lovely souvenir of your trip!

Choose a dictionary to suit your needs. A slimmed-down traveler's dictionary won't help you understand newspaper articles or the lyrics to your favorite song. By the same token, a seven-pound reference book is impractical on a backpacking trip through South America.

Sometimes you'll find several possibilities and no clue to help you choose. The best way to handle this is to look each option up in the opposite section of the dictionary. You'll probably be able to figure out which one you need.

Now let's look up words you don't understand from some sentences in Spanish. Look for context clues within each sentence to help you choose the right English equivalent for the underlined word.

Las fábricas de zapatos de la ciudad de León forman una importante base económica.

*Excerpted from The Oxford Spanish Dictionary, 2nd Edition. Oxford University Press, Inc., New York. 1998.

Nuestro hotel <u>cuenta</u> con gimnasio, spa, centro de negocios, club nocturno y dos restaurantes de alta categoría.

El conocido autor de las esculturas "Piedra" y "Gente" tendrá su próxima <u>instalación</u> en el museo de arte en mayo.

Thanks to your dictionary, you no doubt discovered that *fábricas* is a false cognate that means "factories" rather than "fabrics," that the expression *contar con* has nothing to do with counting but means "has," and *instalación* in the context of an artist's work refers to a showing or exhibit rather than some sort of remodeling.

So, you're off to a good start! With a good dictionary, a good book, and a desire to learn, you'll make great progress on your Spanish journey.

Chapter 2
Pronunciation Review

Unlike English, Spanish is a phonetic language; words are essentially pronounced the way they are spelled. There are no tricky combinations that are pronounced one way in one word and some other way in another. This is great news for you—pronunciation can be the toughest part of language learning. Once you learn how vowels and consonants are pronounced in Spanish, you're on your way to sounding native!

Spanish Around the World: An Introduction to Accents

Spanish is a Romance language, which means its foundation is Latin. Some of the other major Romance languages are French, Italian, Portuguese, Rumanian, and Catalan. Because the Iberian Peninsula (Spain and Portugal) was also colonized for extensive periods of time by Arabic- and Greek-speaking people, Spanish also includes many words and expressions that are Arabic or Greek in origin.

When Spanish explorers brought their language to the Americas in the fifteenth century, local populations added their own linguistic spice, and Spanish began to acquire new dimensions. The Spanish spoken in Mexico, for example, includes words and expressions from native languages including Aztec, Mayan, Zapotec, and Mixtec, among others. The Spanish spoken in much of South America is influenced by the indigenous languages Quechua and Aymara. More recent linguistic ingredients color the Spanish of various South American and Caribbean countries, and include influences from African languages, as well as from Italian and German. The Spanish spoken in the United States is heavily influenced by English. Virtually any time languages come into contact for extended periods, some sort of linguistic evolution takes place, and dialects are formed.

FACT

The word "Spanish," or *español*, refers to the people and the language of Spain. Nevertheless, most Spanish-speakers call the language they speak *español*. Another term that is sometimes used is *castellano*.

As a student of Spanish keep in mind that the core of the language is the same, no matter how colored it may be by other influences. You can speak the Spanish you learn in this book in any Spanish-speaking country and you'll be understood. And, if your accent is good, the locals might just assume you're from some other Spanish-speaking country!

Accents

Spanish is a national language of twenty-one countries in the world, and is spoken "unofficially" by large populations in a number of other countries, like the United States As a result, Spanish is spoken with many accents, and has evolved significant dialectal differences between countries and even from one part of a country to another. This is a completely natural occurrence. Just think for a minute about the range of accents and word use in American English from North to South. Then, think about all the places English is spoken, for example, the United States, Canada, the United Kingdom, South Africa, India, Malaysia, Singapore, Australia, and New Zealand. English is spoken differently in each place. What's especially important to keep in mind, though, is that English speakers can understand most of what people from English-speaking countries say. There may be some miscommunications and misunderstandings, but communication is rarely completely disrupted by the different accents and vocabulary that English speakers use.

ALERT!

Remember that everywhere a language is spoken, it usually has a particular accent and linguistic features that are unique to that place. Just give your ears time to adjust to the Spanish spoken in different locations, and you'll soon discover that it's still Spanish.

No accent or dialect is better than another; think of them as linguistic signatures of people from a particular area. Some Spanish accents are easily identifiable, just like a Bostonian accent is in the United States Take a look at some of the characteristics of just a few of the distinctive accents in the Spanish-speaking world.

- **Spain:** A peninsular accent is easy to identify by the unique pronunciation of the consonants *ll*, *s*, *c*, and z. The letter *ll*, in Spain, is pronounced high on the palate, rather than behind the teeth. It sounds like the double *l* in the English word "million." Speakers from most other countries pronounce *ll* closer to the English *y* sound. The Spanish *s* is typically softer and less sibilant than in Latin American countries. The consonants *z* and the soft *c* (*ce* or *ci*) are pronounced similarly to the *th* in the English word "think."

- **Argentina and Uruguay:** One of the most distinctive features of these two southern cone countries is the pronunciation of the letters *ll* and *y*, which Argentines and Uruguayans pronounce rather like *sh* or *zh*. Speakers from these two countries are also known for their lilting intonation.

- **Cuba and Puerto Rico:** Final consonants and, sometimes, whole syllables can disappear when Cubans and Puerto Ricans speak at a natural pace. Many vowels are highly aspirated, which, in turn, makes the consonants following them fade.

- **Mexico:** The accent of northern Mexico, in particular, is famous for the sing-song intonation of its residents and their tendency to elongate final syllables.

This is just a sampling of the linguistic richness of the Spanish language. Everywhere it is spoken, Spanish has developed a unique rhythm, accent, and vocabulary.

Sounding Native

You've just learned that *everyone* has an accent, so now you can stop worrying about yours. While it's a worthy goal to sound "native," think for a minute what that really means. Which accent and dialect are you going to use as your model—Castilian Spanish, Paraguayan Spanish, Guatemalan Spanish, or the Spanish spoken in the Dominican Republic? It really doesn't matter. You will ultimately acquire an accent and dialectal touches based on your experience with the language among native speakers. If you travel often to Honduras, for example, you will likely pick up typically Honduran pronunciation and vocabulary. If you then begin to spend more time in Bolivia, your Honduran accent will probably give way to Bolivian rhythms and sounds.

So, worry less about sounding "native" and focus more on simply speaking clearly, eliminating as much as possible English overtones in your Spanish. Imitate the ways that native speakers say things, and use any resources available to you. The reality is that, unless you live for an extended period of time in a single Spanish-speaking environment, it is more likely that you'll acquire a fairly generic accent in Spanish. That means that, eventually, no one will be able to guess where you're from!

Imitating native speakers is the best way to refine your own accent. The real key to sounding "native," though, is to diminish the influence of your own accent in English.

Spanish Consonants

Effective communication is the real goal of language learning, so it's important to be aware of what pronunciation mistakes might impede communication. For the most part, the pronunciation of Spanish consonants is quite similar to that of their English counterparts. There are, however, some differences you should be aware of. Let's take a look at the consonants that may surprise you.

The Consonants B and V

For all practical purposes, you can pronounce these two consonants the same way in Spanish—somewhere right in between the two, with your lips together but without a vibration. The consonant *b* should not be as explosive in Spanish as it is in English, and *v* shouldn't vibrate. Both produce a softer *b/v* combination sound. So, for example, the pronunciation of *baca* (luggage rack) and *vaca* (cow) is identical most of the time in Spanish.

The Consonant C

The pronunciation of the consonant *c* depends on the vowel that follows it. Pronounce *c* with a hard "k" sound when it is followed by *a*, *o*, or *u*. Pronounce *c* with a soft "s" sound when it is followed by *e* or *i*. Look at the following examples.

caballo	**kah-BAI-yo**
cosa	**KOH-sa**
cenar	**say-NAHR**
cinema	**SEE-nay-mah**

The Consonants K and Q

The letter *k* only appears in borrowed words in Spanish and retains its "k" sound. *Q*, which is always followed by *u*, also always produces a "k" sound. When *qu* is followed by *a* or *o*, the combination is pronounced "kwa" and "kwo." *Qu* followed by *e* or *i* is pronounced "kay" and "key." Look at the following examples.

kilo	**KEY-low**
quántum	**KWAHN-toom**
queso	**KEH-soh**
Quijote	**key-HO-tay**

The Consonant G

The pronunciation of *g* depends on the vowel that follows it. When *g* is followed by *a*, *o*, or *u*, it has a hard sound like the "g" in the English word "game." When *g* is followed by *e* or *i*, it has a strong "h" sound like the English word "happy." The *g* in Spanish is never pronounced like the "g" in "generic" or the second "g" in "garage."

galería	**gah-lair-EE-ah**
gol	**GOHL**
gustar	**goos-TAHR**
genial	**heh-NEEAHL**
gimnasio	**heem-NAH-syo**

The Consonant H

The Spanish *H* is always silent, though it can be used with *c* to produce *ch*, the same sound as in the English word "chair."

hombre	**OHM-breh**
exhalar	**ex-ah-LAHR**

The Consonant J

The letter *j* is always pronounced like a hard "h" in English.

Javier	**ha-BEEAIR**
masaje	**mah-SAH-heh**

The Consonant LL

Though the single *l* is pronounced the same way it is in English, the double *ll* is pronounced in a variety of ways in Spanish. It can sound like the "ll" in "million," the sounds "sh" or "zh" as in "shush" or "exposure," a hard "j" as in "jack," or, most commonly, the sound "y" as in "yellow."

The Consonant Ñ

The letter *ñ* in Spanish is pronounced "ny" like the word "canyon" in English.

niño	**NEE-nyoh**
champiñón	**chahm-pee-NYOHN**

The Consonants R and RR

The famous trilled or rolled *r* of Spanish is spelled with a single *r* at the beginning of a word and *rr* in the middle of a word. When *r* occurs between two vowels or at the end of a word, it is pronounced similarly to a soft "d" in English.

reloj	**rray-LOH**
barril	**bah-RREEL**
extranjero	**egs-trahn-HEH-roh**
hablar	**ah-BLAHR**

The Consonant X

The *x* in Spanish has a number of pronunciations. Between vowels, a vowel and *h* + a vowel, or in the combinations *exce-* and *exci-*, *x* has a sound like "ks" or "gs." When *x* begins a word or occurs between a vowel and consonant, it has an "s" sound. In some words, *x* is pronounced like a hard "h." In some words of indigenous origin, *x* is pronounced something like "sh."

examen	**eh-KSAH-men**
excelente	**eg-seh-LLEN-the**
exhibir	**eg-see-BEER**
xilófono	**see-LOH-foh-no**
Texas	**TEH-hahs**
Ixtapa	**eesh-TAH-pah**

The Consonant Y

The letter *y* generally produces a "y" sound similar to that in the English word "yellow." In some dialects, it is pronounced nearer the English "j." The letter *y* can also sound like the vowel "i," elongating the sound of the vowel it follows.

apoyo	**ah-POH-yoh, ah-POH-joh**
hoy	**OI**
hay	**AI**

The Consonants D, P, T, and Z

In general, these four consonants are pronounced more softly than their English counterparts: *d*, *p*, and *t* all lose their explosiveness, and *z* loses its vibration. *P* is pronounced with no release of air. *Z* is pronounced like an "s" in Latin America, and like the "th" in "thin" in Spain.

sudar	**soo-DAHR**
madrina	**mah-DREE-nah**
pelea	**peh-LAY-ah**
episodio	**eh-pee-SO-dyoh**

tinto	**TEEN-toh**
tomate	**toh-MAH-teh**
taza	**TAH-sah**
zoológico	**thoh-oh-LOH-hee-koh**

Remember that slight mispronunciations of most consonants will not normally interfere with your communication in Spanish. If you don't roll your *r*'s, or if your *b* or *t* is too explosive, people will still understand what you are saying.

The Consonants

Listen to each example and repeat.

TRACK 1

Let's start with the consonants b and v:
> *baca*
> *vaca*

Next, the consonant *c*:
Hard *c* (before *a*, *o*, or *u*):
> *caballo*
> *cosa*
> *cultivar*

Soft *c* (before *e* and *i*):
> *cenar*
> *cine*

Now listen and repeat the examples of the consonants *k* and *q*:
> *kilo*
> *quántum*
> *queso*

Quijote
Next, try the two sounds of the consonant *g*:
Hard *g* (before *a*, *o*, or *u*):
> *galería*
> *gol*
> *gustar*

Soft *g* (before *e* or *i*):
> *genial*
> *gimnasio*

Now, the silent consonant *h*:
> *hombre*
> *exhalar*

Remember that the consonant *j* makes a hard English "h" sound:
> *Javier*
> *masaje*

The consonant *ll* has a number of possible pronunciations. Listen to the various ways to say this word:
cabello

Remember that the consonant *ñ* sounds like the combination "ny" in English.
niño
champiñón

Now it's time to try the consonants *r* and *rr*:
reloj
barril
extranjero
hablar

Now, try out the various sounds of the consonant *x*:
examen
excelente
exhibir
xilófono
Texas
Ixtapa

The consonant *y* also has a couple of variations. Listen to the two pronunciations of this word:
apoyo

Here are a couple of other *y* sounds:
hoy
hay

Listen and then repeat these examples with the consonants *d*, *p*, *t*, and *z*:
sudar
madrina
pelea
episodio
tinto
tomate
taza
zoológico

Spanish Vowels

The key to Spanish pronunciation is in the vowels. Vowel sounds in Spanish are unchanging, as opposed to vowels in English, which can be pronounced all sorts of ways. In Spanish, if you get the vowels right, people will probably understand what you are saying even if your consonants aren't perfect. So, here's a quick review of the five vowel sounds in Spanish:

- *A*: pronounced like the "a" in "father"
- *E*: pronounced like "ay" in "hay" or the "e" in "hey"
- *I*: pronounced like "ea" in "eat" or "ee" in "seek"
- *O*: pronounced like "oh" and "old"
- *U*: pronounced like "oo" in "cool" or "u" in "rule"

Try pronouncing the following words, each of which contains all five vowels. Then listen to the audio and practice again:

murciélago	**moor-see-EY-la-goh**
comunicante	**koh-moon-ee-KAHN-teh**
meticulosa	**meh-tee-koo-LOH-sah**
repudiado	**reh-poo-DEEAH-doh**

Vowel Pronunciation

Listen to the pronunciation of each vowel and word example. Repeat each after you hear it.

First, the individual vowel sounds:

a
e
i
o
u

TRACK 2

Now try pronouncing these words. Each one contains all five of the vowel sounds:

murciélago
comunicante
meticulosa
repudiado

Diphthongs

When two vowels are blended into a single sound, a diphthong is created. Diphthongs are most commonly formed by a combination of an open (or strong) vowel—*a, e, o*—followed by a closed (or weak) vowel—*i, u*. Diphthongs only occur in combinations of strong and weak vowels; two strong vowels cannot form a diphthong. Look at the following list of diphthongs that occur in Spanish along with examples of words they appear in. Then listen to the audio for additional practice.

Diphthongs

TRACK 3

Listen to each diphthong and word example on Track 3. Repeat each after you hear it.

ai: aislar **(isolate)**	**ays-LAHR**	
au: auto **(car)**	**OW-toh**	
ei: reino **(kingdom)**	**RAY-noh**	
eu: euforia **(euphoria)**	**ayoo-FOR-ya**	
oi: oigo **(I hear)**	**OY-goh**	
ia: farmacia **(pharmacy)**	**fahr-MAH-cyah**	
ie: cielo **(sky, heaven)**	**SYEY-loh**	
io: idioma **(language)**	**ee-DYOH-mah**	
ui: cuidar **(care for)**	**kwee-DAHR**	
ue: rueda **(wheel)**	**RWEH-dah**	

When a vowel combination that would normally form a diphthong is pronounced as two separate vowels, an accent mark is placed over the weaker vowel, as in *frutería* (fruit shop), *laúd* (lute), and *reír* (to laugh), to indicate that it should be pronounced clearly rather than blended into the vowel that precedes it.

ALERT!

Two strong vowels together, *a, e,* and *o,* never form a diphthong. Each vowel is pronounced separately and forms a syllable.

Triphthongs

If a diphthong involves two vowels, can you guess how many a triphthong has? If you said three, you're absolutely right. Triphthongs don't happen often in Spanish, but they do occur on those rare occasions when two vowels are followed by the consonant/vowel *y*, for example in the word *buey* (ox), pronounced BWAY and the names of the countries *Paraguay* (pah-rah-GWAI) and *Uruguay* (oo-roo-GWAI). Other examples of triphthongs can be found in words that include *gu* or *qu* followed by another vowel as in *quiero* (KYEH-roh), *siguiente* (see-GYEHN-teh), and *siquiera* (see-KYEH-rah).

Triphthongs

Listen to the following examples of triphthongs on Track 4. Repeat each one after you hear it.

TRACK 4

ue: buey
uay: Paraguay, Uruguay
uie: quiero, siguiente, siquiera

Accent This: Written and Spoken

All words with more than one syllable are pronounced with a little more emphasis on one of their syllables. This is referred to as the "stress" or "accent" of the word. In Spanish, the rules for which accent to stress are very simple, and any word that breaks the rule has a written accent over the vowel of the syllable that should be stressed. Take a look at the two rules of pronunciation first:

Rule #1: Any Spanish word that ends in a vowel or the consonants *n* or *s* is stressed on the second-to-the-last syllable.

Words Ending in a Vowel *N* or *S*

Look at the following examples and listen to the pronunciation of each word on Track 5. Focus on the stressed syllable. Repeat each example after you hear it.

TRACK 5

comida	**co-MI-da**
estudiante	**es-tu-DIAN-te**
arbusto	**ar-BUS-to**
conversan	**con-VER-san**
palabras	**pa-LA-bras**

Rule #2: Any word that ends in a consonant other than *n* or *s* is pronounced with the stress on the last syllable.

Words Ending in a Consonant Other Than *N* or *S*

Listen to each of the following words on Track 6. Focus on the stressed syllable, and repeat each example after you hear it.

universidad	**u-ni-ver-si-DAD**
reloj	**re-LOJ**
ferrocarril	**fe-rro-ca-RRIL**

When a word is pronounced with the stress on a different syllable than the one indicated by the appropriate rule, a written accent mark is placed over the vowel of the stressed syllable so you know how to pronounce the word. For example, listen to Track 7 on the audio CD and read the following words.

Written Accents

bolígrafo: According to Rule #1, this word should be stressed on the second-to-the-last syllable, but it is pronounced with the stress on the third from the last: bo-lí-gra-fo.

hablábamos: Rule #1 indicates that this word should be pronounced with the stress on the "ba" but the written accent tells you to stress the "bla" instead: ha-blá-ba-mos.

lápiz: Rule #2 tells you to stress the last syllable of this word, but it is, in fact, stressed on the first: lá-piz.

Accent marks are also used to separate vowels that would otherwise form a diphthong. When this occurs, the accent mark is written over the vowel of the syllable that follows the rule.

frutería: Without the accent, the vowel combination *–ia* would be pronounced as a diphthong. The accent mark divides the two vowels into two syllables and the word is pronounced according to Rule #1: fru-te-rí-a.

As you see, it's really quite simple to determine which syllable is stressed in a Spanish word, and, when you know how a word is pronounced, it's easy to remember where to write an accent mark if one is needed. Just test the word with Rule #1 and Rule #2: if it doesn't follow the rule, it needs a written accent.

Accent marks are only written above the vowel of the stressed syllable of a word. They primarily tell you which syllable to emphasize when a word varies from the normal stress pattern outlined in Rule #1 and Rule #2.

Other Occasions for Accents

The written accent has three other uses that have nothing to do with the pronunciation of a word. There is always a written accent on interrogative words to differentiate them from their conjunction form. For example, listen to Track 8.

TRACK 8

Question Words and Conjunctions

¿Qué hace Javier?
(What is Javier doing?)
Javier hace la tarea que tiene.
(Javier is doing the homework that he has.)

¿Dónde está tu mamá?
(Where is your mother?)
Mamá está en la tienda donde hay rebajas.
(Mom is in the store where there is a sale.)

Exclamations are also accented in Spanish, just like interrogative words. Listen to Track 9.

TRACK 9

Exclamations

¡Qué día más hermoso! **(What a beautiful day!)**
¡Cómo me gusta el chocolate! **(How I like chocolate!)**

The written accent is also used to distinguish homonyms, words that are spelled and pronounced the same but which have different meanings. Listen to Track 10 to hear a few common homonyms in Spanish.

TRACK 10

Homonyms

tú **(you)**	*tu* **(your)**
él **(he)**	*el* **(the)**
sólo **(only)**	*solo* **(alone)**
sé **(I know)**	*se* **(one, yourself, himself, herself)**
sí **(yes)**	*si* **(if)**

Practice: The Written Accent

Look at the following list of words and decide whether each should be stressed according to Rule #1 or Rule #2. Then pronounce each word and decide if its stressed syllable is the one indicated by the appropriate rule. If not, add a written accent. After you've finished, listen to Track 11 to check your pronunciation. When you are done, check your answers in Appendix D.

TRACK 11

Written Accent or Not?

1. *mama*
2. *miercoles*
3. *arbol*

4. *vivir*
5. *revista*
6. *periodico*
7. *simpatica*
8. *Mexico*
9. *estudian*
10. *Rodriguez*

Practice: Accent or No Accent?

Listen to Track 12 as you read the following paragraph along with the narrator. Then add as many of the missing written accents as you can find. If you are unsure whether a word needs a written accent or not, follow these easy steps:

1. Underline the word.
2. Review Rules #1 and #2.
3. Listen again to determine whether or not the word is pronounced according to its rule or needs a written accent.

Listen as many times as necessary to complete your editing task. Then check your work in Appendix D.

TRACK 12

Where Do the Accents Go?

Un dia, Esteban, un joven de Panama, pregunta a su amiga Ursula: ¿Que quieres hacer este fin de semana que es fiesta? Ursula, quien recuerda que la fiesta comienza el miercoles, responde que deben hacer una excursion al campo. Primero, los jovenes van al supermercado y compran los articulos necesarios. Despues, visitan la fruteria para llevar platanos y naranjas. Finalmente paran en la drogueria y compran protector solar y proteccion contra los mosquitos y otros insectos. El martes por la tarde ya tienen todo preparado y saben donde van a pasar la fiesta. El miercoles en la madrugada salen. ¡Como se van a divertir!

Chapter 3

Equivalents of the Verb "To Be"

It's pretty simple to "be" in English. One verb does it all. In Spanish, however, "being" is a little more involved. You have to think about all sorts of things like whether you're referring to the existence of something or identifying it; describing an essential characteristic or a state of being; talking about location; or talking about time, weather, or health. It's really not as complicated as it sounds, though. Just put English aside for a while, and try out some other ways of "being" in Spanish.

The First Steps: Ser, Estar, *and* Hay

You probably know that the two most important "to be" verbs in Spanish are *ser* and *estar.* They are both irregular in their conjugation. The good news is that, because these two verbs are used so frequently, you'll memorize their forms in no time. *Ser* is completely irregular; *estar* only has an irregular *yo* form, but you also have to remember to add accents to some of the conjugations. Take a minute to review these two verbs in the simple present tense before we talk about how they are used.

CONJUGATION OF *SER* AND *ESTAR*		
Subject Pronoun	Ser	Estar
yo	*soy*	*estoy*
tú	*eres*	*estás*
él, ella, usted	*es*	*está*
nosotros	*somos*	*estamos*
vosotros	*sois*	*estáis*
ellos, ellas, ustedes	*son*	*están*

Essence or State of Being?

Why on earth would you need two verbs that mean "to be," and how do you know when to use one or the other? Well, *ser* and *estar* have one major distinction that will help you decide which verb to use when. *Ser* primarily refers to the essence of something. It is used to identify and describe essential characteristics. *Estar*, on the other hand, refers to a state of being, and is used to describe physical and emotional conditions as well as to say where things are located. Take a look at some examples:

SER AND *ESTAR*	
Essence	State of Being
Nosotros somos Martín y Luisa.	*Estamos en el parque.*

SER AND ESTAR	
Essence	**State of Being**
We are Martin and Luisa. (identification)	We are in the park. (location)
Martín es amable.	*Luisa está triste.*
Martin is friendly. (essential characteristic)	Luisa is sad. (emotional state)
Los perros son simpáticos.	*Mis perros están gordos.*
Dogs are nice. (essential characteristic)	My dogs are fat. (physical condition)
Soy de Argentina.	*Estoy en Chile de vacaciones.*
I am from Argentina. (identify nationality)	I am in Chile on vacation. (location)

Ser is the verb of choice to tell time in Spanish. You may prefer to think that time is a state of being since it changes constantly, but try to imagine each moment as having its own unique essence. That's the Spanish concept of time. Keep in mind too that, except for one o'clock, Spanish considers the hours to be plural, so you say *Es la una* (It's one o'clock) and *Es la una y diez* (It's one ten), but *Son las doce* (It's twelve o'clock) and *Son las siete y media* (It's seven thirty). The question *¿Qué hora es?* is always singular.

There Is and There Are: Hay

This is one of those great cases where Spanish is simpler than English. All it takes is one little word, *hay*, to refer to the existence of something in the present. *Hay* is singular and plural, so you can use it to say everything from "There is a cup of coffee on the table" (*Hay una taza de café en la mesa*) to "There are a thousand people in the square" (*Hay mil personas en la plaza*) without worrying about any other verb form.

Practice: Hay, Ser, *or* Estar?

Decide if you need *hay*, *ser*, or *estar* to complete each sentence. You can check your answers in Appendix D.

[handwritten: hay = there is / ser = to be / estar = to be in a place]

1. *Yo* __estoy__ *en Caracas, Venezuela.*
2. *Tú* __eres__ *mexicano, ¿verdad?*
3. *No* __hay__ *muchas personas en el restaurante.*
4. *¿Qué hora* __es__ *?*
5. *El museo* __esta__ *en el centro de la ciudad.*
6. *Elena* __esta__ *enferma; va al doctor esta tarde.* *[handwritten: this afternoon]*
7. *Ellos* __son__ *interesantes.*
8. *Nosotros no* __estamos__ *contentos.*
9. __Hay__ *un libro bueno en la mesa.*
10. *Yo* __Soy__ *alta.* *[handwritten: tall]*

Two More Ways to Be: Hacer *and* Tener

Next, let's review how you talk about the weather using the verb *hacer*. For reasons you probably don't want to go into, Spanish uses the combination of *hace* + noun to describe many weather conditions. Have a look at the following examples:

Hace frío. **(It's cold.)**
Hace calor. **(It's hot.)**
Hace buen/mal tiempo. **(It's nice/ bad weather.)**
Hace viento. **(It's windy.)**
Hace sol. **(It's sunny.)**

FACT

The verb *hacer* generally means "to do" and "to make." Obviously, the weather expressions with *hace* don't have these meanings nor can they be translated literally into English. You can also use *hace* with certain expressions of time to say how long someone has been doing something or how long it's been since something happened.

Just like *hacer*, the verb *tener* has a variety of applications, and not all of them translate literally as "to have." Unlike *hacer* in the special case of weather expressions, however, *tener* is conjugated according to the personal subject. Consider these examples of *tener* to describe certain physical conditions:

Tengo frío. **(I am [feel] cold.)**
Tienes calor. **(You are [feel] hot.)**
Tenemos sed/hambre. **(We are [feel] thirsty/hungry.)**

ALERT!

Pay close attention to the uses of *ser, estar, hacer,* and *tener*. Though they all can mean "to be" in English, they are by no means interchangeable. In fact, your message may be misunderstood if you use the wrong verb with some of these expressions. In some cases, it might be embarrassing. For example, if you wanted to say you felt cold but said *Soy frío* instead of *Tengo frío*, you would actually be communicating that you were heartlessly cold, and no one would think you were referring to the temperature!

Practice: Ser, Estar, Hacer, or Tener?

Now it's time to practice a bit with these ways of "being" by translating the following. Write the Spanish translation for each on the blank line. You can check your answers in Appendix D.

1. Alberto is from Ecuador.
2. It's hot in Quito today.
3. I feel hot.
4. Julia is thirsty.
5. We're tired.
6. The coffee is cold.
7. You (*ustedes*) aren't happy.
8. It's not sunny in Santiago.

9. Are you (*tú*) thirsty?
10. They are nice people.

Describing People, Places, and Things

The world is full of all kinds of people, places, and things. Let's review and expand your vocabulary by looking at some words to name people, places, and things.

Person	Place	Thing
la madre/el padre (mother/father)	*la ciudad* (city)	*el libro* (book)
el/la abuelo/a (grandparent)	*el pueblo* (town)	*el periódico* (newspaper)
el/la esposo/a (spouse)	*el campo* (countryside)	*la planta* (plant)
el/la hijo/a (son/daughter)	*la casa* (home/house)	*el coche/el carro* (car)
el/la amigo/a (friend)	*el teatro* (theater)	*la taquilla* (ticket booth)
el/la novio/a (boy/girlfriend)	*el cine* (cinema)	*la película* (movie)
el/la niño/a (child)	*el parque* (park)	*el banco* (bench)
el/la vecino/a (neighbor)	*la vecindad/el barrio* (neighborhood)	*la calle* (street)

Once you've identified the people, places, and things around you, you can come up with all sorts of descriptions using *ser* or *estar* with adjectives. Remember, though, that *ser* + adjective refers to essential characteristics like personality, color, and interest, while *estar* + adjective describes states of being, like how someone or something looks or feels at a particular time. There is a big difference between *Mi novio está triste* (My boyfriend feels sad) and *Mi novio es triste* (My boyfriend is a sad person)!

Adjectives

Essential Characteristic	State of Being	Either
inteligente (intelligent)	*contento/a* (content)	*grande* (big)
pequeño/a (small)	*loco/a* (crazy)	*delgado/a* (slender)
internacional (international)	*sentado/a* (seated)	*gordo/a* (fat)
interesante (interesting)	*interesado/a* (interested)	*aburrido/a* (boring/ bored)
peruano/a (Peruvian)	*cerrado/a* (closed)	*cansado/a* (tiresome/tired)
ruidoso/a (noisy)	*abierto/a* (open)	*(des)ordenado/a* (messy/neat)
natural (natural)	*destrozado/a* (destroyed)	*bonito/a* (pretty)
azul (blue)	*mojado/a* (wet)	*difícil* (difficult)
trabajador/a (hardworking)	*roto/a* (broken)	*limpio/a* (clean)
religioso/a (religious)	*enojado/a* (angry)	*tranquilo/a* (calm)

ALERT!

The use of *ser* to describe essential characteristics and *estar* to identify states of being is a general distinction. There are many dialectal differences from country to country, as well as idiomatic uses of *ser* and *estar* with adjectives that might seem surprising at first. In Mexico, for example, *estar* is used much more than *ser* with adjectives that would seem to describe essential characteristics, a dialectical feature that is less common in other countries.

Most of these categorizations probably seem very clear-cut, but some may be surprising. When a combination strikes you as unexpected, think about why the speaker might have chosen one verb or the other. For example, colors are generally conceived of as essential characteristics. Blue is blue, and once something is blue, the color is considered to be an essential characteristic and would be described using the verb *ser*. Green, however, is both a color and the term used for unripe fruit. Unripeness is a state of being and would be described with the verb *estar*. So it's possible to have a sentence like this: *Las manzanas Granny Smith son verdes y esta manzana está muy verde* (Granny Smith apples are green and this apple is very unripe). Let's look at some other examples to help you get a better feel for the difference between using *ser* and *estar* with some adjectives:

La ciudad de Buenos Aires es grande.
(The city of Buenos Aires is large.)
Tu hijo está grande.
(Your son is big. Your son has grown.)

La novia de Alejandro es bonita.
(Alejandro's girlfriend is pretty.)
Silvia, estás muy bonita.
(Silvia, you look very pretty.)

Size would seem to be an essential characteristic and, in the case of things that don't change size, like cities, that is absolutely true. In those cases, *ser* is the verb you want to use. However, people can change size: kids get bigger as they get older, and people lose and gain weight, becoming heavier or thinner. You can express these changes of state in Spanish simply by using *estar* with adjectives like *grande*, *gordo*, and *delgado*. Notice that smallness doesn't easily fit into this category. Your grandmother may look like she's shrinking, but it would be unusual to describe that change with *estar* and *pequeña*. It could be done, though, and the implication would be precisely that she is getting smaller, not just shorter or thinner!

Practice: Describing People, Places, and Things

Try making sentences from the following cues. Then check your answers with the sample answers provided in Appendix D, paying closest attention to the combination of *ser* or *estar* with the adjective.

1. *madre / pueblo / pequeño*
2. *niño / banco / sentado*
3. *películas / internacionales / interesantes*
4. *vecindad / calles / limpias*
5. *Eliana / hondureña / trabajadora*
6. *La Ciudad de México / ruidosa / grande*
7. *amigo / enojado*
8. *el cine / la taquilla / abierta*
9. *Víctor / aburrido*
10. *casa / tranquila*

Noun and Adjective Agreement

Do you remember than all nouns in Spanish are either masculine or feminine? Most masculine nouns end in *–o*, and most feminine nouns end in *–a*. Other common masculine endings are *–aje*, *–men*, *–gen*, and *–or*. Other common feminine endings are *–dad*, *–ud*, *–ed*, *-ión*, *–umbre*, *–ie*, and *–sis*. Of course, there are exceptions, but these endings are pretty reliable indicators. Look at the following examples of masculine and feminine words:

Masculine Noun Endings

Ending	Example	English	Feminine Exceptions
–aje	*viaje*	journey/trip	none
–men	*examen*	exam	none
–gen	*origen*	origin	*la imagen* (image), *la margen* (margin)
–or	*doctor*	male doctor	*la labor* (work, handwork)
–o	*libro*	book	*la mano* (hand)

Feminine Noun Endings

Ending	Example	English	Masculine Exceptions
–dad	ciudad	city	none
–ud	salud	health	el ataúd (coffin)
–ed	merced	mercy	none
–ión	religión	religion	el gorrión (sparrow)
–umbre	costumbre	custom	none
–ie	serie	series	none
–sis	síntesis	synthesis	el análisis, énfasis
–a	libra	pound, lb.	el mapa, el problema

Knowing the gender of a noun, whether it is masculine or feminine, is important when you describe things because the adjective you use must agree with the noun in gender as well as number (singular or plural). That's why you would say *El pueblo es pequeño* but change *pequeño* to *pequeña* in *La ciudad es pequeña*. Remember than adjectives that end in the vowel *–e* or a consonant remain the same whether they describe a masculine or a feminine noun. For example, *María es una niña muy inteligente y su hermano Xavier es un niño interesante.*

When you describe plural nouns, the adjective must also be plural: *Los pueblos son pequeños* and *Las ciudades son pequeñas*. Adjectives that don't need to change for masculine or feminine will change to plural when you describe plural nouns: *María y Sonia son niñas inteligentes y sus hermanos Xavier y Pedro son interesantes.* Don't worry if you make mistakes, though. Your message will usually be clear even if you mix up noun and adjective agreement.

Practice: Nouns and Adjectives

Now it's time to practice a bit by translating a few sentences into Spanish. Double-check your choice of *ser* or *estar.* Then compare your work to the answers in Appendix D.

1. The customs in Spain are interesting.
2. Quito is an international city.
3. The doctor (fem.) is Chilean.
4. The streets of our town are tranquil.
5. Your problem is difficult.
6. The maps are pretty.
7. The author's (masc.) origin is Cuban.
8. Marisa's boyfriend is hardworking.
9. My hand is broken.
10. The city is beautiful.

The Simple Present

Let's take a moment to review the difference between the simple present tense and the present continuous (also called the present progressive). There are some similarities and some differences between the way these tenses are used in English and Spanish.

Let's start with a quick review of the three categories of verbs and their conjugation in the simple present tense. Remember that all verb infinitives in Spanish end in either –ar, –er, or –ir. In the simple present tense you simply delete the infinitive ending and add the present tense conjugation ending appropriate to that category of verb. It may sound complicated, but it's really very simple. Have a look at the following table to review the simple present endings.

Simple Present of Regular Verbs

Subject Pronoun	Hablar	Comer	Vivir
yo	hablo	como	vivo
tú	hablas	comes	vives
él, ella, usted	habla	come	vive
nosotros	hablamos	comemos	vivimos
vosotros	habláis	coméis	vivís

Simple Present of Regular Verbs

Subject Pronoun	Hablar	Comer	Vivir
ellos, ellas, ustedes	hablan	comen	viven

Notice that there are some similarities across categories for each conjugation. For example, all the *yo* forms end in –*o*, all the *tú* forms end in –*s*, all the third person singular forms end in the vowel –*a* or –*e*, all the *nosotros* forms end in –*mos*, and all the third person plural forms end in –*n*. Notice how the vowels mark the infinitive category. *Hablar* conjugations all have *a*-based endings, and *comer* and *vivir* have *e*- and *i*-based endings. For the most part, –*er* and –*ir* verbs have identical endings. The only conjugations in which –*ir* verb endings revert to *i* are the *nosotros* and *vosotros* forms. Once you get the pattern down, you can conjugate any regular verb. In fact, you might remember that the conjugations of most irregular verbs have some of the elements of the regular conjugation. We'll review those in later chapters though. For now, let's return to regular verbs and the simple present.

Conjugate the verbs indicated according to the subject given. Refer back to the table if you have any doubts, and check your answers in Appendix D.

Practice: Simple Present of Regular Verbs

1. *Tú* _____ *(hablar) con tus amigos todos los días.* (You speak with your friends every day.)
2. *Yo no* _____ *(comer) carne. Soy vegetariana.* (I don't eat meat. I'm a vegetarian.)
3. *Ustedes* _____ *(vivir) en Montevideo, ¿verdad?* (You live in Montevideo, right?)
4. *Susana y yo* _____ *(estudiar) español en la universidad.* (Susana and I study Spanish at the univeristy.)
5. *¿Quién* _____ *(visitar) este fin de semana?* (Who is visiting this weekend?)
6. *Tú* _____ *(aprender) muy rápido.* (You learn quickly.)
7. *Melisa no* _____ *(depender) de sus padres.* (Melissa doesn't rely on her parents.)
8. *¿*_____ *(subscribir) usted al periódico de su pueblo?* (Do you subscribe to your town's newspaper?)

The Meanings of the Simple Present

It's important to keep in mind that the simple present in Spanish actually translates into four different structures in English. For example, *hablo* can be translated into English as "I speak, I do speak, I am speaking," and even "I will speak." The meaning shifts slightly according to the context in which the verb is used. Look at the following examples and English equivalents.

> *Hablo un poco de español.* **(I speak a little Spanish.)**
> *Hablo por teléfono.* **(I am speaking on the phone.)**
> *Te hablo mañana a las nueve.* **(I'll talk to you tomorrow at nine.)**

The Present Continuous

So, you're probably thinking to yourself, "Why do you need another form for the present continuous if the simple present includes it?" Well, when Spanish speakers want to emphasize that an action is going on at this very minute, they use the present continuous. "And why," you add, "are we talking about the present continuous in a chapter about the verb "to be"?" Because the present continuous uses one of the "to be" verbs we've just reviewed: *estar.* There's one more little thing we need to review: the present participle. You probably remember this. The present participles of regular verbs are formed by changing the ending of *–ar* infinitives to *–ando* and changing the ending of *–er* and *–ir* infinitives to *–iendo* (sometimes spelled *–yendo*). Now, let's see how the present continuous looks in action.

> *Los niños están jugando en el parque.*
> **(The children are playing in the park.)**
> *Silencio, por favor, estamos estudiando.*
> **(Quiet, please, we're studying.)**
> *Te hablo más tarde, estoy comiendo.*
> **(I'll call you later. I'm eating.)**
> *La agencia está traduciendo el documento ahora.*
> **(The agency is translating the document now.)**

Two Basic Rules

There are two things to keep in mind with present participles and the present continuous. First, the present participle is *never* used as a noun form the way it can be in English. "Learning is fun" would be translated with the infinitive in Spanish: *Aprender es divertido.* The second important difference between English and Spanish regarding the present continuous is that this form is *never* an equivalent for the future as in "Jorge and I are studying together tomorrow." The present continuous in Spanish is used strictly to express an ongoing action in the present, something that is happening right now rather than something that is going to take place. This is another example of how English and Spanish express things differently. Your best rule of thumb is: When speaking in Spanish, do it the Spanish way!

TRACK 13

The Present Continuous

Imagine you are a detective checking up on a suspect. You record your observations on a tape recorder. Look at and listen to the following cues and use the present continuous to record what is going on at each moment. Then listen to Track 13 and repeat each answer. You can find the answers written out in Appendix D.

1:15 P.M.: *Luis / comer*
2:00 P.M.: *Luis y su esposa / salir del apartamento*
2:25 P.M.: *Luis / sacar dinero del cajero automático*
3:05 P.M.: *La esposa de Luis / entrar a la farmacia*
3:06 P.M.: *Luis / hablar por teléfono*
3:15 P.M.: *Luis / subir al coche de un amigo*
3:20 P.M.: *La esposa de Luis / caminar hacia el parque*
3:27 P.M.: *Luis y su amigo / recoger a su esposa*
3:28 P.M.: *Los tres / escapar*
11:10 P.M.: *Luis y su esposa / volver a casa*

Have some more fun with the present continuous by writing the detective's observations for another day. Then check your work carefully.

Simple Present or Present Continuous?

Let's review when you use the simple present tense and when you use the present continuous. The simple present is commonly used with *ser* and *estar* to identify or describe people, places, and things. The simple present is also used to describe habitual actions and to express what someone does. It is sometimes used as a mild present continuous or future to say what someone is doing or what someone is going to do. The present continuous with *estar* can *only* describe actions that are taking place at a particular time. These uses are summarized in the following chart.

Simple Present and Present Continuous

Use of Simple Present	Example
Identify	*Es un libro.* (It's a book.)
Describe essential characteristics with *ser*	*Es interesante.* (It's interesting.)
Describe location and states of being with *estar*	*La librería está abierta.* (The bookstore is open.)
Express habitual actions	*Estudio en casa.* (I study at home.)
Say what someone does	*Yo no hablo francés pero Silvia sí lo habla.* (I don't speak French but Silvia does.)
Express what someone is doing	*Jorge duerme.* (Jorge's sleeping.)
Say what someone is going to do	*Mañana escribo postales.* (Tomorrow I'm going to write postcards.)

Use of Present Continuous	Example
Express an action in progress	*María y yo estamos bailando.* (Maria and I are dancing.)

It's pretty simple, especially if you remember that the present continuous can only describe actions in progress at a specific moment in time. All other present tense statements use the simple present.

Practice: Simple Present or Present Continuous?

Translate these ideas from English to Spanish. Then check your work with the sample answers in Appendix D. There may be some differences, but focus on the use of simple present or present continuous.

1. My grandmother is a nice person.
2. Our town is in Chile.
3. The children are leaving tomorrow.
4. I eat a lot, but I'm not fat.
5. Your friends are playing soccer right now.
6. José is cooking dinner tonight.
7. Raquel is calling her mother.
8. I don't live in Miami, but my sister does.

Simple Present and Present Continuous in Your Life

The best way to get comfortable with *ser* and *estar* and all these verbs in the two present tenses is to practice. Look around you and identify and describe what you see. Then say what people are doing so you can practice the present continuous. List your daily activities to practice the simple present. Try thinking in Spanish while you're working out at the gym or going for a walk. There are lots of people and things to describe as well as lots of activities to talk about in your daily life.

Chapter 4

Question and Answer Formation

One of the most important skills to acquire when learning a language is asking and answering questions. Think about it: You probably ask and answer hundreds of questions every day. Lots of information is communicated through questions and answers. Now that you've reviewed some verb basics, some adjectives, and the simple present and present continuous tenses, you're ready to start asking questions and getting some answers.

Just a Simple Yes or No

Remember the game "Twenty Questions"? You can get a lot of information just by asking someone yes-or-no questions. In English, yes-or-no questions with the verb "to be" are formed by inverting the position of the subject and verb in a declarative sentence like this: You are tall. > Are you tall?

Yes-or-no questions with verbs other than "be" in English require the helping verb "do," for example: Do you study Spanish?

In Spanish yes-or-no questions generally follow the reversed subject / verb pattern. Auxiliary verbs are not needed for making any questions or answering them. However, questions in Spanish have a unique feature: they are bracketed by an inverted question mark at the beginning and a standard question mark at the end like this:

¿Estudias español? **(Do you study Spanish?)**
¿Visita Juana mucho? **(Does Juana visit a lot?)**

Statements as Questions

The verb + subject formula is the most common one for yes-or-no questions in Spanish. There is another way, though. In both English and Spanish you can convert the standard word order for a statement into a question simply by raising the inflection at the end of the sentence. Listen to and repeat each example of a sentence and question on Track 14. Focus on the different intonation for each.

Statement and Question Intonation

John works in a bookstore. > John works in a bookstore?
Juan trabaja en una librería. > ¿Juan trabaja en una librería?

TRACK 14

Practice: Yes-or-No Question Formation

Rewrite the following statements as yes-or-no questions with the verb before the subject. Then check your work in Appendix D. Though there might be minor variations, look for the placement of the subject and the verb.

1. *Marta es delgada.* (Marta is slender.)
2. *Ellos hablan con su abuela.* (They are talking to their grandmother.)
3. *La Paz está en Bolivia.* (La Paz is in Bolivia.)
4. *Yo soy bonita.* (I am pretty.)
5. *Tú comes mucho.* (You eat a lot.)
6. *Nosotros trabajamos el día de fiesta.* (We work on the holiday.)
7. *Tus amigos viven en Cusco.* (Your friends live in Cusco.)
8. *Javier regresa el lunes.* (Javier comes back on Monday.)
9. *Los niños ven mucha televisión.* (The kids watch a lot of television.)
10. *Yo voy a Paraguay en marzo.* (I go to Paraguay in March.)

Answering Yes-or-No Questions

Now you remember how to ask yes-or-no questions. Let's review how to respond to them. You can always answer with a simple *Sí* or *No* and be done with it. But if you want to answer with a complete sentence, *Sí* or *No* should be followed by a comma (or a pause, if you're speaking) and then the rest of the sentence. Have a look at the following examples and listen to Track 15.

TRACK 15

Yes-or-No Questions and Answers

¿Viven tus amigos en Cusco?
Short answer: *Sí (No)*
Affirmative long answer: *Sí, mis amigos viven en Cusco.*
Negative long answer: *No, mis amigos no viven en Cusco.*

ALERT!

Remember to make the verb negative as well when you answer a question negatively. English requires the auxiliaries "don't" and "doesn't" in front of the verb, but in Spanish you simply put *no* in front of the verb to make it negative: I don't play the guitar > *Yo no toco la guitarra.*

Subject and Verb Changes

Sometimes you have to change the subject and conjugation of the verb when you answer a question. If the subject of the question is "I," for example, the subject in the response will be "you." If someone asks about "you," you'll have to respond with "I." If the question asks about "us," the subject in the response could either be "we" or "you" in the plural. Take a minute to look over the following table:

Subject Changes in Yes-or-No Questions	
Question Subject	**Answer Subject**
I (*yo*)	you (*tú* or *usted*)
you (*tú* or *usted*)	I (*yo*)
he, she (*él, ella*)	he, she (*él, ella*)
we (*nosotros*)	we, you (*nosotros, vosotros, ustedes*)
they (*ellos, ellas*)	they (*ellos, ellas*)

Let's look at a few examples so you feel more comfortable with the changes that may occur when you answer a yes-or-no question in Spanish:

Question: **Do I need money today?**
(*¿Necesito [yo] dinero hoy?*)
Answer: **Yes, you need money today.**
(*Sí, [tú] necesitas dinero hoy.*)

Question: **Are you Colombian?**
(*¿Es usted colombiano?*, *¿Eres tú colombiano?*)
Answer: **No, I'm not Colombian.**
(*No, [yo] no soy colombiano.*)

Omission and Inclusion of Subject Pronouns

You probably remember that the subject pronouns are not necessary in Spanish when the subject is clearly understood, as is usually the case when you answer a question. If I ask you how your friend is, the subject in your answer will undoubtedly be your friend. You don't have to repeat it in your answer. However, you might choose to include a subject pronoun in your answer to emphasize the subject. For example, *¿Estudian ustedes francés?* (Do you study French?) could be answered with: *Elisa estudia francés pero yo estudio chino* (Elisa studies French but I study Chinese). In this case, the subject pronoun *yo* is included, and should be emphasized in speaking, to signal the change of subject.

The subject pronoun is often omitted in Spanish, especially in the *yo, tú, nosotros,* and *vosotros* conjugations because the verb ending makes it clear what the subject is. Subject pronouns are more commonly used for the third-person singular and plural conjugations to clarify what the subject is.

Practice: Answering Yes-or-No Questions

Read each question and respond completely with either *sí* or *no*. Then listen to Track 16 to hear the question as well as model affirmative and negative answers. Repeat them for extra practice. You can find translations of the questions and the Spanish answers written out in Appendix D.

TRACK 16

Answering Yes-or-No Questions

¿Hablas español bien?
¿Vive usted en Latinoamérica?
¿Trabajas todos los días?
¿Hablo muy rápido?
¿Es su ciudad más interesante que Madrid?
¿Hace buen tiempo hoy?
¿Visitas muchos países?
¿Estudia tu hermano en la universidad?
¿Están los museos en el centro?
¿Necesitamos reservaciones para el restaurante?

"Or" Questions

Sometimes a question will give you options to choose from in your response. For example: "Are you tall or short?" To respond, obviously, all you have to do is pick one of the options and change the subject pronoun and verb conjugation to finish the statement like this: "I am short." Another alternative, of course, is to substitute some other option that wasn't included in the question, for example: "I am of medium height." You might even add a phrase to compensate for changing the option, for example: "I am of medium height, but my sister is short." These questions and answers follow exactly the same format in Spanish as in English. The Spanish word for "or" is *o* and the word for "but" is *pero*. Look at the following examples and listen to Track 17. Repeat each example after you hear it, focusing on intonation.

FACT

The word *o* (or) changes spelling to *u* in front of a word that begins with *o*. This is for ease of pronunciation. For example, to ask if someone would like to have some flan, fruit, or something else for dessert, you would say: *De postre, ¿quiere usted flan, fruta u otra cosa?*

TRACK 17

"Or" Questions and Answers

¿Es usted de Guatemala o El Salvador?
(Are you from Guatemala or El Salvador?)
(Yo) Soy de Panamá.
(I'm from Panama.)
¿Juega tu hermano al fútbol o al béisbol?
(Does your brother play soccer or baseball?)
Mi hermano juega al tenis pero mi hermana juega al fútbol.
(My brother plays tennis but my sister plays soccer.)

TRACK 18

Answering "Or" Questions

Listen to the narrative and answer the questions. (The narrative is not shown because this is meant to be a more challenging exercise.) Then listen to and repeat the sample answers. You can find the questions and answers written out in Appendix D. Your answers may vary from the sample answers, but you will be able to confirm the basic structure.

Tag Questions

Questions that end in phrases like ". . . right?", ". . . do you?", "isn't it?," and so forth, are called tag questions. This sort of question really asks the respondent to agree with whatever the speaker has stated. Of course, you don't have to agree, but the question is phrased in such a way as to prompt your response with a little tag, for example: "You go to the movies, don't you?" English tags often include a form of the verb "to be" or the words "do, does, don't," and "doesn't." Tag questions in English indicate the expected affirmative or negative response in a kind of reverse phrasing. The negative tag ". . . don't you?" curiously enough, asks for an affirmative confirmation. It's really rather complicated for someone learning English.

Spanish Tag Phrases

Spanish tags are a lot more straightforward. They are rarely based on the verb in the question. Rather, they are simply set phrases tacked onto the end of the sentence like a question to solicit confirmation of what has already been stated. Here are some of the most common Spanish tags and approximate equivalents in English. Most of the Spanish tags are interchangeable and carry roughly the same meaning as all of the English tag forms.

Spanish	English
¿sí?	Okay?, don't you agree?
¿no?	isn't it?, aren't they?, don't you?, doesn't he/she?, etc.
¿verdad?	right?
¿no crees?	don't you think?
¿no es cierto?	isn't that right?
¿de acuerdo?	Okay?, do you agree?

The following are some examples of Spanish tags in action. Listen to each tag question as you follow along in the text. Then repeat each example, focusing on intonation.

TRACK 19

Tag Questions

Clara toca el piano muy bien, ¿no crees?
(Clara plays the piano very well, don't you think?)
Vamos al parque después del cine, ¿de acuerdo?
(Let's go to the park after the movies, okay?)
Hace mal tiempo en el invierno, ¿no es cierto?
(The weather is bad in the winter, isn't that right?)
Tienes tres hermanos, ¿no es cierto?
(You have three brothers, isn't that right?)

Practice: Tag Questions

Let's try translating some tag questions. Remember that Spanish tags are pretty much interchangeable with all the English tags, so your answers may vary from the sample answers in Appendix D. Just check the structure of your questions to see if you've got things in the right place.

1. Your sister plays the guitar, doesn't she?
2. The stores open at ten o'clock, right?
3. Eduardo and Pedro work in the mornings, don't they?
4. The concerts in the square are good, don't you think?
5. You can eat in the Mexican restaurant, okay?

TRACK 20

Answering Tag Questions

You're all set to practice answering tag questions now, aren't you? Listen to each question on Track 20 and respond with a complete sentence. (The questions are not listed here because this is meant to be a more challenging exercise.) Then repeat the sample answer though it may be a little different from your own. You'll find the questions and sample answers written out in Appendix D.

Using Interrogative Words

As you know from your experience with the game "Twenty Questions," it isn't always very practical to gather all the information you need with yes-or-no questions. Sometimes you just want to cut to the chase and get the facts. These types of questions use interrogative words in front of the verb to specify what sort of information is being requested. The question word "who" requests the identity of a person; "what" identifies things; "when," a time; "where," a location; "how," a way; and "why," a reason. The same kinds of words are used in Spanish informational questions. Look at the following table of Spanish and English question words:

Interrogative Words	
Spanish	**English**
¿Quién...?	Who...?
¿Quiénes...?	Who...? (plural)
¿Qué...?	What...?
¿Cuál...?	Which...?
¿Cuáles...?	Which...? (plural)
¿Cuándo...?	When...?
¿Dónde...?	Where...?
¿Cómo...?	How...?
¿Por qué...?	Why...?
¿Cuánto(a)...?	How much...?
¿Cuántos(as)...?	How many...?

Accents on Interrogatives

Remember that Spanish interrogative words always have an accent mark on the vowel of the stressed syllable, whether the interrogative appears in a direct question or embedded in a question or statement:

¿Quién es? **(Who is it?)**
¿Sabes quién es? **(Do you know who it is?)**
No sé quién es. **(I don't know who it is.)**

The accent mark has nothing to do with pronunciation in these cases; it simply differentiates the interrogatives from the relative pronouns, which we'll learn about in the last section of this chapter.

The interrogatives *quién* and *quiénes* are followed by the singular and plural conjugation of the verb, respectively: *¿Quién vive allí?, ¿Quiénes viven allí?* All the other question words are followed by a verb conjugated according to the subject of the question, for example, *¿Dónde trabaja tu novio?, ¿Cuándo comen los niños?*

Interrogatives and Prepositions

Some interrogatives can be modified with a preposition to alter the questions slightly. For example:

¿A quién(es) . . . ? **(To whom?, For whom . . . ?)**
¿Para quién(es) . . . ? **(For whom . . . ?)**
¿De quién(es) . . . ? **(From whom . . . ?)**
¿A qué hora . . . ? **(At what time . . . ?)**
¿Para qué . . . ? **(For what . . . ?)**
¿En qué . . . ? **(In what . . . ?)**
¿En cuál(es) . . . ? **(In which . . . ?)**
¿Adónde . . . ? **(To where . . . ?)**
¿De dónde . . . ? **(From where . . . ?)**
¿Hasta cuándo . . . ? **(Until when . . . ?)**

ALERT!

Try not to confuse *¿Qué?* and *¿Cuál?* The first can be followed by any verb: *¿Qué es esto?, ¿Qué haces? Qué* can also be followed by a noun: *¿A qué hora . . . ?, ¿De qué color . . . ? ¿Qué tren . . . ?* The interrogative, *cuál,* on the other hand, can only be followed by forms of the verb *ser* or *estar*: *¿Cuál es tu nombre?, ¿Cuál está más cerca?*

Ask Questions

Look at the following answers and write the question that would solicit each response. The hints in bold will help you decide which part of the answer to link to the question. Check your work in Appendix D. There may be some variation, but the answer key should help you confirm your understanding of question formation.

1. *Juan y Martín viven en Guadalajara.*
2. *Yo trabajo en la galería Indigo.*
3. *Para preparar flan necesitas huevos, leche y azúcar.*
4. *Estamos muy bien, gracias.*
5. *La señora Martínez enseña español porque le gusta.*
6. *Creo que mis amigos van al Uruguay en septiembre.*
7. *El cine es más interesante que el teatro.*
8. *La película comienza a las ocho.*
9. *Este regalo es de mi abuelo.*
10. *Para aprender una lengua nueva es importante practicar.*
11. *Mi mamá toma mucho café.*
12. *Hay veinte personas en la clase.*

TRACK 21

Answering Questions

Imagine you have just made a new acquaintance while on vacation in Paraguay. Listen to Track 21 and answer your new friend's questions in complete sentences. (The text is not shown here because this exercise is meant to be a more challenging exercise.) Then listen again as you look at the sample answers in Appendix D.

Embedded Questions

An embedded question is one in which the interrogative is in the middle of what looks like a yes-or-no question. In fact, embedded questions are asking for more than a yes-or-no answer but are phrased more indirectly than a question beginning with an interrogative word. They often begin with such phrases as "Do you know . . . ?" and "Can you tell me . . . ?" You use this sort of question all the time but probably don't think about it very much. Listen to Track 22. Look at each example in the text and repeat each one after you hear it.

TRACK 22

Embedded Questions

¿Sabes dónde está el museo?
(Do you know where the museum is?)
¿Puede usted decirme cuándo sale el tren a Toledo?
(Can you tell me when the train to Toledo leaves?)
¿Quieren ustedes explicar por qué no hay galletas?
(Do you want to explain why there aren't any cookies?)

Use of Embedded Questions

Embedded questions can seem a bit more polite than direct questions. If you approach a stranger to ask about a train schedule, for example, the embedded question is less abrupt than the direct question. Sometimes, though, embedded questions are used to emphasize the question, as in the missing cookies example. Imagine a mother asking this of her kids. It's a pretty strong and direct question in that context.

Practice: Write Embedded Questions

Unscramble the words to write embedded questions. Then check your work against the sample answers in Appendix D.

1. *¿saben / están / ustedes / los libros / dónde?*
2. *¿está / tú / el restaurante / entiendes / por qué / cerrado?*
3. *¿cómo / explicar / usted / quiere / a / la estación de tren / llego?*
4. *¿trabaja / Jaime / decirme / quién / puede / allí?*
5. *¿vosotros / hay / qué / podéis / en el jardín / descubrir?*
6. *¿ellos / saben / va / adónde / Milagros?*
7. *¿usted / comienza / a qué hora / el programa / sabe?*
8. *¿Marisa / cómo / puede / preparar / explicarme / el flan?*

Embedded Interrogatives

Less obvious than embedded questions are embedded interrogatives, which seem to imply a question though they are phrased as statements. For example, *No sé quién viene a la fiesta* (I don't know who is coming to the party) includes the subtle question, "Who might be coming to the party?" Here are a few more examples:

> *Los niños quieren saber adónde vamos.*
> **(The kids want to know where we're going.)**
> *Pregúntale a Rita qué prefiere comer.*
> **(Ask Rita what she prefers to eat.)**
> *No entendemos por qué sales temprano.*
> **(We don't understand why you leave early.)**

Some of the most obvious phrases that lead to these sorts of embedded interrogatives are *querer saber, preguntar a, explicar a*, etc., which suggest a need to know or find out. If you can fairly easily imagine a question closely related to the statement, you are looking at an embedded interrogative. Since they are so closely related to questions, these words have accent marks just like interrogative words.

Relatives

No, this section isn't about your cousins. It's about words that relate one idea to another. The words *que, quien,* and *donde* are the three the most common connectors used to join two sentences into one. When these words are used as connectors, they are called relative pronouns or relative adverbs, depending on their specific function. Refresh your memory with these examples:

> *El pueblo es muy pequeño. Tú vives en el pueblo.* **>** *Tú vives en el pueblo que es muy pequeño.* **or** *El pueblo en que tú vives es muy pequeño.*

Mi abuelo habla mucho. Mi abuelo tiene muchos amigos. **>** *Mi abuelo, quien habla mucho, tiene muchos amigos.*

Voy a Salamanca. Jorge vive en Salamanca. **>** *Voy a Salamanca donde vive Jorge.*

No Accents on Relatives

As you remember, interrogatives always have accent marks. You probably also remember that we said the accent marks differentiated the interrogatives from the relative pronouns, which we would talk about later. Well, here they are. Notice that *que, quien,* and *donde* don't have accent marks when they serve simply to connect two sentences without any overt or implied question.

Practice: Interrogatives and Relatives

Complete the following sentences with an appropriate interrogative or relative word. There may be more than one option to complete the sentence. Then check your responses with the sample answers in Appendix D.

1. *¿Quieres saber _____ trabaja Mario?*
2. *No importa _____ cuesta, voy a comprar esa chaqueta.*
3. *Necesito aprender _____ preparar la paella.*
4. *Juan es el chileno _____ vive en mi calle.*
5. *El museo de arte está en la zona cultural _____ están los otros museos.*
6. *¿Pueden ustedes decirnos _____ cierran las tiendas?*
7. *Necesitamos comprar un regalo _____ es el cumpleaños de Sara.*
8. *Sara es la chica _____ yo tomo clases de español.*
9. *No entiendo _____ no podemos visitar Buenos Aires.*
10. *¿Quién sabe hasta _____ está abierta el correos?*

Chapter 5
Making Comparisons

One of the most natural things human beings do is talk to other people. We introduce ourselves, talk about ourselves, ask about others, compare our ideas and theirs, and compare our world to theirs. This chapter will give you a good foundation to get out there and talk to someone in Spanish.

5

Yours, Mine, and Ours: Expressing Possession

Imagine that you are on a group tour and everyone's luggage has just been dropped off at your hotel in Lima. How are you going to sort out which bag is whose? Well, it's simple. You're going to use possessive adjectives to say things like "My bag is red" and "Your bag is over there." Here's what the possessive adjectives look like:

Possessive Adjectives

English	Spanish
my	*mi, mis*
your	*tu, tus; su, sus; vuestro(a), vuestros(as)*
our	*nuestro(a), nuestros(as)*
their	*su, sus*

Agreement in Possessives

Remember that the possessives are adjective forms. As such they have to agree in number and gender with the object or objects possessed. Agreement in number affects the possessives referring to the subjects *yo, tú,* and *él, ella, usted* and their plural forms *ellos, ellas, ustedes.* Number and gender are reflected in the possessive forms referring to *nosotros* and *vosotros.*

ALERT!

Possessive adjectives agree in number and gender of the object or objects possessed. They do not agree with the number or gender of the possessor. The phrase "his magazines" is translated as *sus revistas* in Spanish. The possessive is plural because it refers to a plural item. It is irrelevant that the magazines belong to only one person, in this case masculine.

Let's look at some examples to refresh your memory about possessive adjectives:

Possessives in Action

Subject Pronoun	Possessive Singular	Possessive Plural
yo	mi libro	mis libros
tú	tu amiga	tus amigas
él, ella, usted	su periódico	sus periódicos
nosotros	nuestro libro y nuestra amiga	nuestros libros y nuestras amigas
vosotros	vuestro libro y vuestra amiga	vuestros libros y vuestras amigas
ellos, ellas, ustedes	su libro	sus libros

ALERT!

The only possessive forms that reflect gender as well as number are the two that refer to *nosotros* (we) and *vosotros* (you familiar plural in Spain). While all possessive adjectives have singular and plural forms, these two also have masculine and feminine forms.

Subject Pronoun or Possessive Adjective?

Be careful not to confuse the subject pronouns *nosotros* (we) and *vosotros* (you) with their masculine plural possessive adjective forms: *nuestros* (our) and *vuestros* (your). They may look very similar, but there is a big difference between the subject and the possessive. Notice too, that the possessive adjective for third person singular and plural, "his, her, your" (singular and plural), and "their" is the same: *su*. The meaning is understood from the context of the sentence in which it is used. If you're talking about

María and then refer to her car, there will be absolutely no confusion about who *su* refers to.

The only difference between the familiar subject pronoun *tú* (you) and its possessive adjective *tu* (your) is the accent mark. The subject pronoun always has an accent mark to differentiate it from the possessive adjective. Both words are pronounced exactly the same.

You, You, and You

Remember that there are several ways to say "you" in Spanish, and each one has its possessive form. If the item possessed belongs to someone you would address as *tú*, the possessive adjectives are *tu* and *tus*. In Spain, the plural of *tú* is *vosotros*, which has four possessive forms, as we've seen: *vuestro, vuestra, vuestros,* and *vuestras.* If you refer to someone as *usted*, the possessive adjectives used are *su* and *sus*.

Practice: Possessives

Practice a bit by translating the following sentences into Spanish. There are hints to guide you through the references to "your." Then check your work in Appendix D.

1. My book is interesting.
2. Your (*tú*) shoes are pretty.
3. Her boyfriend is Puerto Rican.
4. Your (*usted*) ideas are very good.
5. Your (*vosotros*) brothers are working now, aren't they?
6. Your (*ustedes*) glasses are on the table.
7. Our teachers (feminine) are intelligent.
8. Their money is in the bank.
9. Our grandmother is old.
10. Your (*vosotros*) friend (male) is active.

Expressing Possession with De

Let's go back to that scene we described at the beginning of the chapter. You and your tour group have just arrived at your hotel and are facing a jumble of luggage. Obviously, you can't identify everyone's bags by using the possessive adjectives. There would be too many different people represented by *su*! Here is another way: use the word *de*. The formula *de* + possessor is the equivalent of the apostrophe "s" combination in English:

> *La maleta de Rosa* . . . **(Rosa's suitcase . . .)**
> *Las maletas de la señora Olmedo* . . . **(Mrs. Olmedo's suitcases . . .)**
> *Las maletas de mis padres* . . . **(My parents' suitcases . . .)**

Notice that you start with the item possessed in this structure and then use *de* to say who the owner is: *La maleta de Rosa está allí.* (The suitcase of Rosa is there). If you have two owners, you only need to use *de* in front of the first, like this: *El coche de Juan y Rosa es nuevo* (Juan and Rosa's car is new). If you have a string of possessive statements, simply use the formula *de* + owner for each: *Los juguetes de los niños están en el cuarto de Elena* (The children's toys are in Elena's room). To ask whom something belongs to, use *¿De quién(es)* . . .? For example, *¿De quién es la maleta?* (Whose suitcase is it?) –*Es de Rosa.* (It's Rosa's.)

ALERT!

Don't forget to contract *de* + *el* into *del* when these two words occur in sequence. For example, *El libro del maestro está en la biblioteca* (The teacher's book is in the library).

Practice: Possession with De

Look at each of the following sentences and jot down how you would express the same idea in Spanish. Then listen to the answers on Track 23 and repeat each one.

TRACK 23

Possession with *De*

1. Susana's suitcases are green.
2. The room's door is broken.
3. My brother's new friend is Mexican.
4. La Paz is Bolivia's highest city.
5. The students' classes are interesting.
6. Alberto and Mario's photos are on Alberto's computer.

Meeting and Greeting

Meeting and greeting people involves a lot of formulaic language in Spanish, just as in English. And as in English, there are formal and informal phrases suitable to meeting people in different situations. For example, if you are introduced to a business colleague at a meeting, you would use somewhat more formal language than if you were meeting a friend of a friend at a party. Remember that Spanish distinguishes between the formal and informal you: *usted* and *tú*. Though usage varies from country to country, a good rule of thumb is to use *usted* with someone you would address with a title like *señor, señora, señorita, doctor, doctora,* etc. If you would address someone by his or her first name, you would likely use *tú*. In many cases, you can take your cue by which form the people around you are using.

FACT

The honorifics *don* and *doña* are used with first names as a way of addressing someone with particular respect. Though they originally meant "Sir" and "Lady," these terms are now used more with elderly people as a sign of respect as well as affection. For example, you might refer to your friend's grandparents as *don Alberto* and *doña Olivia* rather than using *señor* and *señora* with their last names.

Introductions

Let's use introductions as a starting point. Imagine that someone is introducing you to someone else. Read over the following examples of introductions and watch for clues that indicate why each is formal or informal.

Formal and Informal Introductions

Formal	Informal
Quiero presentarle al señor Martínez.	Quiero presentarte a mi amiga, Elena.
Permítame presentarle a la señora Topete.	Permíteme presentarte a José y Lucero.
Déjeme presentarle a la doctora Sánchez.	Déjame presentarte a mis hermanas, Alba y Tina.
Señora Guzmán, el profesor Blanco.	Sandra, Silvia

Your first clue in each of these is how the person addresses you. If you are addressed with the *usted* form, for example, *permítame* or *déjeme presentarle*, you can be pretty sure that you should respond using the *usted* form. Both of the command forms in the formal examples are *usted* commands, and the object pronoun *le* also refers to *usted*. The informal introductions use the *tú* command forms, *permíteme* and *déjame* and the object pronoun *te*. It is possible that these forms would be used in formal introductions if, for example, a friend of yours were introducing you to someone that you would both address as *usted*, though your own relationship is informal.

The second clue is how each person is named. Notice that the formal introductions all use titles and the person's last name. The informal introductions use first names. Other subtle clues include references like *mi amiga* and *mis hermanas*. If someone is introducing you to their friends or siblings, you would most likely use informal forms of address with them since you are probably being included as a friend or honorary family member. Of course, there may be exceptions where you might address someone formally even though you are introducing a friend or family member and vice versa.

Responding to Introductions

The next step is responding appropriately to introductions. Some responses are completely neutral and can be used in either formal or informal contexts. Some are specifically one or the other. Look at the examples and try to decide why each is considered formal, informal, or neutral.

Responses to Introductions

Formal	Informal	Neutral
Es un gusto conocerlo(la).	Es un gusto conocerte.	Mucho gusto.
Mucho gusto conocerlo(la).	Mucho gusto conocerte.	Un gusto.
Es un placer conocerlo(la).	Es un placer conocerte.	Un placer.

Did you notice that the formal responses mostly include the direct object pronoun *lo* or *la* and the informal responses use the direct object pronoun *te*?

Of course, you might be introduced to more than one person at a time. In those cases, the singular pronouns would change their plural forms, *los, las, os,* and the singular verb to plural, *están.* Or you could simply use a neutral response. Look at the following example of a short formal introduction and response:

Ramón, quiero presentarte a los señores Ramos.
Es un placer conocerlos, señores.

Follow-Up

Most introductions include more than the initial introduction and response. When you say it's a pleasure to meet the person you have just been introduced to, it's common for that person to respond to your response. The easiest response is to use one of the neutral phrases. So, for example, you have just been introduced to Mr. Ramos, who responds with *Es un gusto conocerlo.* You could respond to him with a simple *Mucho gusto* or any of the other neutral phrases. An excellent response in Spanish when someone says one of the "it's a pleasure to meet you" sorts of phrases is to say *igualmente* (likewise).

FACT

The direct object pronouns *lo, los, la,* and *las* are often replaced by the pronouns *le* or *les*. This is a dialectal form that is fairly common, particularly in Spain. *Es un gusto conocerlo* becomes *Es un gusto conocerle.*

TRACK 24

Meeting and Greeting

Are you ready to give it a try? Listen to the introductions on Track 24 and respond with an appropriate formal or informal phrase. (The text is not listed because this is meant to be a more challenging exercise.) Then listen to and repeat the sample responses. You can find the introductions and sample responses written out in Appendix D.

It's All in the Family

Who are the most important people around you? Probably your family, friends, and colleagues. Let's begin by reviewing and expanding your kinship and friendship vocabulary. Then we can describe them a bit and compare some of their characteristics.

Kinship and Friendship Vocabulary

great-grandparents	*los bisabuelos*
grandparents	*los abuelos*
father/mother	*el padre/la madre*
stepfather/stepmother	*el padrastro/la madrastra*
husband/wife	*el/la esposo/a*
son/daughter	*el/la hijo/a*

stepson/stepdaughter	*el/la hijastro/a*
siblings	*los/las hermanos/as*
stepbrother/stepsister	*el/la hermanastro/a*
father-/mother-in-law	*el/la suegro/a*
brother-/sister-in-law	*el/la cuñado/a*
son-/daughter-in-law	*el yerno/la nuera*
grandson/granddaughter	*el/la nieto/a*
uncle/aunt	*el/la tío/a*
cousin	*el/la primo/a*
nephew/niece	*el/la sobrino/a*
godson/goddaughter	*el/la ahijado/a*
godfather/godmother	*padrino/madrina*
great uncle/great aunt	*el tío abuelo/la tía abuela*
pal	*el compadre/la comadre*
partner/buddy	*el/la compañero/a*
friend	*el/la amigo/a*
boy/girlfriend	*el/la novio/a*
colleague	*el/la colega*
associate	*el/la socio/a*

Describing People

In Chapter 3 we practiced a bit with adjectives to describe people, places, and things. Let's expand on that list with some more adjectives. You might want to use the dictionary to make a personal list based on the specific characteristics of your own family and friends.

- *joven* (**young**)
- *viejo/a* (**old**)

- *mayor* **(elderly)**
- *comprensivo/a* **(understanding)**
- *egoísta* **(selfish)**
- *amable* **(kind)**
- *excéntrico/a* **(eccentric)**
- *conservador/a* **(conservative)**
- *liberal* **(liberal)**
- *energético/a* **(energetic)**
- *perezoso/a* **(lazy)**
- *tranquilo/a* **(easy going)**
- *pesado/a* **(annoying)**
- *gentil* **(accommodating)**
- *abierto/a* **(outgoing)**
- *tímido/a* **(shy)**
- *callado/a* **(quiet)**
- *reservado/a* **(reserved)**
- *alto/a* **(tall)**
- *bajo/a* **(short)**
- *de estatura media* **(medium height)**

TRACK 25

Questions about Family and Friends

Imagine you have just met someone during your visit to Peru and you are talking about your family and friends. Listen to your new friend's questions on Track 25 and respond in complete sentences. (The text is not shown here because this is meant to be a more challenging exercise.) Then compare your answers with the sample answers in Appendix D. There are sure to be differences, but you can check the basics.

Compare Using Adjectives

Since you already know how to combine adjectives with *ser* and *estar* to describe people, places, and things, let's talk about how to use adjectives to compare them. You can compare the characteristics of things in three ways: they have the same amount of the characteristic, one thing has more of the characteristic, or one has less of it. Imagine, for a moment, that you want to compare several characteristics of your sweet little grandmother and your pesky teenage brother, Jaime. Let's look at some characteristics you might compare.

Characteristics to Compare

Grandma	Jaime
old	young
short	tall
understanding	annoying
kind	kind
quiet	energetic
reserved	outgoing
lazy	lazy

Think about how you would compare the age of these two people in English. There are several possibilities, for example:

Grandma is older than Jaime.
Jaime is younger than Grandma.
Grandma is less young than Jaime.
Jaime is less old than Grandma.
Grandma isn't as young as Jaime.
Jaime isn't as old as Grandma.

More Than . . .

The two most obvious comparisons, "Grandma is older than Jaime" and "Jaime is younger than Grandma," are comparisons based on more of a quality, in this case, age. In English the most common way to make this sort of comparison is to simply add *–er* to the end of the adjective. Then you follow the formula of "adjective + *–er* + than." When an adjective in English has multiple syllables, it is more common to use the word "more," and the formula changes slightly to "more + adjective + than." Spanish generally uses the latter formula *más* + adjective + *que* to express more of a quality.

TRACK 26

More Than...

Listen to the following examples and repeat each one.

Abuelita es más vieja que Jaime. **or** *Abuelita es mayor que Jaime.*
(Grandma is older than Jaime.)
Jaime es más joven que Abuelita.
(Jaime is younger than Grandma.)

The comparatives "better" and "worse" are irregular in Spanish. Use *mejor* and *peor*. For example, *El chocolate es mejor que los vegetales.* The comparative *más viejo(a)* is a bit abrupt when applied to people, since it implies that something is old and rather worthless. When describing people, *mayor* is a gentle way of saying older. To refer to an "older" or "younger" brother, use *hermano mayor* or *menor*.

Less Than . . .

The second two examples compare on the basis of having less of the quality of oldness or youngness. In English, we use the formula "less + adjective + than," and the same formula is used in Spanish: *menos* + adjective + *que*.

TRACK 27

Less Than...

Listen to the following examples and repeat each one.

Abuelita es menos energética que Jaime.
(Grandma is less energetic than Jaime.)
Jaime es menos viejo que Abuelita.
(Jaime is less old than Grandma.)

Not As . . .

The third set of examples also expresses comparisons of inequality but in a different way. English uses the formula "not as + adjective + as." In Spanish the formula is the same: *no + tan* + adjective + *como*. Of course, in both cases you have to include the verb "to be", which may be either *ser* or *estar* in Spanish depending on whether the quality compared is an essential characteristic or a state of being.

TRACK 28

Not As...

Listen to the examples and repeat each one.

Abuelita no es tan joven como Jaime.
(Grandma isn't as young as Jaime.)
Jaime no es tan viejo como Abuelita.
(Jaime isn't as old as Grandma.)

In each case, we have compared the age of Grandma and Jaime, but in a slightly different way. There is no rule for which formula to use. You can decide which characteristic seems most outstanding and base your comparison on that characteristic. For example, in the case of a teenager and a grandmother, it's more natural to refer to the teenager being younger than the grandmother rather than less old because a teenager isn't old at all. The important thing to remember, though, is that you have to follow the comparative formulas.

Comparisons of Equality

So what if you want to compare a characteristic that each person has in the same measure? Grandma and Jaime are both kind people, and they are both lazy. You've only got one formula to remember in this case. English uses "as + adjective + as," and Spanish uses the same formula: *tan* + adjective + *como*.

TRACK 29

Comparisons of Equality

Listen to each example and repeat.

Abuelita es tan amable como Jaime. **(Grandma is as nice as Jaime.)**
Jaime es tan perezoso como Abuelita. **(Jaime is as lazy as Grandma.)**

Let's take a moment to summarize the different ways you can make comparisons with adjectives.

Comparisons with Adjectives

Different	
more + adjective + than	*más* + adjective + *que*
less + adjective + than	*menos* + adjective + *que*
not as + adjective + as	*no tan* + adjective + *como*
Same	
as + adjective + as	*tan* + adjective + *como*

Practice: Equal and Unequal Comparisons

Practice the different formulas as you compare Grandma and Jaime in as many ways as you can. Refer to the previous table and the following cues. Then write out complete sentences. Remember, there is more than one way to make many of these comparisons. Check your responses against the sample answers in Appendix D.

1. Jaime / *alto* / Abuelita
2. Abuelita / *callada* / Jaime
3. Jaime / *perezoso* / Abuelita
4. Abuelita / *reservada* / Jaime
5. Jaime / *pesado* / Abuelita

6. Abuelita / *comprensiva* / Jaime
7. Jaime / *abierto* / Abuelita
8. Abuelita / *callada* / Jaime

Impersonal Expressions with Infinitives

Family members and friends often live in close quarters and interact on a regular basis. What are some of the things that it's important to do or not do to avoid driving each other crazy? For example, it's important to respect others, it's a good idea to talk about problems you may have, and it's best to communicate clearly. All of these are examples of impersonal expressions followed by an infinitive. They are nice, indirect ways of telling someone what to do without being pushy or using a command form. Spanish uses exactly the same formula.

Impersonal Expressions

Listen to each example and repeat.

TRACK 30

Es importante respetar a los demás.
(It's important to respect others.)
Es una buena idea hablar sobre los problemas que hay.
(It's a good idea to talk about problems that exist.)
Es mejor comunicarse claramente.
(It's best to communicate clearly.)

Impersonal Expressions

There are lots of impersonal expressions you can use to give advice to someone. Many of them are very similar in English. Look at the following list for some good examples:

- *Es importante* **(It's important)**
- *Es una buena/mala idea* **(It's a good/bad idea)**
- *Es mejor* **(It's better/best)**

- *Es recomendable* (**It's advisable**)
- *Es necesario* (**It's necessary**)
- *Es bueno/malo* (**It's good/bad**)
- *Es imprescindible* (**It's imperative**)
- *Es fundamental* (**It's essential**)

FACT

It's easy to turn these impersonal expressions into negatives to give the opposite advice. You might make the expression negative, or you might make the infinitive that follows negative. For example, *Es mejor compartir las cosas* (It's better to share things) can be changed to: *No es mejor compartir todas las cosas* (It's not best to share everything) or *Es mejor no compartir todas las cosas* (It's better not to share everything). Each sentence has a slightly different meaning, but they are all equally subtle in the way they give advice.

Some Good Advice

So what is it that you want your family and friends to do or not do? Here are a few useful infinitives for you to build on:

- *compartir* (**to share**)
- *conversar* (**to talk over**)
- *discutir* (**to argue**)
- *respetar* (**to respect**)
- *permitir* (**to allow**)
- *ayudar* (**to help**)
- *escuchar* (**to listen to**)
- *pensar* (**to think**)
- *considerar* (**to consider**)
- *aconsejar* (**to advise**)
- *convencer* (**to convince**)
- *comprender* (**to understand**)

Practice: Impersonal Expressions with Infinitives

Let's put the pieces together and write out some good advice for getting along with family and friends. Use the cues to get started and then complete each sentence with your own ideas. Check the sample answers in Appendix D when you're done.

1. *Es importante / compartir / hermanos y hermanas*
2. *Es una buena idea / ayudar / los suegros*
3. *Es imprescindible / escuchar / todos*
4. *Es necesario / conversar / los problemas*
5. *Es mejor / pensar*
6. *Es fundamental / respetar*
7. *No es bueno / discutir*
8. *Es recomendable / comprender*

Good Advice

It's important to keep what you're learning fresh by practicing. Of course, it's best to get a friend to collaborate so you can practice together. Describe each other and each other's neighborhood; write e-mails to each other in which you talk about your family and friends; compare yourselves; compare your families and friends; give each other subtle advice. It's ideal to practice orally and in written form every day. And, of course, it's a good idea to use the dictionary or another resource to supplement your vocabulary so your descriptions and comparisons are precise and more interesting. The most important thing, though, is to have fun!

Chapter 6

Out and About: Verbs and Adverbs

Once you identify and describe people, it's likely you'll want to say something about what they do. The more verbs you learn, the more you can talk about what's going on around you. Then you'll probably want to say how often and in what manner people do things. Adverbs are your most important tools for this task. So let's add some action to your Spanish lessons by talking about the fun activities you do, along with how often and in what way you do them.

Leisure Activities

What do you do in your free time, your *tiempo libre*? Besides work and sports, which we'll talk about in coming chapters, what are some of the activities that help define who you are? Take a look at the verbs for some leisure activities:

- *cocinar* **(to cook)**
- *inventar* **(to invent)**
- *arreglar* **(to fix)**
- *pintar* **(to paint)**
- *dibujar* **(to draw)**
- *sacar/tomar fotos* **(to take photos)**
- *coser* **(to sew)**
- *bordar* **(to embroider)**
- *tejer* **(to knit or weave)**
- *trabajar con madera* **(to work with wood)**
- *trabajar de voluntario/a* **(to volunteer)**
- *fabricar* **(to make)**
- *leer* **(to read)**
- *charlar* **(to chat)**
- *tocar* **(to play a musical instrument)**
- *observar pájaros* **(to bird-watch)**
- *coleccionar* **(to collect)**
- *montar* **(to ride)**
- *pasear* **(to stroll, to go about)**
- *andar* **(to walk, to go about)**
- *escuchar* **(to listen to)**

Practice: Who Does What?

Let's practice verb conjugation in the present tense again by saying what people do in their free time. Use the cues to talk about some of your leisure activities and those of your family and friends. Then check your sentences against the models in Appendix D.

1. *yo / coleccionar / sellos*
2. *Tía Susana / pintar / paisajes*
3. *mis abuelos / observar pájaros*
4. *tu prima y yo / charlar*
5. *la madrina de Eva / tejer*
6. *tú / cocinar*
7. *Jorgito / andar en bicicleta*
8. *mi cuñada / pasear con su perro*
9. *vosotros / escuchar música*
10. *ustedes / inventar juegos*

FACT

Leisure time is highly valued in Spain and Latin America. People spend a lot of time visiting with friends and family, chatting in cafes, walking around town, or hanging out in plazas and parks. The evening *paseo* (stroll) is as much a part of most people's day as their morning cup of coffee.

Likes and Dislikes

Remember the verb *gustar*? You can use *gusta* + infinitive to say what people like to do. This verb works a bit differently from the other verbs we've practiced because it literally means that something pleases someone. Because of this, the subject of the verb isn't very often a person the way it is with other sorts of verbs. If there is romance in the air, however, and someone pleases someone else, *gustar* will be conjugated according to who pleases. For example, *Me gustas* means "You please me" or, in standard English, "I like you."

Things are a lot more clear-cut when you talk about activities that you like. When an activity is the subject of *gustar*, you use *gusta* because an activity is considered a singular subject. To say whom an activity pleases, use the object pronouns *me, te, le, nos, os, les*. So, to express that you like to watch movies, you would say: *Me gusta ver películas*, literally, "Watching movies pleases me." To make the sentence negative, simply add *no* in front of the pronoun: *No me gusta ver películas.* Let's look at some more examples with *gusta* in Spanish.

> *Me gusta coleccionar sellos.*
> **(I like to collect stamps.)**
> *Te gusta cocinar.*
> **(You like to cook.)**
> *A la tía Susana le gusta pintar.*
> **(Aunt Susana likes to paint.)**
> *A tu prima y a mí nos gusta charlar.*
> **(Your cousin and I like to chat.)**
> *A mis abuelos les gusta observar pájaros.*
> **(My grandparents like to bird-watch.)**

The object pronouns used with *gustar* can be emphasized or clarified with *a mí, a ti, a él, a ella, a usted, a nosotros, a vosotros, a ellos, a ustedes.* In the case of *me, te,* and *nos*, this additional phrase serves to emphasize the person who enjoys the activity. In the case of *le* and *les*, the purpose is generally to clarify, since these pronouns can refer to so many different subjects.

TRACK 31

What Do You Like to Do?

Listen to the questions on Track 31 and then answer in complete sentences using *gusta* + infinitive. (The text is not shown here because this is meant to be a more challenging exercise.) You can look at Appendix D to see the questions written out along with sample answers to compare with yours.

Comparisons with Verbs

You can use the same comparative phrases you learned for adjectives, *más que* and *menos que,* with verbs to compare activities. The formula is verb + *más que/menos que.* You can compare two activities for the same subject: *Nosotros estudiamos más que jugamos* (We study more than we play), or you can compare one person's activity to another's: *Tú estudias más que yo, pero yo juego más que tú* (You study more than I, but I play more than you). Let's look at a couple more examples:

> *Yo arreglo coches más que cocino.*
> **(I fix cars more than I cook.)**
> *Mi cuñado toca el piano menos que toca la guitarra.*
> **(My brother-in-law plays the piano less than he plays the guitar.)**

Another way of expressing a comparison of inequality is by saying that you don't do one activity as much as another. The formula for that is *no* + verb + *tanto como.* For example:

> *Mi hija no pinta tanto como dibuja.*
> **(My daughter doesn't paint as much as she draws.)**
> *Tu novio no charla tanto como tú.*
> **(Your boyfriend doesn't talk as much as you.)**

Comparisons of Equality

You've probably already guessed that you can use the formula verb + *tanto como* to say that one thing is done as much as another. That's right. Check it out:

> *Alberto monta a caballo tanto como monta en motocicleta.*
> **(Alberto rides horseback as much as he rides a motorcycle.)**
> *Nadie saca fotos tanto como tú.*
> **(No one takes photos as much as you.)**

Comparisons of Equality and Inequality

Let's put all this information together so you can easily see how to make comparisons of equality and inequality with verbs.

Same	
verb + *tanto como*	
Marcia anda tanto como tú.	Marcia walks as much as you.
Different	
no + verb + *tanto como*	
Marcia no escucha música tanto como Juan.	Marcia doesn't listen to music as much as Juan.
verb + *más que*	
Juan escucha música más que Marcia.	Juan listens to music more than Marcia.
verb + *menos que*	
Marcia escucha música menos que Juan.	

ALERT!

Remember that an activity may be expressed with more than a one-word verb; for example, *andar en bicicleta* is a verb phrase. Whether an activity is a single verb or a verb phrase, however, the comparative form comes afterward. Never split a verb phrase in a comparison.

Practice: Compare Activities

Are you ready to compare some activities? Look at the chart of Olivia and Pilar's activities. Then use the cues to write comparisons of what they do.

Olivia	Pilar
pasea mucho (strolls a lot)	*saca fotos poco* (takes pictures a little)
cocina todos los días (cooks every day)	*cocina los fines de semana* (cooks on weekends)
monta mucho en bicicleta (cycles a lot)	*monta poco en bicicleta* (cycles a little)
monta poco a caballo (rides horseback a little)	*monta mucho a caballo* (rides horseback a lot)
fabrica muchas cosas (makes a lot of things)	*fabrica algunas cosas* (makes a few/some things)

Use the information about Olivia and Pilar's activities to write complete sentences comparing them. As you now know, there are several ways to do this. Check your answers with the sample answers in Appendix D.

1. *sacar fotos*
2. *cocinar*
3. *montar en bicicleta*
4. *montar a caballo*
5. *fabricar cosas*

Adverbs of Frequency

You're already familiar with the words *mucho* and *poco*. They are two of the most common adverbs of frequency. Adverbs modify verbs in the same way as adjectives modify nouns—they provide a little descriptive information. In the case of adverbs of frequency, they say how often something is done. Many adverbs end in the suffix –*mente* and are adaptations of the adjective form *frecuente* > *frecuentemente*. But there are plenty of adverbs that don't follow a specific pattern. Look at the following examples:

- *mucho* (**a lot, often**)
- *poco* (**a little, not often**)
- *bastante* (**a lot**)

- *siempre* (**always**)
- *nunca* (**never**)
- *de vez en cuando* (**once in a while**)
- *cada hora, mañana, día, otoño, etc.*
  (**each hour, morning, day, autumn, etc.**)
- *todo el tiempo, el mes, etc.*
  (**all the time, all month, etc.**)
- *toda la mañana, tarde, noche*
  (**all morning, afternoon, night**)
- *todos los días, fines de semana, meses, años*
  (**every day, weekend, month, year**)
- *todas las horas, mañanas, tardes, noches, semanas*
  (**every hour, morning, afternoon, night, week**)
- *diariamente, semanalmente, mensualmente, anualmente*
  (**daily, weekly, monthly, annually**)
- *(in)frecuentemente* (**[in]frecuently**)
- *raramente* (**rarely**)
- *periódicamente* (**periodically**)

FACT

Notice that *todo* agrees in number and gender with the nouns that follow: *todo el mes, toda la mañana, todos los días, todas las semanas.* The adverb *cada*, however, remains the same regardless of the word or phrase that follows. *Casi* (almost) can precede many adverbs to modify their meaning slightly: *casi siempre* > almost always.

Placement of Adverbs of Frequency

Most adverbs of frequency are placed after the verb in Spanish. Say what you do and then say how often: *Mis amigos y yo cocinamos bastante* (My friends and I cook quite a lot). *Mucho* and *poco* always follow the verb except in deliberately poetic usage. There are some exceptions to this after-the-verb placement norm, however. For example, the adverbs *siempre*, *nunca*, and *raramente* usually precede the verb: *Elena siempre prepara pizza los viernes* (Elena always prepares pizza on Fridays). Most adverbial phrases like *de vez en cuando* can either precede or follow a verb. In some cases, this is done to emphasize the frequency over the activity or vice versa. Let's look at some examples of adverb placement:

> *Nuestros primos cantan en el coro todos los domingos.*
> **(Our cousins sing in the choir every Sunday.)**
> *Todos los domingos, nuestros primos cantan en el coro.*
> **(Every Sunday, our cousins sing in the choir.)**
> *Yo bailo poco, pero toco el violín mucho.*
> **(I dance little but I play the violin a lot.)**
> *Jaime siempre habla con su mamá cuando tiene un problema.*
> **(Jaime always talks to his mother when he has a problem.)**

The adverb *nunca* can precede the verb—*Mis padres nunca montan en motocicleta* (My parents never ride motorcycles)—or it can be placed at the end of the sentence for greater emphasis. In this case, you must make the verb negative as well: *Mis padres no montan en motocicleta nunca* (My parents don't ever ride motorcycles).

Practice: How Often?

Use the cues to make sentences saying how often each of these people do the activity specified. Use the answer key in Appendix D to check your work.

1. *Nuestros tíos / salir al cine / todos los sábados*
2. *Mi sobrina / tejer / nunca*
3. *Tus nietos / no visitar / mucho*
4. *Mi esposo / trabajar con madera / de vez en cuando*
5. *La abuela / tomar su medicina / cada hora*
6. *Los niños / ver televisión / casi todos los días*

7. *La novia de Alejandro / llamar por teléfono / cada noche*
8. *Mi madrina / pinta / todos los fines de semana*

Adverbs of Quality

Many adverbs describe the way in which something is done; for example, *Mi madrina pinta muy bien, pero dibuja mal* (My godmother paints very well but draws badly). All adverbs of quality in Spanish can be enhanced by the word *muy*, for example, *Tú manejas muy distraídamente* (You drive very distractedly). Let's look at some more examples of adverbs of quality:

- *bien* (**well**)
- *mal* (**badly**)
- *rápidamente* (**rapidly**)
- *lentamente* (**slowly**)
- *felizmente* (**happily**)
- *tristemente* (**sadly**)
- *afortunadamente* (**fortunately**)
- *desafortunadamente* (**unfortunately**)
- *ricamente* (**richly**)
- *pobremente* (**poorly**)
- *locamente* (**crazily**)
- *tranquilamente* (**calmly**)
- *distraídamente* (**distractedly**)
- *emocionalmente* (**emotionally**)
- *cuidadosamente* (**carefully**)
- *atentamente* (**attentively**)

ALERT!

Adverbs of quality are often replaced by their related adjective forms in speech. Though this is incorrect, it is becoming more common. For example, *Usted corre rápidamente* (You run quickly) will often be expressed as *Usted corre rápido* (You run fast).

Formation of Adverbs of Quality

You probably noticed that most of the adverbs of quality end in *–mente*, and you may have noticed than many of them look like they might be based on adjective forms. For example, the adverb *absolutamente* is related to the adjective *absoluto*. Just take off the *–o* at the end of the masculine singular form of the adjective, drop in an *–a*, and then add the suffix *–mente*. If the adjective ends in the vowel *–e* like *inteligente* or a consonant like *natural*, simply add the suffix *–mente* without changing a thing: *inteligentemente* and *naturalmente*.

Of course, not all adjectives can be turned into adverbs. Colors, for example, don't have adverb forms in Spanish; there's no such thing as "yellowly."

ALERT!

When an adjective with an accent is changed to an adverb by adding *–mente*, the accent should stay in the original location. For example: *distraído > distraídamente* and *fácil > fácilmente*.

Practice: Adjective to Adverb

Change the following adjectives into adverbs. Then check your work in Appendix D.

1. *artístico* (artistic) _____
2. *callado* (quiet) _____
3. *furioso* (furious) _____
4. *metódico* (methodical) _____
5. *delicado* (delicate) _____
6. *cómico* (funny, comical) _____
7. *libre* (free) _____
8. *básico* (basic) _____
9. *general* (general) _____
10. *religioso* (religious) _____

For some extra fun, use each of these adverbs in a sentence to talk about how you, your family, friends, and/or colleagues do things. Make up some more adverbs and check your inventions in a dictionary.

Comparisons with Adverbs

We're always told that we can't compare apples and oranges. But we've seen that we can compare qualities (adjectives) and activities (verbs). We can also compare the frequency or the manner in which activities are done using adverbs and comparison forms. Imagine that you're comparing two candidates, Alán and Sonia, for a promotion at work. You know what they are like and you know what they do, so now you've decided to compare the way they work to see if you can make a decision. Let's review the notes you made:

Alán	Sonia
trabaja rápidamente (works quickly)	*trabaja lentamente* (works slowly)
trabaja metódicamente (works methodically)	*trabaja cuidadosamente* (works carefully)
comunica efectivamente (communicates effectively)	*comunica muy claramente* (communicates very clearly)
presenta sus reportes artísticamente (presents reports artistically)	*presenta sus reportes detalladamente* (presents reports in a detailed manner)
colabora bien con los demás (collaborates well with others)	*colabora muy bien con los demás* (collaborates very well with others)
llega a tiempo todos los días (arrives on time every day)	*nunca pierde un día de trabajo* (never misses a day of work)

Comparative Forms with Adverbs

According to your notes, *Alán trabaja más rápidamente que Sonia, pero Sonia trabaja más cuidadosamente que Alán* (Alan works more quickly than Sonia, but Sonia works more carefully than Alan). It isn't going to be easy to decide who the better candidate is based on that. Let's look at a few more examples:

> *Alán no colabora tan bien con los demás como Sonia.*
> *Sonia presenta menos artísticamente, pero más detalladamente que Alán.*

> *Sonia no llega tan puntualmente como Alán.*

> *Alán comunica tan efectivamente como Sonia.*

Don't those comparative forms look familiar? The formulas are the same ones that you used for comparing with adjectives, except that the adjective is replaced by an adverb:

Comparison of Equality
tan + adverb + *como* (as . . . as)

Comparisons of Inequality
no tan + adverb + *como* (not as . . . as)
más + adverb + *que* (more . . . than)
menos + adverb + *que* (less . . . than)

The comparative forms for the adverbs *bien* and *mal* are irregular in Spanish. Use *mejor* and *peor* just like you did when you compared the adjectives *bueno* and *malo*. To say that Alan speaks Chinese better than Sonia but Sonia speaks Spanish better, for example, say *Alan habla chino mejor que Sonia, pero Sonia habla español mejor que Alán.*

Practice: Compare with Adverbs

Well, what are you going to do about Alan and Sonia? Answer the following questions and try to reach some conclusion. Check your responses with the sample answers in Appendix D. You'll also find translations of the questions in case you need them.

1. *¿Quién trabaja menos rápidamente?*
2. *¿Cuál de los dos trabaja más cuidadosamente?*
3. *¿Quién colabora mejor con los demás?*
4. *¿Quién comunica mejor?*
5. *¿Quién llega más puntualmente?*

So, who would you hire and why? See how important adverbs can be?

TRACK 32

Adverbs Make the Difference

Practice with adverbs as you compare your activities to those of some other people. Look at and listen to the prompts, and make a comparative sentence for each set. Then listen to and repeat the sample answers. You can find the model answers written out in Appendix D.

tú / tu hermano / leer
tus padres / tus abuelos / ver televisión
tú / tu pareja / cocinar
tu hermano / tu sobrino / andar en bicicleta
ustedes / sus hijos / usar la computadora

Chapter 7
Reflexive and Transitive Verbs

This chapter is about routines, all those little activities that you do almost every day at home, at work, and as you unwind after a long day. You get up, maybe exercise, shower and get dressed, have breakfast, go to work, and then unwind with friends, a relaxing stroll, a nice dinner, a movie, TV, or a good book. Sound familiar? Well, this is the chapter where you're going to learn how to do it all in Spanish!

Reflexive Verbs

Lots of verbs in Spanish are reflexive, meaning that the action of the verb reflects back on the subject. For example, "I look at myself in the mirror" is a reflexive form in English. The Spanish equivalent of "to look at oneself" is *mirarse*. Reflexive verbs in Spanish use pronouns in place of the words "myself, yourself, ourselves," etc. Let's start by having a look at the complete conjugation of *–ar*, *–er*, and *–ir* verbs in Spanish: *mirarse*, *ponerse*, and *vestirse*.

FACT

The infinitive form of a reflexive verb takes the pronoun *se*. For example, if you look for "wake up" in the dictionary, you'll find the Spanish translation listed as *despertarse*. In constructions that take a conjugated verb plus a reflexive infinitive, use the pronoun that relates to the subject of the conjugated verb: *Voy a levantarme, Vas a despertarte, etc.*

Reflexive Conjugations

Subject Pronoun	Mirarse (to look at oneself)	Ponerse (to put on)	Vestirse (to get dressed)
yo	me miro	me pongo*	me visto*
tú	te miras	te pones	te vistes*
él, ella, usted	se mira	se pone	se viste*
nosotros	nos miramos	nos ponemos	nos vestimos
vosotros	os miráis	os ponéis	os vestís
ellos, ellas, ustedes	se miran	se ponen	se visten*

*Remember the stem change in these conjugations: e > i

Notice that the verbs themselves are conjugated like any other verb. The only difference is that reflexive verbs include reflexive pronouns. Because the reflexive pronoun and the verb conjugation make it very clear who the subject is, you rarely use subject pronouns as well. However, it is common to include the subject pronouns for the third-person singular and plural conjugations for clarification since they all have the same reflexive pronoun: *se*. Remember that you can always use subject pronouns in any conjugation for emphasis: *Tú te pones mucho perfume, pero yo nunca me pongo perfume* (You put on a lot of perfume, but I never put on perfume).

Reflexive Verbs in Your Daily Life

Many of your daily activities are expressed with reflexive verbs in Spanish. Let's have a look at some more of them:

- *despertarse** (**wake up**)
- *levantarse* (**get up, stand up**)
- *lavarse* (**wash oneself**)
- *bañarse* (**take a bath**)
- *ducharse* (**take a shower**)
- *secarse* (**dry oneself**)
- *cepillarse los dientes* (**brush one's teeth**)
- *afeitarse* (**shave oneself**)
- *peinarse* (**comb one's hair**)
- *maquillarse* (**put on makeup**)
- *arreglarse* (**get ready**)
- *sentarse** (**seat oneself**)
- *quitarse* (**take off**)
- *acostarse** (**go to bed**)
- *dormirse** (**fall asleep**)

*These verbs are stem-changing verbs like *vestirse. Despertarse* and *sentarse* change from *e > ie, acostarse* and *dormirse* change from *o > ue*. Remember that stem-changing verbs change in all conjugations of the simple present except the *nosotros* and *vosotros* forms.

Reflexive Verbs

Listen to the examples of reflexive verbs in action as you look at them in the text. Repeat each sentence after you hear it.

Me levanto todos los días a las 5:30.
(I get up every day at 5:30.)
Tú siempre te arreglas muy bien.
(You are always well put together.)
Mi mamá se sienta para maquillarse.
(My mother sits down to put on her makeup.)
Nos cepillamos los dientes tres veces al día.
(We brush our teeth three times a day.)
¿A qué hora se acuestan ustedes?
(What time do you go to bed?)

You don't need to use possessive adjectives with reflexive verbs like *lavarse*. To say you wash your hands or hair, simply say *Me lavo las manos (el pelo).* The reflexive pronoun makes it obvious whose hands are being washed.

Practice: Reflexive Verb Conjugations

Now it's your turn. Use the cues to make complete sentences using reflexive verbs. Check your answers in Appendix D when you're done.

1. *Carmen / generalmente / despertarse / muy temprano*
2. *bañarse / yo / y lavarse el pelo / cada mañana*
3. *Anita / maquillarse / cuidadosamente / y entonces / vestirse*
4. *Mi hermano y yo / afeitarse / todos los días*
5. *¿lavarse los dientes / tú / después de desayunar?*
6. *Adán / siempre / vestirse / elegantemente*

7. *¿ustedes / quitarse / los lentes de contacto / antes de ducharse?*
8. *los niños / ponerse / ropa cómoda / para jugar* .
9. *yo / sentarse / en el medio / cuando / ir al cine*
10. *ellos / normalmente / acostarse / temprano*

ALERT!

When the adverbial phrases *antes de* (before) and *después de* (after) are followed by a verb, the verb is in the infinitive form: *A veces me duermo en el sofá antes de acostarme* (Sometimes I fall asleep on the sofa before going to bed). In the case of reflexive verbs, remember to attach the appropriate reflexive pronoun to the infinitive.

Por *and* Para: *Part 1*

In Spanish, you'll need to learn the difference between *por* and *para*. These two little words may have driven more Spanish students bonkers than all of the reflexive verbs put together. But they're really not that hard to use. Take a look:

¿Por qué vas a trabajar?
(Why do you go to work?)
Voy a trabajar porque me gusta.
(I go to work because I like it.)
También voy a trabajar para ganar dinero.
(I also go to work in order to earn money.)
Voy a trabajar para mejorar el mundo.
(I go to work to make the world a better place.)

That wasn't so bad, was it? Use *por* with *qué* to ask "why?"; answer with *porque*, "because," or give a reason with *para* + infinitive. Here are some more uses of *por* and *para*:

Por

- Reason or Cause: *A veces llego tarde por el tráfico.*
  (Sometimes I arrive late due to traffic.)
- Movement Through or By a Place:
  Caminamos por el estacionamiento.
  (We walk through (by) the parking lot.)
- Length of Time, Duration of an Action or Event:
  Trabajo por* ocho horas cada día.
  (I work for eight hours each day.)
- In Place Of:
  Cuando mi colega está enfermo trabajo por él.
  (When my colleague is sick, I work in his place.)

*Por is often omitted in this context.

Para

- Destination, Movement Toward a Place:
  Voy para la oficina.
  (I'm heading to the office.)
- Intention or Use for Something:
  La computadora es una herramienta para trabajar.
  (The computer is a tool for work.)
- For Whom Something is Intended or Done:
  Este reporte es para mi jefe.
  (This report is for my boss.)

Using Por and Para Together

Is the difference between *por* and *para* crystal clear now? Hang in there; don't let *por* and *para* send you over the edge! Let's look at some more examples so you get more comfortable.

Martín tiene su puesto por sus conexiones familiares; trabaja para su suegro.
(Martín has his job because of his family connections; he works for his father-in-law.)

Después del trabajo camino por el parque para relajarme.
(After work, I walk through the park to relax.)

A veces uso mi celular para una llamada personal, pero sólo hablo por unos minutos.
(Sometimes I use my cell phone for a personal call but I only speak for a few minutes.)

Silvia está enferma por lo tanto voy para el restaurante para trabajar por ella.
(Silvia is sick so I'm heading to the restaurant to work for her.)

F A C T

Even if you mix up *por* and *para*, your message will almost always be understood. One case where there might be confusion is if you say *Trabajo por mi cuñado* (I work in place of my brother-in-law) when you meant to say that you work as his employee: *Trabajo para mi cuñado.*

TRACK 34

Por or *Para*?

It's your turn now! Answer the questions you hear on Track 34 using either *por* or *para*. (The questions are not shown here because this is meant to be a more challenging exercise.) You can find the questions written out in Appendix D. Then compare your responses to the model answers in Appendix D.

Por *and* Para: *Part 2*

You may have learned at some point that the simplest direct translation of both *por* and *para* is "for." However, we've already seen that "for" doesn't nearly cover the bases. *Por* and *para* aren't that simple to translate, but they aren't really all that hard to get straight either. Let's look at some additional uses of these two Spanish prepositions:

Por

- Exchange or Substitution:
  El banco me da cuatro pesos por dólar.
  (The bank gives me four pesos per dollar.)
  Quiero cambiar el lápiz por una pluma.
  (I want to exchange the pencil for a pen.)
- Rate or Unit of Measure:
  Escribo cincuenta palabras por minuto.
  (I write fifty words per minute.)
  El banco cobra el veinte por ciento de interés.
  (The bank charges twenty percent interest.)
- Purpose of an Errand:
  Voy por café.
  (I'm going for coffee.)

Para

- Perspective or Opinion:
  Para el jefe, somos muy importantes.
  (We're very important to the boss.)
- For:
  Trabajamos aquí para las vacaciones.
  (We're working here for our vacation.)

Idiomatic Uses of Por

There are quite a few idiomatic expressions in Spanish that use *por*. In fact, you already know some of them. *Por ejemplo . . .*

- *por favor* **(please)**
- *por eso* **(for/because of that, so)**
- *por fin* **(finally, at last)**
- *por ahora* **(for now)**
- *por el momento* **(for the moment)**
- *por lo menos* **(at least)**
- *por cierto* **(by the way, in fact)**
- *por supuesto* **(of course)**

- *por si acaso* (**in case**)
- *por la mañana, tarde* (**in the morning, afternoon**)
- *por la noche* (**at night**)

Some of these may make perfect sense to you, given what you already know about the uses of *por*. But, like any good idiomatic expression, there are plenty that don't seem to have any reason at all to include *por*. Not to worry, though. Once you learn them, you'll realize just how handy they are. Look at some more examples and try to work these expressions into your daily conversations. Practice is the best way to internalize new material, *¡por supuesto!*

Juan normalmente trabaja por la tarde pero, por el momento, no llega.
(Juan normally works in the afternoon but, for now, he hasn't arrived.)
Por si acaso Juan no llega, ¿puedes tú quedarte y trabajar por él?
(In case Juan doesn't arrive, can you stay and work for him?)
Bueno, puedo quedarme por lo menos tres horas.
(Well, I can stay at least three hours.)
Tengo una cita por la noche; por eso me voy a las cinco.
(I've got a date at night, so I'm taking off at five.)
Por cierto, hay una fiesta en la casa de Melinda. ¿Quieres ir con nosotros?
(By the way, there's a party at Melinda's house. Do you want to go with us?)

Practice: Por *and* Para

Now, *por el bien de todos*, for everyone's good, let's have one more little practice with *por* and *para*. Complete each sentence with either *por* or *para*, and then check your answers with the answer key in Appendix D.

1. *No me gusta este libro; voy a cambiarlo _____ otro.*
2. *¿Tienes hambre? ¿Vamos _____ un sándwich?*
3. *Javier siempre se acuesta temprano _____ levantarse temprano.*
4. *Tu propuesta es muy interesante. _____ mí es mejor que las otras.*
5. *Necesitamos _____ lo menos tres personas _____ equipo.*

Reflexive and Transitive Verbs

It's pretty hard to say much in Spanish without using reflexive and transitive verbs. Remember that the action of a reflexive verb reflects back on the subject. In a transitive (nonreflexive) verb, the action usually affects someone or something else. Often this is very obvious. Let's look at some examples:

mirar: Miramos los animales en el zoológico.
mirarse: Nos miramos en el espejo después de vestirnos.
lavar: Martina lava su coche cada sábado por la tarde.
lavarse: Me lavo el pelo con un champú especial para estar bonita.
acostar: Las mamás acuestan a sus niños después de la cena para descansar.
acostarse: ¿A qué hora te acuestas?
llamar: Llamo a mi novio todas las noches.
llamarse: Hola, me llamo Sandra; ¿cómo te llamas tú?

To say what people's names are, Spanish speakers generally use the reflexive verb *llamarse* (to call oneself) rather than *Mi nombre es.* To find out what someone's name is, ask the question *¿Cómo te llamas?* or *¿Cómo se llama?*

Practice: Transitive or Reflexive?

Translate the following sentences using a transitive verb or its reflexive counterpart as appropriate. Remember that a transitive verb normally affects someone or something other than the subject while the action of a reflexive verb reflects back onto the subject. Then compare your work to the answers in Appendix D.

1. José usually puts his books on the table.
2. María puts on good clothes to go to a restaurant.
3. I don't like to bathe; I shower.

4. Sometimes we give the dog a bath.
5. You wash your windows a lot to enjoy the view.
6. You wash your hands before eating, don't you?
7. We generally take off our shoes when we enter the house.
8. My grandparents take things off the chair and I sit down.

Of course, not all transitive verbs have reflexive counterparts, so don't get carried away! Think about whether or not the action is directed toward someone or something else or whether it directly affects the subject. Verbs like *andar, tejer,* and *visitar,* for example, are only transitive with no reflexive option: you walk somewhere or with someone; you knit or weave something; you visit people or places.

Let's look at some more after-hours activities. Pay attention to which ones are transitive and which are reflexive.

- *reunirse con amigos* **(to get together with friends)**
- *salir* **(to go out)**
- *divertirse* **(to enjoy oneself, to have a good time)**
- *pasarlo bien* **(to have a good time)**
- *tomar algo* **(to have a drink or snack)**
- *hacer ejercicio* **(to exercise)**
- *relajarse* **(to relax)**
- *dar un paseo* **(to go for a stroll)**
- *jugar a las cartas* **(to play cards)**
- *descansar* **(to rest)**
- *quedarse en casa* **(to stay home)**

Verbs that Change Meaning

Some verbs actually change meaning when used as reflexives. Sometimes the change is slight, sometimes it's fairly significant. Let's look at a few examples:

- *dormir* **(to sleep or put to sleep as in rock or sing a child to sleep)**
- *dormirse* **(to fall asleep)**
- *ir* **(to go)**

- *irse* (**to take off in a hurry**)
- *volver* (**to return**)
- *volverse* (**to become, to turn into**)
- *hacer* (**to do or to make**)
- *hacerse* (**to make for oneself, to become**)
- *comer* (**to eat**)
- *comerse* (**to gobble up**)
- *cambiar* (**to change or exchange**)
- *cambiarse* (**to change oneself or to change clothes**)
- *perder* (**to lose**)
- *perderse* (**to get lost, to miss a bus, train, etc.**)
- *quedar* (**to remain, to be left**)
- *quedarse* (**to stay**)

TRACK 35

Transitives and Reflexives

Listen carefully to the use of transitive and reflexive verbs in the examples on Track 35. (The examples are not shown here because this is meant to be a more challenging exercise.) Think about the meaning of each and then write an English translation. Compare your sentences to the answers in Appendix D. There may be slight variations, but you should be able to see if you understand the way transitive and reflexive verbs differ in meaning.

Special Applications of Reflexives

Reflexive verbs are sometimes used in ways that aren't particularly reflexive. One of the most common nonreflexive uses of reflexive verbs is to emphasize an action as we've seen with the verb *irse*. Though the transitive verb *ir* has pretty much the same meaning, the reflexive form makes the movement of going more abrupt or quick. Other common verbs that can be made reflexive for emphasis include verbs of eating and drinking like *comerse* and *tomarse*, and some other verbs of movement like *caminarse* and *subirse*.

Cuando mamá hace un pastel me como tres pedazos porque es tan rico.

(When Mom makes a cake, I gobble up three pieces because it's so good.)

Después de hacer ejercicio me tomo varios vasos de agua.

(After exercising, I drink several glasses of water.)

Es una buena idea tener cuidado cuando te subes al metro.

(It's a good idea to be careful when you hop on the subway.)

Idiomatic Expressions with Reflexives

There are also plenty of idiomatic expressions that use reflexive verbs. Take a look at some of them.

- *salirse con la suya* **(to get one's own way)**
- *estarse quieto* **(to keep still)**
- *llevarse bien / mal con* **(to get along well / badly with someone)**
- *olvidarse de* **(to forget)**
- *reírse de* **(to laugh at)**
- *preocuparse por* **(to worry about)**
- *quejarse de* **(to complain about)**
- *enojarse de* **(to get angry about)**
- *alegrarse de* **(to be happy about)**
- *ponerse a* **(to set oneself to)**

Here are some examples of these idiomatic reflexives in action:

El presidente siempre se sale con la suya.

(The president always gets his own way.)

Elena y yo no nos llevamos bien.

(Elena and I don't get along well.)

A veces te preocupas por detalles insignificantes.

(Sometimes you worry about insignificant details.)

Me río mucho de los chistes de Jaime.

(I laugh a lot at Jaime's jokes.)

Mañana ustedes se ponen a trabajar duro.

(Tomorrow you're getting down to work.)

Chapter 8

The Future Tense

We're always looking ahead and wondering what the future will bring. Sometimes we make predictions or concrete decisions about what's going to occur or what we are going to do. Sometimes, the future involves hypothesis: "if this happens, I'll . . ." Occasionally, we use the future in a rather determined way to say what changes we're going to make. "What were your New Year's resolutions, by the way?"

Parts of the Body

We've all said things like this: "I'm going to eat better," "I'm going to lose weight," "I'll exercise more." As a culture, we are rather obsessed with our physical appearance and condition, and spend small fortunes and a great deal of energy on improving them. Let's start with a quick look at the human body, inside and out.

La Cabeza (The Head)
- *los ojos* (eyes)
- *las orejas* (ears)
- *el oído* (inner ear)
- *la nariz* (nose)
- *la boca* (mouth)
- *los labios* (lips)
- *los dientes* (teeth)
- *la frente* (forehead)
- *las mejillas* (cheeks)
- *el cerebro* (brain)
- *el cuello* (neck)
- *la garganta* (throat)

El Torso (The Torso)
- *el pecho* (chest)
- *las costillas* (ribs)
- *los pulmones* (lungs)
- *el corazón* (heart)
- *los brazos* (arms)
- *los hombros* (shoulders)
- *las manos* (hands)
- *los dedos* (fingers and toes)
- *el estómago* (stomach)
- *la cintura* (waist)
- *las caderas* (hips)
- *las nalgas* (buttocks)

El Resto (The Rest)
- *las piernas* (legs)
- *las rodillas* (knees)
- *los tobillos* (ankles)
- *los pies* (feet)
- *los huesos* (bones)
- *los músculos* (muscles)
- *la sangre* (blood)
- *las venas* (veins)

Practice: Parts of the Body

You might try writing these words down on index cards, mixing them up, and trying to categorize them again. You could also play pin the card on your partner, and identify parts of the body on a live subject. (It's best to pin the card to clothing as much as possible, and use tape on skin!) At any rate, the more comfortable you are with this vocabulary, the easier things will be as we move along. For some quick practice, try to identify the body part in each group below that doesn't seem to fit. Then write a short sentence to explain how the other terms are related. When you're done, check your responses with those in Appendix D.

1. *corazón*	*músculo*	*sangre*	*manos*
2. *boca*	*dientes*	*costillas*	*estómago*
3. *cerebro*	*pulmones*	*pecho*	*costillas*
4. *manos*	*pies*	*dientes*	*dedo*
5. *ojos*	*rodillas*	*oídos*	*lengua*

The Five Senses

The five senses, *los cinco sentidos,* are:

- *la vista* (sight)
- *el oído* (hearing)
- *el olfato* (smell)
- *el gusto* (taste)
- *el tacto* (touch)

To say that Carla has good or bad eyesight you can say: *Carla tiene buena (mala) vista* or *Carla ve bien (Carla no ve bien, ve mal)*. If Carla has good or bad hearing, say: *Carla tiene buen (mal) oído* or *Carla oye bien (Carla no oye bien, oye mal)*. Careful, though: the sentence *Carla tiene buen gusto* means that Carla has good taste. If you want to say she has a good or bad sense of taste, use *Carla (no) tiene buen paladar*. We don't often talk about people's sense of touch, so you will most often use *tacto* in the following ways: If you say *Carla tiene tacto* you are saying that Carla is tactful. If you say *Carla no tiene tacto*, you are saying she is tactless!

Describing Parts of the Body

It's a fine thing to know some of the parts of the body, but what do we do with them? You can do quite a lot, as a matter of fact. You can describe people more completely, for example: *Elena tiene ojos verdes muy exóticos* (Elena has very exotic green eyes); *Simón tiene piernas muy largas* (Simon has very long legs); *Arnold tiene músculos grandes y es muy fuerte* (Arnold has big muscles and is very strong). You can also say what you do with different parts of the body: *Escuchamos con los oídos* (We listen with our inner ears); *Bailas con las caderas* (You dance with your hips); *Respiramos con la nariz y los pulmones* (We breathe with our nose and lungs). You can also describe problems you have with different parts of the body, but let's save that for a little later.

Physical and Mental Condition

What kind of shape are you in? What about your physical and mental condition? Are you starting to get a little creaky, a little slower, a little less flexible? Or are you one of those marvelously fit people that the rest of us envy? In Chapter 3 you learned that the verb *estar* is often used to describe physical and emotional states. Let's look at some examples in this particular context:

Estoy bien/mal.
(I am (feel) well/ill.)
Estoy enfermo(a), flojo(a), delgado(a), gordo(a).
(I am (feel) sick, weak, thin, fat.)

Gloria está en buena (mala) condición.
(Gloria is in good (bad) condition.)
Eloy está en buen/mal estado físico.
(Eloy is in good/bad physical shape.)
Para su edad, los abuelos están en forma.
(For their age, the grandparents are in shape.)

Another way to talk about how you feel is with the verb *sentir* and its reflexive form *sentirse*. The verb *tener* is also used to describe many physical conditions. Look at how these three verbs are used:

Siento/tengo un dolor en el pecho.
(I feel/have a pain in my chest.)
Marta tiene dolor de garganta y dolor de cabeza.
(Marta has a sore throat and a headache.)
¿Cómo se sienten ustedes?
(How do you feel?)

TRACK 36

What's the Matter?

The verbs *doler (o > ue)*, *molestar*, and *preocupar* use indirect object pronouns just like the verb *gustar* to express what is hurting, bothering, or worrying someone. Listen to the following questions and answers on Track 36 as you look at each example in the text. Repeat each after you hear it.

¿Qué te duele? Me duele mucho la cabeza.
(What hurts [you]? –My head hurts [me] a lot/–I have a terrible headache.)
¿Qué les molesta? Nos molestan los pies.
(What is bothering you? –Our feet are bothering us.)
¿Qué le preocupa? Me preocupa mi peso.
(What are you worried about? –I'm worried about my weight.)

A Visit to the Doctor

The last thing you want when you're traveling is to get sick and have to see a doctor. This can be particularly intimidating when you don't speak the language well. Medical professionals tend to use lots of formulaic language and euphemisms for parts of the body and bodily functions, expressing many things so academically or delicately that they can be difficult to understand. If you do happen to need a doctor while you are visiting a Spanish-speaking country, don't be shy about reminding her that you don't speak the language well and would like her to speak slowly and clearly: *No hablo bien (el) español; por favor hable despacio y claramente.* Don't be reluctant to say you don't understand: *Perdone, no comprendo*, and insist that the doctor explain things again: *Por favor, explique eso otra vez.* It may be awkward, but it's best in the long run for you and the doctor to understand each other as well as possible.

English uses the verb "to feel" quite loosely as a synonym for verbs like "to believe, to think," and "to have an opinion." Spanish does not. Be careful to avoid the use of *sentir* and *sentirse* in any way other than to describe physical and emotional states.

TRACK 37

A Visit to the Doctor

Listen to Track 37 to hear a few more common health issues that may come up during a visit to the doctor. Read the following as you listen.

¿Tiene fiebre, mareos, vómitos, diarrea?
(Do you have a fever, dizziness, vomiting, diarrhea?)
¿Está embarazada?
(Are you pregnant?)
¿Cuando fue al baño la última vez?
(When did you last go to the bathroom?)

¿Tiene alergia a algún medicamento?
(Are you allergic to any medication?)
Voy a ponerle una inyección de antibióticos.
(I'm going to give you an injection of antibiotics.)
Voy a darle una receta para antihistaminas, un anti-inflamatorio, algo para calmarle el estómago, algo para bajarle la fiebre.
(I'm going to give you a prescription for antihistamines, an anti-inflammatory, something to calm your stomach, something to lower your fever.)

FACT

In many Hispanic countries, common ailments are often treated with herbs. Most households keep a supply of such things as *té de manzanilla* and *yerbabuena* (chamomile and mint tea) among others for calming upset stomachs, lowering fevers, treating digestive complaints, and relieving tension. A town may have as many *botánicas* (herbal shops) as pharmacies.

The Future with Ir

You've already seen how the simple present can be used as a very subtle future tense. The most common structure, though, is the same one as in English: "going to + infinitive." The Spanish version is a conjugated form of *ir* + *a* + infinitive. For example, to say "I'm going to exercise more" in Spanish, you would say: *Voy a hacer más ejercicio.* With reflexive verbs you can either place the pronoun in front of the conjugated form of *ir* or attach it to the infinitive of the main verb like this: *Te vas a levantar más temprano, ¿no es cierto?* or *Vas a levantarte más temprano, ¿no es cierto?* (You're going to get up earlier, aren't you?).

ALERT!

When you use a reflexive verb in the *ir + a +* infinitive structure, don't forget the reflexive pronoun. You can attach the pronoun to the infinitive or place it in front of the conjugation of *ir.* There is no preference for one form over the other.

Practice: Talk about the Future with Ir

Use the following cues and the structure *ir + a +* infinitive to write sentences about your plans for the future. Then check your work against the answer key in Appendix D. You're going to have fun with this—*¡Te vas a divertir con esto!*

1. *yo / correr / tres veces por semana*
2. *nosotros / reunirse con amigos / para jugar al tenis*
3. *tú / descansar / después del trabajo*
4. *mi tía / ponerse en forma / ir al gimnasio*
5. *Raquel / consultar con el doctor / para saber qué le pasa*
6. *vosotros / tomarse las vitaminas / todos los días*
7. *los niños / lavarse los dientes / después de cada comida*
8. *mi amiga y yo / preocuparse menos por el peso / pensar más en alimentarse mejor*

Sports and Fitness

Your good intentions to get in shape may inspire you to take up *un deporte* or engage in some other fitness activity *para mejorar tu estado físico.* Which of these might be on your list of interests?

- *correr* **(to run)**
- *caminar / andar* **(to walk)**
- *nadar* **(to swim)**
- *bucear* **(to scuba / skin dive)**
- *surfear* **(to surf)**

- *escalar*
  (to rock climb)
- *jugar al tenis, béisbol, baloncesto, fútbol*
  (to play tennis, baseball, basketball, soccer)
- *practicar la tabla de vela, el ciclismo, la natación, yoga*
  (to windsurf, cycle, swim, practice yoga)
- *levantar pesas*
  (to lift weights)
- *bajar/aumentar de peso*
  (to lose/gain weight)
- *mejorar el estado físico*
  (to improve one's physical condition)
- *cambiar de actitud*
  (to change one's attitude)

You've certainly got a lot of activities to choose from. Which ones appeal most and why? Use the verb *interesar*, which is another *gustar*-type verb, to say what interests you, and use *preferir (e > ie)* to express a preference. For example, *¿Te interesa correr? -No, prefiero caminar o nadar.* (Does running interest you? –No, I prefer to walk or swim.)

FACT

The most popular sport in the Spanish-speaking world is soccer, *el fútbol*. It's played by young and old everywhere—in empty lots, in streets and parks, on beaches, and, of course, in professional stadiums. In Mexico, Venezuela, and the Caribbean islands, *el béisbol* is also enormously popular. How many Hispanic baseball players can you name?

TRACK 38

What Interests You?

Listen to Track 38 and answer some questions about some of your activities, interests, and preferences. You'll also hear sample answers for each one. (The text is not shown here because this is meant to be a more challenging exercise.) Of course, your answers may be quite different and still be perfectly correct. You can see the questions and the answers written out in Appendix D.

I'm Going to Quit . . . and Start . . .

Sometimes getting back in shape involves changing habits. You might have to stop smoking, eating fast food, or watching too much TV. You might start eating better and exercising more. In Spanish these structures are a bit different from English. To say you are going to stop smoking, you would say: *Voy a dejar de fumar.* If your friend regularly gives up eating fast food, you would say: *Clara deja de comer comida rápida regularmente.* The formula to stop doing something in Spanish is: *dejar de* + infinitive. To start doing something else instead, you would use the formula: *empezar + a* + infinitive. For example, to say you are going to start exercising every day, you would say: *Voy a empezar a hacer ejercicio todos los días.* What bad habits are you going to change? What are you going to do instead? Look at the following examples and then make your own list of resolutions.

The formulas *dejar de* + infinitive and *empezar a* + infinitive can be conjugated in any tense or in combination with other verbs. For example, you can talk about what you do every year: *Cada año dejo de . . .* or *empiezo a . . .,* what you are doing right now: *estoy dejando de . . .,* what you're going to do in the future: *voy a empezar a . . .,* as well as what you want to or prefer to do: *quiero / prefiero dejar de. . . .*

Es importante dejar de comer comida rápida y empezar a alimentarse bien.
It's important to stop eating fast food and to start eating well.)
Nosotros no queremos levantar pesas; vamos a empezar a practicar yoga.
(We don't want to lift weights; we're going to start practicing yoga.)
Juan dice que va a correr un maratón cada año.
(Juan says he's going to run a marathon every year.)

Voy a hablar con mi doctora porque me siento muy cansada.
(I'm going to talk to my doctor because I feel very tired.)
Quiero estar en forma, por eso voy a practicar más deportes.
(I want to be in shape, so I'm going to practice more sports.)

Resolutions

Listen to Track 39 to hear some example resolutions. (The text is not shown here because this is meant to be a more challenging exericise.) Then repeat each example after you hear it.

TRACK 39

The Future Tense

You're probably familiar with the old song, *Qué será, será*. That's an example of another future tense in Spanish. While English expresses the future using "will" + infinitive, in Spanish you add special endings to the infinitive. It's so simple that you don't even have to learn different endings for the different categories of verbs. All infinitives use exactly the same endings. So, have a quick look at the future:

The Future Tense

Subject Pronoun	*Dejar*	*Comer*	*Vivir*
yo	*dejaré* (I'll stop)	*comeré* (I'll eat)	*viviré* (I'll live)
tú	*dejarás* (you'll stop)	*comerás* (you'll eat)	*vivirás* (you'll live)
él, ella, usted	*dejará* (he, she, you will stop)	*comerá* (he, she, you will eat)	*vivirá* (he, she, you will live)
nosotros	*dejaremos* (we'll stop)	*comeremos* (we'll eat)	*viviremos* (we'll live)
vosotros	*dejaréis* (you'll stop)	*comeréis* (you'll eat)	*viviréis* (you'll live)
ellos, ellas, ustedes	*dejarán* (they, you will stop)	*comerán* (they, you will eat)	*vivirán* (they, you will live)

And that's it! What could be simpler than one set of endings for all verbs in the future? You're probably wondering why all the tenses don't share endings. Well, in Chapter 12 we'll see one more that does. For now, though, let's look a bit more carefully at the future.

FACT

English uses the auxiliary verb "will" plus an infinitive to express the future. The subject pronoun and "will" are often contracted into "I'll," "you'll," "we'll," etc. In Spanish the future is formed by a single word: the infinitive with a future ending. Whether or not you choose to use the subject pronoun as well, there is nothing to contract in Spanish.

The endings for the future tense are all regular, as we've seen. However, there are a few verbs that change slightly before you add the future ending:

hacer: har–		decir: dir–	
haré, harás, hará, haremos, haréis, harán		diré, dirás, dirá, diremos, diréis, dirán	
poder: podr–	**saber: sabr–**	**querer: querr–**	
podré, podrás,	sabrá, sabremos	querréis, querrán	
poner: pondr–	**venir: vendr–**	**tener: tendr–**	**salir: saldr–**
pondré, pondrás	vendrá, vendremos	tendréis	saldrán

Three Ways to Talk about the Future

As you have seen, there are many ways to talk about the future. You can use the simple present and a word referring to the future for a very subtle future tense; you can use the formula *ir + a +* infinitive to refer to a more immediate future; and you can use the future tense for expressing very definite ideas about what will happen. Review the following examples to remind yourself of the differences. Notice how similar Spanish and English are in the three ways you can refer to the future.

Mañana comemos con Marisa.
(Tomorrow we eat with Marisa.)
Voy a vestirme bien para la fiesta.
(I'm going to dress up for the party.)
Tú llamarás al doctor, ¿verdad?
(You will call the doctor, won't you?)

The future tense can predict or project; it can even be rather commanding. For example, imagine a mother telling her little boy: *Te lavarás las manos antes de comer.* She's not really predicting or talking about what will happen; she's telling her son exactly what to do.

Cause and Effect

Another use of the future tense in Spanish is to express the outcome in a cause and effect statement like this: *Si como menos y hago más ejercicio, perderé peso.* (If I eat less and exercise more, I will lose weight.) The formula is simple: *si* + present tense + future. You can also turn the formula around and begin with the result. Let's look at a few more examples:

Si me levanto tarde, perderé el tren.
(If I get up late, I'll miss the train.)
Si te alimentas bien, estarás sano.
(If you eat well, you'll be healthy.)
Jugaremos mejor si practicamos más.
(We'll play better if we practice more.)

Notice that reflexive verbs still have their pronoun in the future tense. Be sure to place them before the verb in this form.

Conjecture

The future tense is also used in a very interesting way in Spanish to express conjecture. Imagine that someone knocks at your door and you wonder aloud who it could be. In Spanish you would say: *¿Quién será?* You wonder about what the doctor might tell you at your appointment: *¿Qué dirá el doctor?* You can also use the future this way to draw conclusions based on certain evidence. Imagine that you see a really muscular guy and you figure that he probably lifts weights. In Spanish you would say: *Ese chico levantará pesas.* You feel hot and cold so your wife tells you that you probably have a fever: *Tendrás fiebre.*

Practice: What Will the Future Bring?

Complete each sentence using the future tense of the verb in parentheses. Then check your responses and understanding of each statement in Appendix D.

1. *Si tú nos invitas, nosotros _____ (ir) a tu casa la semana que viene.*
2. *Juan hace mucho ejercicio; _____ (estar) en muy buena forma.*
3. *Mañana yo _____ (empezar) a correr cada día con Ramón.*
4. *Tú tienes mucha fiebre; ¿ _____ (llamar) al doctor?*
5. *¿Qué _____ (hacer) Maro y Estéban si dejan de jugar al fútbol?*

Chapter 9

Using the Past Tenses

How did things use to be; what happened when; who did it; and what was the outcome? What else was going on at the time? Have you ever experienced anything similar? The past and present perfect tenses are the primary tools of narration. So let's find out how to tell the story in Spanish.

The Imperfect Tense

At some point in your life, you have undoubtedly heard people describe what things were like in the "good old days" when they were younger. Spanish has a specific past tense dedicated to this sort of descriptive narrative: the imperfect. Now, keep in mind that there is nothing imperfect about it. *Imperfecto* is a grammatical term which refers to the ongoing nature of the past action described rather than its completeness or perfectness. We'll talk more about the differences between the two in a bit. For now, let's focus on what things were like in times gone by. The first step is to learn the conjugation of the *imperfecto.* It's very simple.

	The Imperfect Tense		
Subject Pronoun	*Jugar*	*Tener*	*Vivir*
yo	jugaba	tenía	vivía
tú	jugabas	tenías	vivías
él, ella, usted	jugaba	tenía	vivía
nosotros	jugábamos	teníamos	vivíamos
vosotros	jugabais	teníais	vivíais
(ellos, ellas, ustedes)	jugaban	tenían	vivían

Not surprisingly, the –*er* and –*ir* verbs share the same conjugation endings. Additionally, notice that these verbs all have an accent mark on the stressed *í* of the ending. The –*ar* verbs only have an accent on the *nosotros* conjugation. You probably also noticed that, for each verb category, the first- and third-person singular conjugations are identical, and you might wonder if that will be confusing. Keep in mind that, in most cases, context makes it clear who the subject of the verb is, but remember that you can always use the subject pronoun if there is any possibility of miscommunication.

Irregular Verbs in the Imperfect

Like any good verb tense, the imperfect has a few verbs that are irregular in their conjugation. These aren't very tricky though, since they follow the regular pattern after you make the irregular change. You'll probably learn them as easily as you learned the regular conjugations.

Irregular Verbs in the Imperfect

Subject Pronoun	Ir	Ser	Ver
yo	iba	era	veía
tú	ibas	eras	veías
él, ella, usted	iba	era	veía
nosotros	íbamos	éramos	veíamos
vosotros	íbais	erais	veíais
ellos, ellas, ustedes	iban	eran	veían

TRACK 40

The Imperfect

So, how is the imperfect used? Well, we've seen one context already: Spanish uses this tense to describe how things used to be in the past. For example, listen to Track 40, which has some examples of how you might talk about what your life was like when you were ten years old. Repeat each sentence after you hear it, paying close attention to the placement of the accent.

Cuando yo tenía diez años, era muy tímida.
(When I was ten years old, I was very shy.)
Mi familia y yo vivíamos en Acapulco.
(My family and I lived in Acapulco.)
Papá trabajaba en un hotel.
(Dad worked in a hotel.)

A veces mis hermanos y yo nadábamos en la piscina del hotel. **(Sometimes, my siblings and I would swim in the hotel pool.)**
Mucha gente famosa se quedaba en el hotel.
(Lots of famous people stayed in the hotel.)

Have a look at the following list for a summary of the uses of the imperfect:

- Description: *Tú eras muy delgado cuando eras niño.*
  (You were very slender as a boy.)

- States of Being: *Yo no estaba enojada ayer; estaba triste.*
  (I wasn't angry yesterday; I was sad.)

- Habitual Actions: *José siempre se levantaba temprano y salía a caminar.*
  (José always used to get up early and go out for a walk.)

- Ongoing Actions at a Past Time: *Tú jugabas mientras yo trabajaba.*
  (You were playing while I was working.)

- Age: *Mi abuela tenía veinte años cuando conoció a mi abuelo.*
  (My grandmother was twenty when she met my grandfather.)

- Time: *Eran las tres de la tarde y no había nadie en casa.*
  (It was three in the afternoon and there was no one in the house.)

- Dates: *Era el seis de agosto . . .*
  (It was August sixth . . .)

The English phrases "used to" and "would" that describe habitual actions in the past are expressed with the imperfect in Spanish. For example, "When I was little, I would always walk to school" would be translated into Spanish as: *Cuando era pequeño, siempre andaba a la escuela.*

Practice The Imperfect

Translate the following sentences into Spanish and then check your answers in Appendix D. There may be some slight differences, but you should be able to tell if you've got the idea.

1. My brother was very funny when he was a boy.
2. Susana and I used to be good friends.
3. When you were sixteen you worked in a restaurant, didn't you?
4. I liked to go to bed late when I was younger.
5. Martin and Clara used to play the piano together at parties.

Introduction to the Preterite

Spanish has another past tense called the *pretérito*. This is the tense you use to talk about everything else in the past. For example, you use the imperfect to describe habitual or ongoing actions, but use the preterite to relate non-habitual actions or a sequence of actions in the past. Let's review the preterite conjugations, and then we can talk more about when and how this past tense is used.

Regular Verbs in the Preterite

Subject Pronoun	Hablar	Comer	Vivir
yo	hablé	comí	viví
tú	hablaste	comiste	viviste
él, ella, usted	habló	comió	vivió
nosotros	hablamos	comimos	vivimos
vosotros	hablasteis	comisteis	vivisteis
ellos, ellas, ustedes	hablaron	comieron	vivieron

You may have noticed that the *nosotros* forms of the *–ar* and *–ir* verb categories are identical in the preterite and the simple present. Don't let it throw you. The context will usually make it clear whether the verb refers to a past or present event.

ALERT!

The first- and third-person conjugations of regular verbs in the preterite all have an accent mark on the last vowel. Don't get lazy and leave it off! This little accent makes a big difference between, for example, *habló* (he, she, you spoke) and *hablo* (I speak).

Most verbs with stem changes in the present tense are completely regular in the preterite. For example, the stem-changing verb *acostarse*, which changes from *o > ue* in all the present tense conjugations except the *nosotros* and *vosotros* forms, retains the *o* of the stem in all of the preterite conjugations: *me acuesto* (I go to bed) but *me acosté* (I went to bed), *te acostaste, se acostó, nos acostamos, os acostasteis, se acostaron.*

Practice: Regular Preterite

Before we go any further, let's practice what you've learned about the regular preterite conjugations. Complete each of the following sentences with the preterite of the verb in parentheses. Then check your work in Appendix D.

1. *Alberto _____ (levantarse) a las siete, _____ (bañarse) y _____ (desayunar) antes de ir al trabajo.*
2. *Yo _____ (ver) a Alberto a las nueve y nosotros _____ (tomar) un café.*
3. *Alberto y sus colegas _____ (hablar) varias horas sobre un problema. Finalmente _____ (decidir) votar por una solución.*
4. *¿Por qué _____ (llegar) tú tarde al trabajo ayer? ¿ _____ (comer) con Alberto después de la reunión?*
5. *Yo _____ (salir) con Eliana y ella me _____ (llevar) a un restaurante salvadoreño muy bueno.*

Preterite Stem and Spelling Changes

Remember that we said most stem-changing verbs were regular in the preterite? Well, a few stem-changers have special stem changes in the preterite. These vowel changes occur only in the third-person singular and plural: *él, ella, usted* and *ellos, ellas, ustedes.* Look at these examples:

o > u: dormir(se)	*morir*
(se) durmió, (se) durmieron	*murió, murieron*
e > i: divertir(se)	*vestir(se)*
(se) divirtió, (se) divirtieron	*(se) vistió, (se) vistieron*

Additionally, verbs that end in *–car, –gar,* and *–zar* have minor spelling changes in the preterite. These changes occur in the first-person singular and are made for pronunciation purposes. Look at the following examples:

c > qu: buscar   Yo busqué el libro. **(I looked for the book.)**
g > gu: jugar   Yo jugué al fútbol con Sonia. **(I played soccer with Sonia.)**
z > c: almorzar   Yo almorcé en la cafetería. **(I ate lunch in the cafeteria.)**

The reason for the spelling change is obvious for *busqué* and *jugué.* You have to add the *u* before the *é* to retain the pronunciation of the hard /k/ and /g/ sounds. Without the change you would have to pronounce the *yo* form of these two verbs in the preterite something like "boo say" and "hoo hay," neither of which would communicate effectively. The change from *z* to *c* has an historic origin that doesn't have much to do with the modern phonetics of the language. Nevertheless, the change continues to be made.

A Few Irregular Preterite Verbs: **Ser, Ir, Hacer, Estar, Tener**

No verb tense in Spanish is complete without some irregular verbs, and the preterite tense actually has quite a few. The good news is that many of the irregular preterites fall into categories of similar irregularities. Let's start with five of the most common irregular verbs: *ser, ir, hacer, estar, tener.*

FACT

The preterite of the expression *hay* is *hubo*. To say "There was a cat" or "There were some cats," for example, you would say: *Hubo un gato* or *Hubo unos gatos*. It would be more common, however, to use the imperfect: *había.*

Subject Pronoun	Ser	Ir	Hacer	Estar	Tener
yo	fui	fui	hice	estuve	tuve
tú	fuiste	fuiste	hiciste	estuviste	tuviste
él, ella, usted	fue	fue	hizo	estuvo	tuvo
nosotros	fuimos	fuimos	hicimos	estuvimos	tuvimos
vosotros	fuisteis	fuisteis	hicisteis	estuvisteis	tuvisteis
ellos, ellas, ustedes	fueron	fueron	hicieron	estuvieron	tuvieron

Let's review some of the unique features of these irregular conjugations. First, in contrast with the regular forms, there is no accent mark on the first- or third-person singular conjugation in the irregulars. Next, *ser* and *ir* have identical irregular conjugations in the preterite. As always, context will enable you to distinguish one from the other. Now, look at the stem change for *hacer, estar,* and *tener.* The *ha–* of *hacer* changes to *hi–*; *est–* and *ten–* change to *estuv–* and *tuv–*; and all three verbs take *–er/–ir* type endings even though *estar* is an *–ar* verb. In summary, these five verbs have the following irregular characteristics in the preterite:

- First- and third-person singular conjugations are without accents.
- *ser* and *ir* have identical conjugations
- *hacer > hi–*: hice, hiciste, hizo, hicimos, hicisteis, hicieron
- *estar* and *tener > estuv–* and *tuv–*
- *estar* takes *–er/–ir* type endings

You'll learn more irregular preterite in future chapters. Some of them fall into these same categories; some are in categories all their own. Stay tuned!

The third-person singular conjugation of *hacer* in the preterite is spelled with a *z: hizo*. This spelling change is to maintain the soft */s/* sound. As you know, the combination *–co* would result in a hard */k/* sound.

TRACK 41

Irregular Preterite

Listen to Track 41 and answer the questions using the preterite. (The text is not given here because this is meant to be a more challenging exercise.) You can find a translation of each question as well as a sample answer in Appendix D.

A great way to get more practice with the preterite is to keep a journal. Tuck a small spiral notebook in your pocket or purse and jot down what you, your friends, family, and colleagues did throughout the day. If you don't know the verb in Spanish, write it down in English and then look it up. Do this for about a week and you'll know more verbs in the preterite than you could ever imagine!

Narrate Using Imperfect and Preterite

As you know, the imperfect is primarily used to describe actions in the past without reference to beginnings or endings. In a sense, the imperfect takes you back to the past so you can experience it again. The preterite, on the other hand, is used to describe events in their completeness. If the imperfect takes us back to past events in progress, the preterite relates events that are more specifically over and done with. Don't worry if you're not completely clear on the distinction yet; it just takes practice, and there's plenty of that coming up.

Meaning Changes

Some verbs actually change meaning depending on whether you use them in the imperfect or the preterite. Well, to put it more accurately, their translated meaning changes since English uses different verbs rather than different tenses to express the two concepts. The two verbs in Spanish that seem to have the most obvious change of meaning in English are *saber* and *conocer.* You probably remember that both of these verbs in the present tense mean "to know" in English, but *saber* means to know factual information while *conocer* refers to knowing or being familiar with a place or person. When these verbs are conjugated in the past, knowing takes on different aspects in the imperfect and preterite. For example:

Sabíamos donde estabas. **(We knew where you were.)**
Supimos donde estabas. **(We found out/learned where you were.)**
Yo no conocía a Beto. **(I didn't know Beto.)**
Yo conocí a Beto la semana pasada. **(I met Beto last week.)**

These shifts of meaning may seem very strange until you remember that the imperfect describes ongoing actions or states in the past and the preterite expresses changes of state and beginnings and endings. So, *sabíamos* describes the ongoing state of knowledge while *supimos* describes the beginning of the state of knowing, which in English is expressed with the verbs "to find out" and "to learn." Likewise, *no conocía* describes the ongoing state of not being familiar with Beto, and *conocí* refers to the moment when your familiarity began, when you "met" in English translation.

Look at the following table to see how some other verbs shift meaning in the imperfect and preterite.

Imperfect	Preterite
ir: Ibas a la fiesta, ¿verdad?	*Fuiste a la fiesta, ¿verdad?*
You were going to (had the intention of going to) the party, right?	You went to the party, right?
querer: Quería hablar con Matilde.	*Quise hablar con Matilde.*

Imperfect	Preterite
I wanted (had the desire) to speak to Matilde.	I tried to speak to Matilde (but was unable to).
no querer: No quería hablar con Matilde.	*No quise hablar con Matilde.*
I didn't want to speak to Matilde.	I refused to speak to Matilde.
poder: Ellos (no) podían ver.	*Ellos (no) pudieron ver.*
They were (un)able to see.	They were (un)successful at seeing.
costar: La blusa costaba treinta dólares.	*La blusa costó treinta dólares.*
The blouse cost (was priced at) thirty dollars.	The blouse cost (and someone paid) thirty dollars.
tener que*: Alán tenía que limpiar su cuarto.	*Alán tuvo que limpiar su cuarto.*
Alán had to (was supposed to) clean his room.	Alán had to (was obliged to) clean his room.

*Other verbs of obligation like deber *and* necesitar *follow the same pattern of meaning shifts as* tener que.

Practice: Imperfect or Preterite?

Complete the following narrative using the imperfect or preterite of the verbs in parentheses according to the context. When you're done, compare your responses to those in Appendix D. You'll find a translation into English there as well to help you resolve doubts.

_____ (ser) sábado y Alfredo _____ (querer) dormir tarde. Él _____ (estar) muy cansado después de una semana de trabajo. Pero, a las ocho _____ (sonar) el teléfono y Alfredo _____ (despertarse). _____ (ser) su amigo, Juan, quien _____ (llamar) para invitar a Alfredo a jugar al fútbol. Alfredo no _____ (querer) decir que no, así que _____ (levantarse) rápidamente, _____ (bañarse) y _____ (vestirse). En quince minutos, cuando Juan _____ (llegar) en el coche, Alberto _____ (estar) listo. Los chicos _____ (jugar) hasta el mediodía y _____ (divertirse) mucho.

The Present Perfect

The last past tense is the present perfect. As in English, this tense uses two verbs in combination: a form of "to have" and the past participle of the main verb, for example: "We have finished supper." In Spanish, the auxiliary verb used is *haber*. Look at the next two charts to learn how to conjugate *haber* and form the past participle of each verb category.

The Conjugation of *Haber*

(yo) he (I have)

(tú) has (you have)

(él, ella, usted) ha (he or she has, you have)

(nosotros) hemos (we have)

(vosotros) habéis (you have)

(ellos, ellas, ustedes) han (they, you have)

The Past Participle

Hablar	Comer	Vivir
hablado	comido	vivido

Most one-syllable verbs like *ser, dar,* and *ir* are regular: *sido, dado, ido.* There are, of course, some irregular past participles. Look at the following list:

- *decir: dicho* (**said**)
- *hacer: hecho* (**done**)
- *romper: roto* (**broken**)
- *ver: visto* (**seen**)
- *poner: puesto* (**put, placed**)
- *volver: vuelto* (**returned**)
- *abrir: abierto* (**opened**)
- *escribir: escrito* (**written**)
- *cubrir: cubierto* (**covered**)
- *morir: muerto* (**dead**)

Interestingly, the present perfect generally refers to something in the past, even though it seems to describe a present state. For example, "I have been to Spain many times" (*Yo he ido a España muchas veces.*) refers to many past visits to Spain but describes the present condition of having many experiences Spain. Think about the following examples for a minute.

> *He desayunado.* **(I have had breakfast.)**
> *Has vivido en muchos países.* **(You have lived in many countries.)**
> *No hemos abierto el paquete.* **(We haven't opened the package.)**

ALERT!

The verb *haber* cannot be used in place of *tener* to mean "to have." Likewise, *tener* cannot be used in place of *haber* to form the present perfect in Spanish.

Already and Yet: Ya and Todavía

Sentences in the present perfect often include the words "already" or "yet." The Spanish equivalents are *ya* and *todavía*. But these words are not direct translations between English and Spanish. Use *ya* in affirmative sentences or questions; use *todavía* in negative statements like this:

> *Ya he comido.* **(I have already eaten.)**
> *¿Ya has tomado el café?* **(Have you had coffee yet?)**
> *No, todavía no he tomado el café.* **(No, I haven't had coffee yet.)**

The placement of *ya* and *todavía* in Spanish is somewhat flexible. It's most common to put these words in front of the verb, but you can also put them at the end of the sentence. However, you cannot put them in between the form of *haber* and the past participle.

> *He comido ya.*
> *¿Has tomado el café ya?*
> *No, no he tomado el café todavía.*

ALERT!

The English expression "to have just done something" is not present perfect in Spanish. Use the formula *acabar de* + infinitive. For example, to say "Javier has just left the house" you would say: *Javier acaba de salir de casa.*

TRACK 42

Present Perfect

Listen to each question on Track 42 and answer in a complete sentence using the present perfect. (The questions are not shown here because this is meant to be a more challenging exercise.) You can see the questions and sample answers written out in Appendix D.

Chapter 10
Casual Etiquette Using Infinitives

Many of our daily encounters involve making requests of other people. At work, at play, at home, we often find ourselves in the position of asking people to do things for us. Spanish has command forms equivalent to "do this" and "don't do that" in English, but Spanish speakers tend to use less direct expressions for making requests. Read on and you'll find out how.

Polite Requests Using Verb + Infinitive

You've already seen the formula verb + infinitive in action in several different contexts. You've used *ir + a* + infinitive to express the future; you've used *gustar* + infinitive to say what you like to do; and you've used impersonal expressions with infinitives to give indirect recommendations. You can also use certain verbs with infinitives to make polite requests in Spanish. One of the most common of these combinations is *poder* + infinitive. When phrased as a question like *¿Puede ayudarme?* (Can you help me?), this formula yields a polite request. Add *por favor* to the beginning or end, and your wish will be their command!

> *Por favor, ¿puede ayudarme?*
> *¿Puede ayudarme, por favor?*

Though this sort of request is phrased as a yes-or-no question, you aren't really seeking a yes-or-no answer. This is just a polite way of asking someone to do something for you. Let's look at a few more verb + infinitive combinations for making polite requests.

- *querer: ¿Quiere decirme dónde está el jefe?*
  (Do you want to tell me where the boss is?)
- *permitir: ¿Me permites pasar, por favor?*
  (Will you let me by, please?)
- *hacer el favor de: ¿Nos hace el favor de llamar antes de venir?*
  (Will you do us the favor of calling before you come?)

Of course, tone is a critical element in making polite requests. These same phrases can sound quite obnoxious if you use a demanding tone. Be careful of your intonation to ensure that your request is received as you intended.

Another Polite Request Strategy

Another very common way to make requests politely is to phrase them as simple questions. Instead of telling your colleague to send a fax for you, for example, you can soften the command by saying: *¿Me mandas este fax,* *por favor?* (Will you send this fax for me please?). You're really using the same strategy as the verb + infinitive combination but simplifying the grammar. This is a very common approach in many contexts in which a command form would be too imperious and the verb + infinitive combinations a bit too lengthy. The simple question is direct but polite because it is still a request rather than a command. Notice that, although the English translation uses "will," you are not using the future tense in Spanish. These requests are always made with the simple present.

When making a request, be careful to conjugate the verb appropriately. If you are making a request of someone you don't know well, use the *usted* form. When you make requests of friends, use *tú, vosotros,* or *ustedes.* Remember that the second verb is always in the infinitive.

Polite requests are always appropriate, but particularly so in more formal situations, for example, when you are speaking with someone you don't know well. They are especially appropriate between an employer and employee because they maintain a tone of respect even though one person is telling the other what to do.

TRACK 43

Polite Requests

Let's imagine a parent giving instructions to a babysitter, a middle-aged woman named Elena. Listen to each example as you follow along in the text. Then repeat each polite request after you hear it. Pay close attention to intonation.

Elena, ¿nos hace el favor de preparar algo para cenar?
(Elena, will you do us the favor of preparing something for dinner?)
Elena, ¿puede bañar a Susanita después de cenar, por favor?
(Elena, can you bathe Susanita after eating, please?)
Elena, ¿quiere leer un cuento a Susanita cuando se acueste?
(Elena, do you want to read Susanita a story when she goes to bed?)

Elena, ¿nos llama si tiene una pregunta, por favor?
(Elena, will you call us if you have a question, please?)

Notice that the requests all use the *usted* form to show respect for Elena's age. The parents could also show respect by addressing the sitter as *señora Elena* or *señora* + Elena's last name. If the sitter were a teenager, the *tú* form would be perfectly appropriate as would the use of first names.

Responding to Polite Requests

So, how does one respond to a polite request? Of course, most responses will be in the affirmative, but you might have to say "no" in a polite manner. A simple *sí* or *no* just won't do. Let's look at a few examples of affirmative and negative responses that will maintain the appropriately polite tone.

Affirmative Responses
- *Sí, con mucho gusto.*
  (Yes, with pleasure.)
- *Por supuesto.*
  (Of course.)
- *Como no.*
  (Certainly.)

Negative Responses
- *Lo siento, no puedo.*
  (I'm sorry, I can't.)
- *Lamentablemente, no tengo tiempo.*
  (Unfortunately, I don't have time.)
- *Me gustaría ayudar, pero no puedo.*
  (I'd like to help, but I can't.)

The affirmative responses are pretty straightforward. All you need to do is say *sí* and add an appropriately enthusiastic phrase. To soften the blow of a negative response, though, it is best to include *lo siento* and some sort of reason for your inability to carry out the request.

Practice: Polite Requests and Responses

Shall we try out some of these strategies? Use the cues to write polite requests and responses. The check your answers with the models in Appendix D.

1. *¿poder / usted / llamar mañana / por favor?*
2. *por supuesto / llamar mañana / con mucho gusto*
3. *¿querer / tú / explicarme / cómo funciona esto?*
4. *lo siento / no sé / preguntar a Melena*
5. *¿hacerme el favor de / usted / mandar este paquete?*
6. *cómo no / con mucho gusto*
7. *¿por favor / avisarme / tú / cuando llegue / el señor Gallardo?*
8. *no poder / yo / salir temprano / tengo cita con el médico*

Demonstratives

There are many situations in which you need to refer to "this," "that," and "the other thing." These words are called "demonstratives" because they demonstrate which thing or things you are referring to. Demonstratives can be used to point out specific items or to refer to abstract concepts or unknown things. Because they are adjectives, they agree in number and gender with the item they refer to. There are also neuter forms to refer to abstracts. Let's have a quick look.

Demonstratives

Masculine	Feminine	Neuter
este libro	*esta revista*	*esto*
this book	this magazine	this (thing or idea)
estos libros	*estas revistas*	*estos*
these books	these magazines	these (things or ideas)
ese libro	*esa revista*	*eso*
that book	that magazine	that (thing or idea)

Demonstratives

Masculine	Feminine	Neuter
esos libros	*esas revistas*	*esos*
those books	those magazines	those (things or ideas)

Demonstratives help to communicate a sense of nearness or distance from the speaker to the object(s) in question. In addition to physical distance, demonstratives can communicate temporal distance. Because of this, their use is rather subjective. There isn't a hard-and-fast rule to determine when you would use "this" or "that"; it generally depends on the perspective of the speaker. There are some norms, however. For example, if the speaker is holding a book in his hand, it is more likely that he will say *este libro* (this book) rather than *ese libro* (that book) because of his proximity to the book. Once the item is out of reach of the speaker, though, there just isn't a concrete rule for his choice of demonstrative. When the speaker is referring to abstract concepts like "this idea" or "that notion," the distance is even more relative.

If that isn't enough for you, Spanish has a third demonstrative that communicates a greater spatial or temporal distance than "that." This third form is more or less equivalent to the English ideas "that over there" or "that way back when."

Aquel libro es fascinante.
(That book [that book over there, or that book that I read a long time ago], is fascinating.)
Aquella mujer es interesantísima.
(That woman [that over there, or that woman from the past], is very interesting.)
Aquello no me gusta.
(I don't like that [that thing over there, or that idea from the past].)
Aquellos barcos son muy bonitos.
(Those boats [those boats in the distance, or those boats from the past], are very beautiful.)

Aquellas casas son muy caras.
(Those houses are very expensive.)
¿De dónde son aquellos?
(Where are those things over there from?)

Practice by looking around you and jotting down sentences using demonstratives to talk about things near and far.

This and That in the Garden

To clarify, let's take this lesson about demonstratives into the garden. First, start with a garden vocabulary tour, and then practice with demonstratives as you make polite requests of landscape professionals.

Plants
- *la planta* (**plant**)
- *el árbol* (**tree**)
- *el arbusto* (**bush**)
- *el césped, el pasto* (**lawn, grass**)
- *la hierba* (**grass**)
- *la mala hierba* (**weed**)
- *la flor* (**flower**)
- *la rama* (**branch**)
- *el tronco* (**truck, stem**)
- *la hoja* (**leaf**)
- *la semilla* (**seed**)
- *el fruto* (**fruit or nut**)

Tasks
- *plantar* (**plant**)
- *sembrar* (**sow seed**)
- *cortar* (**cut, mow**)
- *recortar* (**trim**)
- *podar* (**prune**)
- *regar e > ie* (**water**)
- *cuidar* (**take care of**)

- *recoger* (**gather up, [***hojas***] rake leaves**)
- *barrer* (**sweep**)
- *quitar la mala hierba* (**pull weeds**)
- *echar abono, insecticida* (**put on fertilizer, insecticide**)
- *tirar* (**throw away**)

Tools
- *la maceta* (**pot**)
- *la regadera* (**watering can**)
- *la manguera* (**hose**)
- *la pala* (**shovel**)
- *la escoba* (**broom**)
- *el rastrillo* (**rake**)
- *la podadora* (**pruning tool**)
- *la sierra* (**saw**)
- *la carretilla* (**wheelbarrow**)
- *la tierra* (**soil**)
- *la arena* (**sand**)
- *el barro* (**mud, clay**)

Take a minute to look around your garden and jot down the things that need doing. Here are some likely jobs awaiting you:

- *cortar el césped* (**cut the grass**)
- *recortar los arbustos* (**trim the bushes**)
- *regar las macetas* (**water the potted plants**)
- *quitar la mala hierba* (**pull weeds**)
- *plantar o sembrar flores* (**plant some flowers**)
- *recoger las hojas* (**rake up the leaves**)
- *barrer el patio* (**sweep the patio**)

Now let's imagine you've got someone coming by to help you out whose first language is Spanish. How can you politely express what you would like him to do and where? Remember those polite request formulas from the first section of this chapter and the demonstratives from the second section? It's time to put them to a very practical use. Complete each sentence with an appropriate demonstrative to clarify your wishes. You can find the answers in Appendix D.

Practice: Demonstratives in the Garden

1. *¿Puede recortar* _____ (these) *arbustos, por favor?*
2. *¿Quiere cortar el césped y recoger* _____ (those) *hojas?*
3. *¿Me hace el favor de plantar* _____ (these) *flores?*
4. *¿Puede regar* _____ (those over there) *macetas, por favor?*
5. *¿Me quita* _____ (this) *árbol muerto, por favor?*

Demonstrative Pronouns

Demonstrative adjectives are always used with a noun. However, some demonstratives that work like pronouns, replacing the nouns they refer to. For example, you might say something like: "Can you please prune this tree and that one?" "This" is the demonstrative adjective *este*, but "that" doesn't have a noun to modify; it's a pronoun referring back to the word "tree," allowing the speaker to avoid repeating the word. In Spanish, it's very easy to change a demonstrative adjective to a pronoun: just add an accent to the stressed vowel: *éste, ése, aquél, ésta, ésa, aquélla, éstos, éstas, ésos, ésas, aquéllos, aquéllas.* Look at the following examples of demonstrative adjectives and pronouns in action:

¿Puede podar este árbol y ése, por favor?
(Can you please prune this tree and that one?)
Estas ramas están bien, pero aquéllas están secas.
(These branches are fine, but those are dead.)
¿Conoce usted esta planta? ¿Y ésa?
(Are you familiar with this plant? And that one?)

There is absolutely no difference in pronunciation between the demonstrative adjectives and pronouns. The only difference is that the pronoun forms all have a written accent over the vowel of the stressed syllable to distinguish them from the adjective forms.

Express Obligation with Hay que

Unless your home is brand new and you have just finished moving in, you probably have a thousand things on your indoor "to do" list. It's also likely that you are most successful getting your family to do things around the house if you ask politely rather than issuing commands. The same thing is true if you hire a professional. The only difference is the conjugation of the verbs: use *tú, vosotros,* or *ustedes* with your family members (since you're all practicing Spanish now!) but use *usted* or *ustedes* with hired help.

Before you get started on those pesky household chores, though, you need to review some home vocabulary.

Rooms
- *la sala* (**living room**)
- *la cocina* (**kitchen**)
- *el dormitorio* (**bedroom**)
- *el baño* (**bathroom**)
- *el estudio* (**study**)
- *la oficina* (**office**)

Furnishings and Appliances
- *los muebles* (**furniture**)
- *el sofá* (**sofa**)
- *el sillón* (**easy chair**)
- *la mesa, la mesita* (**table, nightstand**)
- *la silla* (**straight chair**)
- *la librería* (**bookcase**)
- *el estante* (**shelf**)
- *la lámpara* (**lamp**)
- *la cama* (**bed**)
- *el escritorio* (**desk**)
- *la cómoda* (**dresser**)
- *el espejo* (**mirror**)
- *la alfombra* (**rug, carpet**)
- *el piso, el suelo* (**floor**)
- *la ventana* (**window**)

- *el inodoro* (**toilet**)
- *el lavabo* (**wash basin**)
- *el fregadero* (**kitchen or utility sink**)
- *la lavadora* (**washing machine**)
- *la secadora* (**dryer**)
- *el refrigerador* (**fridge**)
- *el lavaplatos* (**dishwasher**)
- *la cafetera* (**coffeemaker**)
- *la aspiradora* (**vacuum cleaner**)

Housekeeping Verbs
- *limpiar* (**clean**)
- *lavar* (**wash**)
- *fregar* (**scrub, mop**)
- *sacar brillo* (**wax**)
- *quitar el polvo* (**dust**)
- *pasar la aspiradora* (**vacuum**)
- *ordenar* (**put things in order**)
- *guardar* (**put away**)
- *arreglar* (**fix, fix up**)
- *planchar* (**iron**)
- *colgar o > ue* (**hang, hang up**)
- *doblar* (**fold**)

You can expand on this list by walking around your house and jotting down what you see. Look new words up in the dictionary and then practice making sentences, or make a scrapbook by cutting out pictures from magazines and labeling them in Spanish.

Indirect Requests with Hay que

If you have hired someone to help you with chores, a semi-indirect approach is the most polite. You've already learned several ways to make polite requests. Another one for your repertoire is *hay que* + infinitive. This structure is completely impersonal, so it isn't directed toward anyone in particular. When directed toward a person, this sort of expression functions as a polite request.

TRACK 44

Household Chores

Listen to each example on Track 44 as you follow along in the text. Repeat each polite request after you hear it.

Hay que limpiar la cocina.
(The kitchen needs cleaning.)
Hay que quitar el polvo de los muebles.
(The furniture needs dusting.)
Hay que ordenar la sala y pasar la aspiradora.
(The living room needs straightening and vacuuming.)

These are pretty subtle; chances are that if you used these phrases with your family, they would simply nod and wander off. You might have to be more direct with them. On the other hand, if you have hired someone to help out, this structure is a very polite way of saying what needs doing. The implication is, of course, that he or she will complete the tasks you have identified.

ALERT!

The expression *hay que* is rarely accompanied by *por favor* because it is completely impersonal. Use *hay que* + infinitive to outline tasks, and use *por favor* with other polite requests that are directed at specific people.

Practice: Polite and Indirect Requests

Use the cues to politely ask the following people to lend a hand. Then compare your examples to the sample answers in Appendix D.

1. *Señora Álvarez / lavar y planchar esta ropa*
2. *tu esposo (mi amor) / arreglar la lavadora*
3. *tus hijos / ordenar su dormitorio / guardar esos juguetes*

4. *Señora Álvarez / limpiar los baños*
5. *tu hija (m'hija) / fregar el piso de la cocina*

The Parent/Teacher Conference

Another very delicate situation in which you might have to make requests diplomatically is in a parent/teacher conference. You're the teacher, teacher's aid, social worker, or principal at a school, and you are speaking with the parent of a child who is having a hard time in class. You'd like to get the parent more involved in helping the child with homework and discipline issues, but you cannot phrase these things directly. Think about how you might feel if a teacher told you bluntly to read more often to your child. You might be a lot more inclined to do so if the request is phrased like this: *¿Tiene usted tiempo de leer más con su hijo?* (Do you have time to read more with your son?) or *¿Puede usted llevar a su hijo a la biblioteca para la hora de cuentos?* (Can you take your son to the library for story time?). Let's start with a list of school-related vocabulary that might be useful in a parent/teacher conference.

Subject Areas and Skills
- *la tarea* (**homework**)
- *la lectura* (**reading**)
- *la escritura* (**writing**)
- *las matemáticas* (**math**)
- *la ciencia* (**science**)
- *las ciencias sociales* (**social sciences**)
- *el arte* (**art**)
- *la música* (**music**)
- *los deportes* (**sports**)
- *la geografía* (**geography**)
- *la ortografía* (**spelling**)
- *la comprensión* (**comprehension**)
- *la retención* (**retention**)
- *el enfoque* (**focus**)
- *la atención* (**attention**)

- *la habilidad* (**ability**)
- *la aptitud* (**aptitude**)
- *el conocimiento* (**knowledge**)
- *las relaciones interpersonales* (**interpersonal relationships**)
- *la disciplina* (**discipline**)
- *el comportamiento* (**behavior**)
- *las pruebas* (**tests**)
- *las calificaciones* (**scores**)
- *el entusiasmo* (**enthusiasm**)

Verbs
- *estudiar* (**study**)
- *enfocarse* (**focus**)
- *retener, e > ie* (**retain**)
- *comprender* (**understand**)
- *comportarse* (**behave**)
- *llevarse con* (**get along with**)
- *aprender* (**learn**)
- *repasar* (**review**)
- *aprobar, o > ue* (**pass**)
- *repetir, e > i* (**repeat**)
- *sacar buenas/malas notas* (**make good/bad grades**)
- *confundirse* (**get confused, make a mistake**)
- *progresar* (**progress**)
- *avanzar* (**advance**)
- *adelantar* (**get ahead**)

You'll want to use diplomacy when discussing children with their parents, especially if you need the parents' cooperation in resolving any problems. Review your tools: impersonal expressions with infinitives, polite requests with infinitives, and *hay que* followed by infinitives. Another strategy is to balance praise of a child's strengths with gentle suggestions for the improvement of their weaknesses.

TRACK 45

Polite Requests with Parents

Listen to each polite request on Track 45 as you follow along in the text. Repeat each example after you hear it.

Jaime comprende mucho, pero no siempre retiene las cosas bien.
(Jaime understands a lot, but he doesn't always retain things well.)
A Jaime le gusta mucho aprender. ¿Puede usted ayudarlo a repasar sus tareas?
(Jaime really likes to learn. Can you help him review his homework?)
Jaime es un niño bueno, pero a veces no se comporta muy bien. ¿Puede usted ayudarnos con la disciplina?
(Jaime is a good boy, but he doesn't always behave well. Can you help us with discipline?)
Hay que inspirar a Jaime a hacer más esfuerzo. ¿Tiene usted alguna recomendación?
(Jaime has to be inspired to make more of an effort. Do you have any recommendations?)

So now you have an idea of how to make your requests politely. Keep practicing and you'll soon be very adept at getting people to do what you want and making them feel good about it!

What Comes Next: Sequencing

You've already learned a little bit about sequencing in Spanish. Remember the expressions *antes de* (before) and *después de* (after)? You learned that these phrases are followed by the infinitive to say what you do before and after doing something else, but you can also shorten them to *antes* and *después* to talk about what you do before and after. You can also sequence things by using ordinals: *primero, segundo,* and *tercero,* for example, or talk about what you do in the first, second, or third place: *en primer, segundo, tercer lugar.* You can also sequence with words like "then" and "next": *después* and *luego.*

The ordinals *primero* and *tercero* lose their *o* when they are used in front of any singular masculine noun: *en primer lugar* (in the first place), *el tercer árbol* (the third tree). You saw this same change with *bueno* and *buen*: *un chico bueno* (a good boy) > *un buen chico*.

Check out these two examples, one using *antes de* + infinitive and the other using *despues de* + infinitive:

Voy a limpiar el dormitorio antes de fregar la cocina.
(I'm going to clean the bedroom before scrubbing the kitchen.)
Después de regar, ¿quieres barrer?
(After watering, do you want to sweep?)
And here are a few examples using ordinals:
Primero hay que recoger la sala, segundo, sacudir.
First, the living room needs to be picked up, second, dusted.
En primer lugar, es importante escuchar.
In the first place, it's important to listen.
Primero, vas a lavar la ropa, después plancharla y luego guardarla.
First, you're going to wash the clothes, then iron them, and next put them away.

You can get all the help you need and in the order that you want it done; just ask nicely!

Chapter 11

Office and Work: More Formal Etiquette

The workplace presents another range of interpersonal communication requirements. You may work in a very informal sort of place where everyone is on a first-name basis or a formal one in which hierarchies are maintained and respected. Many work environments are somewhere in between these two extremes. In this chapter you'll learn more about how to use the right tone and appropriate sorts of expressions to communicate effectively with all your colleagues.

Expressing Obligation with Tener que, Deber, Necesitar

Spanish has three more verb + infinitive combinations that you'll find very helpful: *tener que* (to have to), *deber* (should), and *necesitar* (to need). The most common, and probably least formal of the three is *tener que* + infinitive. This is the form you would most likely use with colleagues you are chummy with, people to whom you can say what they have to do without offence. The other two verbs, *deber* and *necesitar*, are a bit more instructional, and you might use them more with a new colleague or someone with whom you have a less informal relationship.

TRACK 46

Sequencing

Listen to each example on Track 46 as you follow along in the text. Repeat each statement after you hear it.

Jaime, primero tienes que completar ese reporte.
(Jaime, first you have to complete that report.)
Señora Olmedo, antes de archivar estos documentos, debe revisarlos.
(Mrs. Olmedo, before filing these documents, you should review them.)
Los nuevos socios necesitan reunirse con Personal la primera semana de empleo.
(New associates need to meet with Personnel their first week of employment.)

Notice that *tener que* is quite direct, while *deber* and *necesitar* can be used to make suggestions and give instructions without being quite so direct. As always, the tone in which these expressions are used determines the formality or informality of the statements.

Impersonal Expressions with Se

You've already learned lots of impersonal expressions as well as the structure *hay que* and know how to use them with infinitives to tell people what to do politely. *Tener que*, *deber*, and *necesitar* can also be used to politely indicate what people have to do. There is another structure that is the most indirect of all, which can be especially diplomatic when you have to tell someone what to do or make requests. The formula is: *se* + third person singular of the simple present + infinitive. For example, *Se tiene que mandar ese reporte cada día* (That report has to be sent every day). Though the implication is that someone in particular has to send the report, the expression itself is impersonal and thus more polite.

TRACK 47

Impersonal Expressions with *Se*

Listen to each example on Track 47 as you follow along in the text. Repeat each statement after you hear it.

No se debe archivar un expediente sin la firma del gerente.
(No file should be filed without the manager's signature.)
A veces se necesita usar el escáner en vez de la copiadora.
(Sometimes the scanner needs to be used instead of the copier.)
Se tiene que reparar el proyector.
(The projector has to be fixed.)

Remember that, as a general rule, the more indirect a request is in Spanish, the more polite it is. Tone is also a key element in keeping a request polite, but your primary tools are the many formulas for indirect expression available to you in Spanish.

Office Vocabulary

Now that you have learned many different ways to express requests and tell people what to do, let's expand your office vocabulary and then talk more about specific tasks and who has to do them.

Office Furnishings and Equipment
- *el escritorio* **(desk)**
- *el archivo, el archivero* **(file cabinet)**
- *el mueble* **(cabinet, credenza)**
- *la computadora* **(computer)**
- *la pantalla* **(screen, monitor)**

- *el teclado* (**keyboard**)
- *el escáner* (**scanner**)
- *el fax* (**fax machine**)
- *la [foto]copiadora* (**photocopier**)
- *el cuaderno* (**notebook**)
- *el expediente* (**file, dossier**)
- *la carpeta, el folder* (**folder**)
- *el proyector* (**projector**)
- *el tablero* (**message board or whiteboard**)
- *el marcador, el lapicero* (**marker**)

Office Activities
- *mandar* (**send**)
- *[foto]copiar* (**photocopy**)
- *archivar* (**file**)
- *imprimir* (**print**)
- *atender, e > ie* (**attend to**)
- *dirigir* (**direct**)
- *coordinar* (**coordinate**)
- *colaborar* (**collaborate**)
- *pedir, e > i* (**request**)
- *investigar* (**research**)
- *confirmar* (**confirm**)
- *documentar* (**document**)

Add to these lists as you look at the furnishings and equipment in your own office and undertake your specific work activities.

Office Who's Who and What's What

Now that you know a little more about typical things and activities in an office, take a minute to think about the different people and departments in a company. Who's who and where do they work?

Job Titles

- *el/la dueño/a* (**owner**)
- *el/la presidente* (**president**)
- *el/la vice-presidente* (**vice president**)
- *el/la director/a* (**director**)
- *el/la sub-director/a* (**sub-director**)
- *el/la [sub]gerente* (**[assistant] manager**)
- *el/la contador/a, el/la contable* (**accountant**)
- *el/la asistente* (**assistant**)
- *el/la secretario/a* (**secretary**)
- *el/la recepcionista* (**receptionist**)
- *el/la socio/a* (**employee, associate**)
- *el/la archivero/a* (**file clerk**)

Departments

- *gerencia* (**management**)
- *contabilidad* (**accounting**)
- *personal* (**personnel**)
- *recursos humanos* (**human resources**)
- *administración* (**administration**)
- *marketing* (**marketing**)
- *investigación* (**research**)
- *producción* (**development, production**)
- *legal* (**legal**)
- *finanzas* (**finance**)
- *manufactura* (**manufacturing**)
- *diseño* (**design**)
- *análisis* (**analysis**)
- *control de calidad* (**quality control**)
- *informática* (**information technology**)

That's just the beginning! Use your dictionary to keep going, keeping in mind that business organization can be quite different from one country to another, so a particular position may or may not exist or may be merged under another job title or within another department. When you're stuck, a good tactic is to describe job responsibilities or the workings of a particular department. Look at the following examples and identify the job title or department described.

> *Reviso la condición financiera de la empresa.*
> **(I review the financial state of the company.)**
> *Contesto el teléfono, escribo cartas y hago citas para el director.*
> **(I answer the phone, write letters, and make appointments for the director.)**
> *Trabajo en el departamento responsable de diseñar productos nuevos.*
> **(I work in the department responsible for designing new products.)**
> *Nosotros nos encargamos de todos los aspectos legales de la empresa.*
> **(We are in charge of all the legal aspects of the company.)**

Did you come up with *contador/a, secretario/a, diseño,* and *legal*? Lots of business vocabulary is similar to English, so you can often make intelligent guesses. Here are a few more helpful words:

Business Terms
- *la empresa, la compañía* **(company)**
- *el/la empresario/a* **(entrepreneur)**
- *la inversión* **(investment)**
- *invertir* **(invest)**
- *ganar* **(earn)**
- *el sueldo* **(salary)**
- *las ganancias* **(earnings)**
- *las pérdidas* **(losses)**
- *las acciones* **(stock)**
- *encargar* **(make responsible for)**
- *encargarse de* **(be responsible for)**
- *manejar* **(manage)**
- *dirigir* **(direct, oversee)**
- *revisar* **(review, audit)**
- *investigar* **(research)**
- *contratar* **(hire)**
- *despedir, e > i* **(fire)**
- *subir* **(move up)**

- *ascender, e > ie* (**move up**)
- *transferir, e > ie* (**transfer**)
- *jubilarse, retirarse* (**retire**)
- *los beneficios* (**benefits**)

Many job titles are gender specific in Spanish, for example, *jefe* and *jefa* (boss) and *secretario* and *secretaria* (secretary). Many titles, though, are gender neutral: the terms *recepcionista* (receptionist) and *gerente* (manager) can refer to a man or a woman.

Practice: Job Ads

Let's take a minute to practice some of this new terminology. Imagine you are looking for a job in the Dominican Republic. Read through these job notices and answer the questions. You'll find translations of each ad and sample answers in Appendix D.

Empresario en el área de la informática busca socios con experiencia extensa en todos los aspectos de la informática. Deben ser creativos y flexibles y necesitan saber colaborar en grupo. Toda persona interesada debe mandar su curriculum por correo electrónico a sramírez@ ecuador.net.ec.

1. *¿Qué tipo de empresa es?*
2. *¿Qué experiencia deben tener los candidaos?*

Empresa internacional busca secretaria bilingüe. Debe tener dominio perfecto del inglés además del español. Necesita encargarse de la correspondencia y los archivos de tres departamentos. Buenos beneficios y sueldo competitivo. Debe llamar por la mañana al 203-43-09.

1. *¿Qué tipo de empresa es?*
2. *¿Cuáles son las responsabilidades del puesto?*

Additional Professions and Trades

Obviously, the business world is only one work arena. There are many other professions and trades. Think about some of the possibilities, and then compare your list to this one.

Professions and Trades
- *el/la artista* **(artist, performer)**
- *el/la actor* **(actor)**
- *el/la arquitecto/a* **(architect)**
- *el/la abogado/a* **(lawyer)**
- *el/la biólogo/a* **(biologist)**
- *el/la carpintero/a* **(carpenter)**
- *el/la dentista* **(dentist)**
- *el/la enfermero/a* **(nurse)**
- *el/la electricista* **(electrician)**
- *el/la geólogo/a* **(geologist)**
- *el/la ingeniero/a* **(engineer)**
- *el/la joyero/a* **(jeweler)**
- *el/la juez* **(judge)**
- *el/la lingüista* **(linguist)**
- *el/la maestro/a* **(teacher)**
- *el/la piloto/a* **(pilot)**
- *el/la plomero/a* **(plumber)**
- *el/la psicólogo/a* **(psychologist)**
- *el/la radiólogo/a* **(radiologist)**
- *el/la sociólogo/a* **(sociologist)**
- *el/la traductor/a* **(translator)**

You can probably expand this quite a bit just by writing down what your friends and family members do. Then you might want to add some of your dream jobs for extra fun!

Giving Instructions

You've learned a lot about different ways to tell people what to do in Spanish. Another context in which you may find yourself in that position is when you give someone instructions. Think about all the things you have to tell a new employee and all the ways you have learned how to do so, for example, impersonal expressions, polite requests, *hay que, tener que, deber,* and *necesitar.* Two other constructions that you already know can also be used to give instruction: the simple present and *ir + a +* infinitive. Let's imagine that you are volunteering at a work-training facility or have offered to give computer classes in Spanish at your local library. Your particular task is to explain how to use a computer and the Internet.

You've already learned some basic computer vocabulary. Let's add to that list:

Computer and Internet Vocabulary
- *el portátil, el laptop* **(laptop computer)**
- *el ratón* **(mouse)**
- *el inalámbrico* **(wireless)**
- *el botón* **(button)**
- *el cable* **(cable)**
- *la conexión* **(connection)**
- *apretar, e > ie* **(press)**
- *tocar* **(touch, strike)**
- *mover* **(move)**
- *la red, el Internet* **(Web, Internet)**
- *buscador* **(browser)**
- *hacer una búsqueda* **(do a search)**
- *la página, el sitio web* **(Web page, Web site)**
- *la página de entrada* **(home page)**
- *avanzar, retroceder* **(scroll down/up, go forward/back)**
- *abrir/cerrar una página* **(open/close a page)**
- *instalar un programa* **(install a program)**
- *hacer clic, seleccionar* **(click on, select)**
- *borrar* **(erase, delete)**
- *el servidor* **(server)**

Computer How-To

You probably don't give much thought to the steps involved in using your computer and surfing the Internet; it might be a challenge to explain it to someone who is inexperienced. The verb *hacer* comes in very handy to tell someone how to do something: *Entonces, haces esto* (Then you do this) and *Después, vas a hacer esto* (After that, you're going to do this). You can give a lot of instruction using only the simple present and *ir + a +* infinitive, but don't forget about all the other structures you've learned to tell people what and how to do things too. Let's try out a few instructions for getting started.

Primero, aprietas este botón para encender la computadora.
(First, you press this button to turn on the computer.)
Ahora tienes que esperar un momento. La computadora va a cargar los programas.
(Now you have to wait a moment. The computer is going to load the programs.)
Para conectar al Internet, debes hacer clic en este icono.
(In order to connect to the Internet, you should click on this icon.)

All of these instructions use the *tú* form for teaching a friend or child. Just change the verbs to the *usted* or *ustedes* form to address someone you don't know well or a group.

FACT

Many computer and business terms in Spanish are taken directly from English. Some are translated directly; some are used in English. Usage may vary widely from country to country. For example, the word "computer" in Latin America is *computadora*. In Spain, however, the word is *ordenador*.

You've Got Mail

Think for a minute about all the ways you get mail these days: e-mail, surface mail, inter-office correspondence, courier. You use your computer, mail boxes, the post office, and other delivery services. You get letters, promotional materials, notices, memos, and packages. Let's start with some basic mail vocabulary in Spanish and then some of the ways you send and receive mail.

Mail Terminology
- *el correo* (**mail**)
- *el correo electrónico, el email* (**e-mail**)
- *la carta* (**letter**)
- *el sobre* (**envelope**)
- *la tarjeta postal* (**postcard**)
- *el sello, la estampilla, el timbre* (**postage stamp**)
- *el paquete* (**package**)
- *el franqueo* (**postage**)
- *el correos* (**post office**)
- *mandar* (**send**)
- *asegurar, seguro* (**insure, insurance**)
- *recoger* (**pick up**)

E-mail

Let's start with e-mail. There is some specialized vocabulary associated with e-mail for you to learn in Spanish, so let's go through your morning mail together and see what you do.

TRACK 48

Managing E-mail

Listen to each example on Track 48 as you follow along in the text. Repeat each statement after you hear it.

Bajo mi correo electrónico cada mañana.
(**I download my e-mail every morning.**)
Primero, elimino los mensajes que no me interesan.
(**First, I delete the messages that don't interest me.**)
Entonces, abro y leo los mensajes importantes.
(**Next, I open and read the important messages.**)

A veces adelanto un mensaje a mis amigos o colegas.
(Sometimes I forward a message to my friends or colleagues.)
Guardo y archivo los mensajes que quiero ver otra vez.
(I save and file the messages that I want to see again.)
Respondo a los correos que lo requieren.
(I respond to the e-mails that require it.)
Escribo y mando muchos correos electrónicos cada día.
(I write and send many e-mails every day.)

Some of the key verbs for talking about e-mail are *eliminar* (delete), *abrir* (open), *adelantar* (forward), *guardar* (save), *archivar* (file), *responder* (respond), and *mandar* (send). You've learned some of them before in other contexts, and some are cognates, so you won't have much trouble remembering them.

Surface Mail

Even though a lot of our communication nowadays is handled electronically, there is just no substitute for surface mail. Let's look at some of the things you might say regarding mail while you're on a business trip in Chile.

¿Hay correo para mí hoy?
(Is there mail for me today?)
Necesito mandar unas cartas y un paquete; ¿dónde está el correos? **(I need to mail some letters and a package; where is the post office?)**
¿Dónde puedo comprar tarjetas postales?
(Where can I buy postcards?)
¿Cuánto cuestan los sellos para Estados Unidos?
(How much do stamps for the United States cost?)
¿Cuánto es el franqueo para este paquete? ¿Y con seguro?
(How much is the postage for this package? And with insurance?)

That should help you take care of most of your surface mail needs while you're traveling. Don't forget your address book!

Business Correspondence Formulas

Do you ever have to correspond with colleagues in Spanish? You probably have no trouble with day-to-day sorts of information now, but you may find yourself stumped as to how to phrase such things as greetings and closings. Do you address a business associate as "Dear"? You certainly don't want to sign off with "hugs and kisses." And what about some handy transitional phrases for everything in between? Here are some common formulas you can use in business letters and e-mails.

Greetings
- *Estimado/a señor/a . . .* (**Esteemed Mr./Ms . . .**)
- *Estimados señores/as* (**Esteemed Sirs/Madams**)
- *Señores/señoras* (**Gentlemen/ladies**)
- *[Estimados] Colegas* (**[Esteemed] Colleagues**)

Transitional Phrases
- *respecto a . . .* (**regarding . . .**)
- *en vista de . . .* (**in light of . . .**)
- *a pesar de . . .* (**in spite of . . .**)
- *gracias a . . .* (**thanks to . . .**)
- *además* (**additionally, furthermore**)
- *sin embargo* (**nevertheless**)
- *por un lado* (**on one hand**)
- *por el otro lado* (**on the other hand**)

Closings
- *Cordialmente* (**Cordially**)
- *Sinceramente* (**Sincerely**)
- *Atentamente* (**Attentively**)
- *Respetuosamente* (**Respectfully**)

Remember that these expressions are equivalents, not exact translations, of formulas used in English. For example, the expression *estimado* and its variants sound very formal in English, but the translation of "dear" would be completely inappropriate in Spanish business communication.

Though you can begin a formal letter in English with "Dear," and we talk about this "on the one hand" and that "on the other hand," don't try to do the same thing in Spanish! You'll be happy to see, though, that the closings used in formal Spanish correspondence are very similar to expressions used in English. Add the word *muy* in front of the Spanish expressions for greater formality: *Muy atentamente* (Very attentively). Use a comma or a colon after business greetings in Spanish, and a comma after the closing, as in English.

Phone Etiquette

Sometimes an e-mail or letter just isn't quick enough or personal enough to handle a situation. Sometimes you have to make a call. Certain elements of phone conversation are as formulaic as written communication: greetings, asking who is calling, asking what the call is regarding, and asking about leaving a message, for example. Take a minute to think about how you phrase these things in English, and then take a look at how it's done in Spanish.

FACT

Mobil or cell phones are extremely common in Latin America and Spain. Service is reliable and often comparatively inexpensive. The most common terms for mobile phones are *el celular* and *el móvil*. If you need a new battery, ask for *una pila* or *una batería*.

Business phone etiquette usually stipulates that phones are answered with the name of the company, the identity of the speaker, and a general greeting ranging from "good morning" or something similar to any number of formulaic phone greetings. When you answer your phone at home, however, you probably only say "hello." Phone greetings vary from country to country, and include expressions like *bueno, sí, aló,* and *diga* or *dígame.* It is not especially common to answer the phone in Spanish with *hola,* though it would be an acceptable informal greeting. The next step when you call is to ask for the person you wish to speak to. The most common way to do so in Spanish is with a question like *¿Está la señora Alba, por favor?* (Is Mrs. Alba there, please?) If you are calling for Mrs. Alba at a place of business, it is likely that you will be asked *¿De parte de quién?* (Who is calling?), to which you would respond with your name and, if appropriate, your company affiliation. Review the following phrases and then practice making a phone call in Spanish.

Greetings
- *Bueno*
- *Aló*
- *Sí*
- *Diga, Dígame*

Speakers
- *¿De parte de quién?   ¿Quién [lo/la] llama?*
  (Who is calling [him/her]?)
- *Con quién hablo?*
  (With whom am I speaking?)
- *¿Quién habla?*
  (Who is speaking?)

Messages
- *¿Quiere dejar un recado/mensaje?*
  (Would you like to leave a message?)
- *¿Puedo dejarle un recado/mensaje?*
  (Can I leave him/her a message?)
- *¿Puedo darle un recado/mensaje?*
- **(Can I give him/her a message?)**
- *Dígale, por favor, que me llame de vuelta.*
  (Please ask him/her to call me back.)

Finishing a phone call is very similar in Spanish and English. You can simply thank the person and say good day or goodbye. You might include one of the following phrases to be extra polite: *Muy amable* (You've been very kind) or *Gracias por su ayuda* (Thank you for your help).

Chapter 12

Conditional and Commands

Where in the Spanish-speaking world would you like to go? Taking your Spanish on the road is one of the most exciting and rewarding ways to practice. In this chapter you'll learn how to use the conditional to state preferences and manage travel surprises, as well as how to give advice and get things done using command forms. So let's make some travel plans!

State Preferences Using the Conditional

Where would you like to go? What would you do there? Who would you prefer to travel with? How long would you stay? English uses the auxiliary verb "would" in front of the main verb to make statements in the conditional. Spanish uses the conditional tense. Remember how the future tense was formed in Spanish by simply adding endings to the infinitive? The conditional is formed exactly the same way—only the endings are different.

The Conditional Tense

Subject Pronoun	visitar	ver	ir
yo	visitaría	vería	iría
tú	visitarías	verías	irías
él, ella, usted	visitaría	vería	iría
nosotros	visitaríamos	veríamos	iríamos
vosotros	visitaríais	veríais	iríais
ellos, ellas, ustedes	visitarían	verían	irían

Notice that the conditional endings are identical for –ar, –er, and –ir verbs, and all the conditional endings have an accent over the stressed *i*. And, would you believe it? All the verbs that have stem changes in the future have the same changes in the conditional.

Stem Changes in the Conditional
- *hacer: haría, harías, haría, haríamos, haríais, harían*
- *decir: diría, dirías, diría, diríamos, diríais, dirían*
- *poder: podría, podrías*
- *saber: sabría, sabríamos*
- *querer: querríais, querrían*
- *poner: pondría, pondrías*
- *venir: vendría, vendríamos*
- *tener: tendríais*
- *salir: saldrían*

The conditional can be used in two-verb combinations or as a stand-alone conjugation. It generally implies a hypothetical situation whether or not an actual hypothesis is stated. Let's look a bit more closely at these two ways of using the conditional.

ALERT!

All the conditional endings are based on combinations of *ía*, even for −*er* and −*ir* verbs. There is only one set of endings to learn for all three verb categories!

Conditional Verb + Infinitive

The conditional is often used with verbs like *gustar, preferir,* and *optar por* in verb + infinitive combinations to express preferences.

TRACK 49

Conditional

Listen to each example on Track 49 as you follow along in the text. Repeat each statement after you hear it.

Me gustaría mucho visitar los castillos de España.
(I would very much like to visit the castles of Spain.)
Mi esposo preferiría viajar por Sudamérica.
(My husband would prefer to travel through South America.)
Creo que tú optarías por explorar las islas del Caribe, ¿verdad?
(I think you would choose to explore the Caribbean islands, wouldn't you?)

The verb *querer* presents a special case in this context. Rather than using the conditional form *querría* + infinitive to say what you would like to do, use the imperfect subjunctive: *Quisiera pasar una semana en la playa de Huatulco* (I'd like to spend a week on the beach at Huatulco). In fact, *me gustaría* and *quisiera* are essentially synonymous in this sort of statement. The difference between the two expressions is so minimal that they can be used interchangeably.

Remember that, in Spanish, when two verbs go walking, the first one does the talking. In other words, the first verb is conjugated and the second remains in the infinitive, present, or past participle form: *Te gustaría hablar; estás hablando; has hablado.*

Other verbs commonly used in the conditional with infinitives are *poder* and *saber* to express what you would be able to do and what you would know how to do in certain circumstances. All the impersonal expressions and verbs of obligation that you have learned can also be used in the conditional with infinitives. Look at the following examples to see how flexible this structure is:

Tú y yo podríamos salir para Lima el sábado.
(You and I could leave for Lima on Saturday.)
Ellos no sabrían escoger un destino.
(They wouldn't know how to choose a destination.)
Sería una buena idea buscar descuentos en los hoteles.
(It would be a good idea to look for discounts on hotels.)
Yo tendría que pedir vacaciones inmediatamente.
(I would have to ask for vacation immediately.)
Habría que comparar las tarifas de las aerolíneas.
(The airline rates would have to be compared.)
Tu hermano debería ayudarte.
(Your brother should help you.)*

*Notice that *deber* doesn't appear to change meaning in the conditional tense. The English translation is "should" whether *deber* is conjugated in the present tense or conditional. However, the tone shifts in Spanish. The statement is gentler when *deber* is used in the conditional rather than the present tense. There may also be an implication that the obligation is hypothetical. English has no equivalent variation for "should."

The Conditional as Hypothesis

You can also conjugate stand-alone verbs in the conditional to make hypothetical statements expressing what someone would do in given circumstances. For example, *Con tres semanas de vacaciones, yo iría al Perú* (With three weeks of vacation, I would go to Peru); *¿Qué harías tú con tanto tiempo?* (What would you do with so much time?); *Para mí, las mejores vacaciones serían no hacer nada* (For me the best vacation would be to do nothing).

The word for "vacation" in Spanish is plural, *vacaciones*, and any verbs associated with the word should be conjugated in the plural. If this strikes you as odd, remember that English has the equivalent plural "holidays" which, though uncommon in the United States, is used in many English-speaking countries.

Would you rather go to the mountains or the beach, the desert or the plains? Make your list and then see if any of your ideal locations appear in the following list.

- *las montañas* **(the mountains)**
- *la costa* **(the coast)**
- *la playa* **(the beach)**
- *el desierto* **(the desert)**
- *el llano* **(the plain)**
- *el lago* **(the lake)**
- *el río* **(the river)**
- *el bosque* **(the forest)**
- *la selva* **(the jungle)**
- *el campo* **(the countryside)**
- *el parque nacional* **(the national park)**
- *el norte* **(the north)**

- *el sur* (**the south**)
- *el este* (**the east**)
- *el oeste* (**the west**)

Practice: The Conditional

Now answer the following questions to practice the conditional. You can find a translation of each question as well as a sample answer in Appendix D.

1. *¿Adónde te gustaría ir de vacaciones?*
2. *¿Por qué preferirías ir allí?*
3. *¿Con quién viajarías?*
4. *¿Qué tendrían que hacer en preparación para el viaje?*
5. *¿Qué podrían hacer allí que no pueden hacer aquí?*
6. *¿Cuánto tiempo pasarían allí?*
7. *¿Sacarías muchas fotos o no llevarías una cámara?*
8. *¿Cúanto costaría el viaje?*

Schedules, Reservations, and Rentals

So, you've made up your mind where you would like to go. Now you have to decide how to get there and how to travel around once you're there. Understanding schedules, making reservations, buying tickets, managing car rentals, and handling surprises on the road will serve you well as you plan your trip. Let's look at some general vocabulary first:

Vehicles
- *el avión* (**plane**)
- *el tren* (**train**)
- *el metro* (**metro, subway**)
- *el autobús* (**bus**)
- *la camioneta* (**van**)
- *el carro* (**car**)
- *el tranvía* (**tram**)

- *el barco* (**boat**)
- *el ferry* (**ferry**)

Odds and Ends
- *el horario* (**schedule**)
- *la reservación* (**reservation**)
- *el boleto* (**ticket**)
- *el asiento* (**seat**)
- *el pasillo* (**aisle**)
- *la ventanilla* (**window**)
- *la llegada* (**arrival**)
- *la salida* (**departure**)
- *la puerta* (**gate**)
- *el aeropuerto* (**airport**)
- *la estación* (**train station**)
- *la terminal* (**bus station, ferry terminal**)
- *el andén* (**train, bus platform**)
- *el vagón* (**train car**)
- *el cochecama* (**sleeper car**)
- *a tiempo* (**on time**)
- *adelantado/a* (**ahead of schedule**)
- *atrasado* (**behind schedule**)

Verbs
- *hacer una reservación* (**make a reservation**)
- *cambiar* (**change**)
- *cancelar* (**cancel**)
- *subir* (**get on, in**)
- *bajar* (**get off, out**)
- *avisar* (**notify**)
- *trasbordar* (**transfer**)
- *alquilar* (**rent**)
- *entregar, devolver* (**turn in, return**)

It's important to keep in mind that some of this vocabulary may be different from one country to another. For example, a "bus" can be called *autobús, camión, colectivo,* or *gua-gua,* depending on the country you're in. You might go to rent a *carro* and discover that it's called a *coche* or *auto* where you are. Most terms are fairly universally understood, though, even if local usage varies, and you'll quickly learn which words are preferred wherever you happen to be.

FACT

Most Spanish-speaking countries use a 24-hour clock for official schedules. 12:00 is twelve noon; 24:00 is midnight. 1:00 is one o'clock in the morning. If your train leaves at 14:07, it leaves at 2:07 P.M.

A Change of Plans: Managing Travel Surprises

You've got your plane tickets, made train reservations, and you're going to rent a car for short excursions. What if your plane arrives late and you miss your train, your train reservations have mysteriously been cancelled, or your preferred rental car isn't available? Experienced travelers know that even the best-laid plans sometimes go awry. The best solution is usually to simply adapt to the changing circumstances. Let's look at a few problems and potential solutions.

TRACK 50

Managing Travel Surprises

Listen to each example on Track 50 as you follow along in the text. Repeat each after you hear it.

Late plane, missed train: *Mi avión llegó retrasado y perdí el tren. ¿Cuándo sale el próximo tren a León?*
(My plane arrived late and I missed the train. When does the next train to Leon leave?)

Reservation change: *¿Me hace el favor de cambiar la reservación?*
(Will you do me the favor of changing the reservation?)

Hotel: *Necesito encontrar un hotel económico para esta noche. ¿Podría recomendar uno?*
(I have to find a reasonably priced hotel for tonight. Could you recommend one?)

Cancel reservation: *Tengo que cancelar unas reservaciones. ¿Dónde hay un teléfono público o una agencia de viajes?*
(I have to cancel some reservations. Where is there a public telephone or a travel agency?)

Wrong model car: *Éste no es el modelo que yo reservé. ¿Hay otro similar al mismo precio?*
(This isn't the model I reserved. Is there a similar one for the same price?)

Extend hotel stay: *Quisiera quedarme dos noches más o ¿puede usted recomendar otro hotel?*
(I would like to stay two nights longer or can you recommend another hotel?)

Problem, request help: *Tengo un problema ¿Podría usted ayudarme?*
(I have a problem. Could you help me?)

Review Automobile Vocabulary

If you plan to rent a car on your trip, take the time to review automobile basics in Spanish and learn how to explain simple problems that may arise like a flat tire (*una llanta pinchada*), a broken belt (*un cinturón roto*), or an empty gas tank (*se me acabó la gasolina*). Ask someone to direct or take you to the nearest garage: *¿Por favor, puede decirme dónde está el garaje más cercano?* or *¿Por favor, puede llevarme a un garaje?* You might find it helpful to keep a copy of the automobile page from a picture dictionary handy as well as a list of useful phrases in the event of car trouble on the road.

Affirmative Commands

You've learned lots of strategies for making polite requests, but sometimes the simplest and most direct approach to getting something done is a command form. Tell someone in no uncertain terms what to do without beating around the bush. Keep in mind that commands can always be softened by simply adding *por favor* and using a polite rather than a demanding tone of voice. Let's divide command forms into three groups: *tú*, *usted* and *ustedes*, and *vosotros* because they are formed differently. Then we'll have a look at the small number of irregular command forms.

Affirmative *tú* commands are very simple. They look just like the third-person singular of the simple present tense.

Regular Affirmative *Tú* Commands

Visitar	Ver	Subir
visita	ve	sube

That's all there is to it! To tell a friend to visit a particular place, see something special, and to go up somewhere, you would say:

Regular Affirmative *Tu* Commands

Read aloud each of the following examples.

Visita el parque nacional.
(Visit the national park.)
Ve la exposición en el Centro de Visitantes.
(See the exhibit in the Visitors' Center)
Sube la montaña en tranvía.
(Go up the mountain in the tram.)

The *usted* and *ustedes* commands are based on the *yo* form of the simple present. Most of the irregular changes occur in this form, so they are incorporated into the commands. Remove the final –*o* from the *yo* conjugation and add the appropriate command ending as outlined in the following chart:

Regular Affirmative *Usted* and *Ustedes* Commands

Subject Pronoun	*Visitar > –e,–en*	*Ver > –a, –an*
usted	visite	vea
ustedes	visiten	vean

The *vosotros* commands are based on the infinitive. Just delete the final –*r* and add –*d*.

Regular Affirmative *Vosotros* Commands

Visitar	*Ver*	*Subir*
visitad	ved	subid

You can make *nosotros* commands by using *vamos a* + infinitive. To say "Let's take the train," for example, you would say: *Vamos a tomar el tren.* The context will make it clear whether you are talking about the future or making a suggestion.

Affirmative Commands with Reflexive Verbs

When you make a *tú, usted,* or *ustedes* command with a reflexive verb, you attach the reflexive pronoun to the end of the command, making one word. When you do this, you generally have to add an accent mark to the vowel of the stressed syllable because you have changed the syllable count. The affirmative *vosotros* commands with reflexive verbs drop the –*d* of the command form when you add the pronoun –*os*. You will usually have to add an accent to the *vosotros* command forms as well. Look at these examples:

levántate (tú)	*levántese (usted)*	*levántense (ustedes)*	*levantáos (vosotros)*
vístete (tú)	*vístase (usted)*	*vístanse (ustedes)*	*vestíos (vosotros)*

FACT

You can use subject pronouns or not with command forms. For example you can say *¡Levántate!* or *¡Levántate tú!* The command that includes the subject pronoun is a bit more emphatic, especially in the case of a reflexive verb.

Remember that command forms can be a bit abrupt in Spanish, so you might want to add *por favor* to commands to make them more polite: *Vístete, por favor* (Please get dressed).

Irregular Affirmative Commands

There are a number of irregular affirmative *tú* commands. For the most part, they are simply truncated forms of the infinitive, generally the first syllable. Look at the following list:

- *poner: pon*
- *salir: sal*
- *tener: ten*
- *venir: ven*
- *hacer: haz*
- *decir: di*
- *ir: ve*
- *ser: sé**

*The *tú* command *sé* has an accent to differentiate it from its homonym *se*, which you've seen in impersonal expressions and as a reflexive pronoun.

There are only three verbs with irregular *usted* and *ustedes* commands: *ir, ser,* and *saber.*

- *ir: vaya, vayan*
- *ser: sea, sean*
- *saber: sepa, sepan*

Verbs that end in *–car, –gar, –zar,* and *–ger* will have slight spelling changes in the *usted* and *ustedes* commands. These changes are to preserve the proper pronunciation of the word. Look over the following examples:

- *sacar: saque, saquen*
- *pagar: pague, paguen*
- *comenzar: comience, comiencen*
- *recoger: recoja, recojan*

TRACK 51

Affirmative *Usted* and *Ustedes* Commands

You might use these commands in a travel context, like the following examples. Listen to each example on Track 51 and repeat.

Saquen ustedes los boletos varios días antes de viajar.
(Get the tickets several days before traveling.)
Pague con tarjeta de crédito o en efectivo.
(Pay by credit card or with cash.)
Comience a prestar más atención al entrar al bosque.
(Start to pay more attention when you enter the forest.)
Recojan sus maletas en la terminal.
(Pick up your suitcases in the terminal.)

Practice: Affirmative Commands

You're ready to start telling people what to do now! Complete each command with the form indicated of the verb in parenthesis. Then check your answers in Appendix D.

1. *Para tener más flexibilidad, _____ (alquilar, tú) un coche.*
2. *_____ (sentarse, usted) al lado de la ventanilla para ver el paisaje.*
3. *Si quieren una experiencia inolvidable, _____ (hacer, ustedes) un viaje en barco por el río Amazonas.*
4. *Por favor, _____ (cambiar, vosotros) de asiento.*
5. *_____ (explicar, usted) qué pasó, señora.*

Use the vocabulary you've learned in this lesson and continue practicing commands by making up sentences to tell your friends what to do regarding their travel plans.

Negative Commands

You can probably think of lots of things to tell people not to do as they plan a trip too. You do this in English by simply putting the word "don't" in front of the command. The negative *usted* and *ustedes* commands in Spanish are just as easy. Just put *no* in front of the verb, for example, *No entregue el coche tarde o tendrá que pagar un día más* (Don't return the car late or you'll have to pay for another day). In the case of reflexive verbs, put the reflexive pronoun in between *no* and the command: *No se olviden de hacer las reservaciones* (Don't forget to make the reservations).

ALERT!

Pronouns are attached to the affirmative commands in Spanish, but they are placed between *no* and the verb for negative commands: *Levántense a tiempo; no se levanten tarde o perderán el tren.*

Things are a little more complicated for negative *tú* and *vosotros* commands because the negative command takes a different verb form altogether. Negative *tú* commands look just like affirmative *usted* commands but they end in *–s*. For example, *¡No te quedes en hoteles caros!* (Don't stay in expensive hotels!). As you remember, the *usted* command is formed by removing the final *–o* of the *yo* form of the simple present tense and adding

–e or *–a*. The negative *tú* commands end in *–es* or *–as*. Let's take a moment to summarize:

Negative *Tu, Usted* and *Ustedes* Commands of Regular Verbs

Subject Pronoun	*Visitar*	*Ver*	*Subir*
tú	*No visites.*	*No veas.*	*No subas.*
usted	*No visite.*	*No vea.*	*No suba.*
ustedes	*No visiten.*	*No vean.*	*No suban.*

The negative *tú* command for the irregular verbs *ir, ser,* and *saber* also looks just like the *usted* command with an *–s*:

No vayas al bosque solo. **(Don't go to the forest alone.)**
No seas tímido. **(Don't be shy.)**
No sepas nada.* **(Don't know anything.)**

*It's very unusual to tell someone not to know something, so it is unlikely you will use this command often.

The *usted* command form is also the basis for the negative *tú* command for the verbs that are irregular in the affirmative. Just add *–s* to the end. These verbs are only irregular in the affirmative *tú* command. Let's review:

- *poner: no ponga (usted); no pongas (tú)*
- *salir: no salga (usted); no salgas (tú)*
- *tener: no tenga (usted); no tengas (tú)*
- *venir: no venga (usted); no vengas (tú)*
- *hacer: no haga (usted); no hagas (tú)*
- *decir: no diga (usted); no digas (tú)*

Likewise, the verbs that have slight spelling changes in the *usted* and *ustedes* commands have the same spelling changes in the negative *tú* command form:

No saques tu dinero en el autobús.
(Don't take out your money on the bus.)
No pagues antes de ver el horario.
(Don't pay before seeing the schedule.)
No comiences a preparar las maletas hasta hacer la reservación.
(Don't start packing your suitcases until you make the reservation.)
No recojas la maleta de otra persona por descuido.
(Don't pick up someone else's suitcase by mistake.)

And *vosotros*? Well, *no perdáis la paciencia*, the negative *vosotros* commands have a few more steps! Start with the *yo* form of the simple present just like you did for the *usted* and *ustedes* commands. Drop the final *–o*. Then add *–éis* or *–áis*.

No visitéis todos los museos.
(Don't visit all the museums.)
No veáis todas las iglesias.
(Don't see all the churches.)
No subáis a las montañas.
(Don't go up the mountains.)
No vayáis al aeropuerto en metro.
Don't go to the airport by metro.)

Negative Commands

TRACK 52

Listen to each statement or question on Track 52 and respond with an appropriate negative command. (The text is not shown here because this is meant to be a more challenging exercise.) If you'd like extra practice, make alternate suggestions using affirmative commands. For example, you may hear something like this: *Voy a hacer una reservación para mañana.* And you may answer with something like this: *No hagas una reservación para mañana. Haz una reservación para el viernes.* You can find the questions and sample answers written out in Appendix D.

Chapter 13

Direct Object Pronouns

There are many types of lodging avail-able in the Spanish-speaking world, from hotels and luxury resorts to sim-ple *pensiones* and campgrounds. You may even consider renting a home-away-from-home. In this chapter, you'll learn to make reservations, request ser-vices and advice, and manage minor inconveniences whatever your lodging preferences.

Check In and Check Out: Hotel Reservations

Checking into a hotel for which you have reservations is very similar to checking into a hotel anywhere in the world: identify yourself, provide a credit card, sign some paperwork, and request the number of keys that you need. As an international traveler, you may be asked to show your passport as well. On the other hand, if you have arrived without reserved lodging, finding a comfortable place to stay may involve extra steps. You might want to compare two or more options, for example, so you'll have to check availability, request room rates, ask to see a room, and find out about any other special services you may require like Internet availability. It may take a bit of time, but you'll probably be much happier in lodging that suits your needs and budget. Take a minute to jot down a list of questions you would ask and then compare your ideas to the following examples.

TRACK 53

Hotel Reservations

Listen to each example on Track 53 as you follow along in the text. Repeat each question after you hear it.

¿Hay una habitación disponible para esta noche?
(Is there a room available for tonight?)
¿Cuánto es?
(How much is it?)
¿Incluye el desayuno?
(Is breakfast included?)
¿Hay otra tarifa si me quedo varias noches?
(Is there another rate if I stay several nights?)
¿Puede mostrarme la habitación?
(Can you show me the room?)
¿Hay acceso al Internet en el hotel?
(Is there Internet access in the hotel?)
¿Hay ascensor, agua caliente, calefacción, aire acondicionado?
(Is there an elevator, hot water, heat, air conditioning?)

You may wish to ask about some additional room features, for example, a room with a view or a quieter room. Let's look at some of the possibilities:

¿Hay una habitación/baño. . . ? **(Is there a room/bath . . . ?)**
con vista de la plaza **(with a view of the square)**
que dé al jardín **(that looks out on the garden)**
que no dé a la calle **(that doesn't overlook the street)**
más grande **(larger)**
más tranquila/menos ruidosa **(quieter/less noisy)**
con una cama doble **(with a double bed)**
con dos camas **(with two beds)**
con ducha/bañera **(with a shower/bathtub)**

FACT

In some places, it's very unusual to locate any nonsmoking rooms in the Spanish-speaking world. You can ask, *¿Hay habitaciones para no fumadores?*, but don't be surprised if the answer is *no*.

Let's look at a conversation between a hotel reception clerk in Guadalajara, Mexico, and a potential guest. As you read through the dialog, think about what you might have said in the same circumstances.

Clerk: *Buenas tardes. ¿En qué puedo servirle?* (Good afternoon. How can I help you?)
Guest: *Buenas tardes. Necesito una habitación para esta noche. ¿Hay algo disponible?* (Good afternoon. I need a room for tonight. Is there anything available?)
Clerk: *Sí, tenemos varias habitaciones disponibles esta noche.* (Yes, we have several rooms available tonight.)
Guest: *¿Cúanto cuestan?* (How much do they cost?)
Clerk: *Una habitación sencilla cuesta cuatrocientos cincuenta pesos.* (A single room costs four hundred and fifty pesos.)
Guest: *¿Incluye el desayuno?* (Is breakfast included?)

Clerk:	*Sí, incluye un desayuno continental.* (Yes, it includes a continental breakfast.)
Guest:	*¿Aceptan tarjeta de crédito?* (Do you take credit cards?)
Clerk:	*Sí, aceptamos todas las tarjetas principales.* (Yes, we accept all major cards.)
Guest:	*Muy bien. Me quedo esta noche.* (Good. I'll stay tonight.)
Clerk:	*¿Me hace el favor de rellenar esta hoja, por favor?* (Will you do me the favor of filling out this form please?)
Guest:	*Cómo no.* (Of course)
Clerk:	*¿Me permite su tarjeta de crédito un momento, por favor?* (Will you let me have your credit card for a moment, please?)
Guest:	*Aquí la tiene.* (Here you are.)
Clerk:	*Firme aquí, por favor. Y aquí tiene su llave.* (Sign here, please. And here is your key.)
Guest:	*¿Por dónde queda la habitación?* (Which way is the room?)
Clerk:	*El ascensor está a la derecha y su habitación está en el tercer piso, saliendo a mano izquierda.* (The elevator is to the right and your room is on the third floor, to the left as you leave the elevator.)
Guest:	*Muchas gracias.* (Thank you very much.)
Clerk:	*A sus órdenes.* (At your service.)

Hotel Categories

Hotel ratings are based on a scale of one to five stars. The most elegant hotels have five stars, *hoteles de cinco estrellas*, and would include such amenities as a spa and salon, pool, exercise room, business center, and one or more fine restaurants. In general, the fewer the stars, the fewer the amenities, but don't discount the potential of lodging with only one or two stars or no stars at all. You may be perfectly comfortable in a family-run hotel (*hotel familiar*) or *pension*, which are often unrated. If you find a place online, it's easy enough to get an idea of whether or not it will suit your needs by looking at its Web site. Otherwise, a simple e-mail or phone call should get you answers to your questions.

Direct Object Pronouns

A pronoun takes the place of a noun or noun phrase. They help you avoid repeating the same information again and again in a conversation. For example, once you have asked if a room is available, you might ask to see it. The pronoun "it" replaces the word "room."

> *¿Hay una habitación disponible?*
> *¿Puedo verla?*

Direct objects are the people, places, or things that are immediately influenced by the verb. They often answer the questions, "who" or "what." In the case of the example, *una habitación* is the noun directly influenced by the verb *ver*, answering the question, "What can I see?"

Look at the following chart of direct object pronouns in Spanish and English.

Direct Object Pronouns

English: I see...	Spanish: *Yo veo* ...
me, myself	*me*
you (*tú*)	*te*
he, she, you (*usted*)	*lo, la*
us	*nos*
you (*vosotros*)	*os*
they, you (*ustedes*)	*los, las*

You probably noticed that the pronouns *me, te, nos,* and *os* look just like the reflexive pronouns. The only pronouns that are different are the third-person singular and plural. It's also important to notice that these pronouns are gender and number specific unlike the English pronouns "it" and "they." Let's look at a few examples of direct object pronouns in action.

¿Me permite su tarjeta de crédito, por favor?
(May I have your credit card, please?)
Cómo no. Aquí la tiene.
(Certainly. Here it is.)
Llene este formulario, por favor.
(Fill out this form, please.)
Puede entregarlo más tarde.
(You can turn it in later.)
¿Me da dos llaves, por favor?
(Will you give me two keys, please?)
Con mucho gusto. Aquí las tiene.
(With pleasure. Here they are.)

Object pronouns, like reflexive pronouns, should be placed in front of a conjugated verb or attached to an infinitive or present participle. If a sentence presents both options, you can choose either one. There is no preference for one placement over the other. Remember that, in the case of affirmative commands, however, any object or reflexive pronoun must be attached to the command.

Tenemos dos habitaciones muy bonitas. ¿Quiere verlas?
(We have two very pretty rooms. Would you like to see them?)
Tenemos dos habitaciones muy bonitas. ¿Las quiere ver?
No podemos ver ésta; la camarera está limpiándola.
(We can't see this one; the maid is cleaning it.)
¿Sus maletas? Déjelas allí con el botones.
(Your suitcases? Leave them there with the bellhop.)

There is no preference for attaching pronouns to the infinitive or present participle or putting them in front of the conjugated verb. It really has more to do with the speed at which a person tends to speak. Fast speakers often prefer to attach pronouns and slower speakers are more likely to leave them detached.

Practice: Direct Object Pronouns

Let's practice using direct object pronouns. Complete each statement with a direct object pronoun in place of the direct object that is highlighted for you. Then check your answers in Appendix D.

1. *No tenemos reservaciones todavía. Debemos hacer _____ hoy mismo.*
2. *El gerente del hotel es el tío de Margarita. ¿ _____ quieres llamar?*
3. *Hay una revista con información turística. Revísa _____ para saber adónde debemos ir.*
4. *¿Hablas a mí? Sí, _____ hablo.*
5. *Esa señora miró de una manera rara a nosotros. Está mirándo _____ otra vez.*

Direct object pronouns, like reflexive pronouns, are placed either in front of a conjugated verb or attached to the infinitive or present participle, but never in between a two-verb construction. They are always attached to affirmative commands.

Requesting Changes

Sometimes, no matter how nice the hotel, you might need to request a room change. Keeping in mind that hotels want to keep their guests happy, you shouldn't be too intimidated to request a change. Besides, it's an opportunity to practice all those polite request forms you've learned. You can soften your request even further with a nice greeting and an expression like *disculpe* or *perdone* (excuse me). Then just identify the problem and politely ask for a different room. Have a look at this conversation:

Guest: *Buenas tardes. Disculpe; estoy en la habitación 302 y hay un pequeño inconveniente.* (Good afternoon. Excuse me; I'm in room 302 and there is a small problem.)

Clerk: *Dígame, por favor.* (Tell me about it, please.)

Guest: *La habitación está muy cerca de los ascensores y hay bastante ruido.* (The room is very near the elevators and there is quite a bit of noise.)

Clerk: *¿Quiere cambiar de habitación?* (Would you like to change rooms?)

Guest: *Si es posible, gracias. ¿Hay una habitación que dé al jardín? Hay mucho ruido de la calle también.* (If possible, thank you. Is there a room that overlooks the garden? There is a lot of street noise too.)

Clerk: *Lo siento, no hay. Pero tengo una que da a la alberca y la alberca cierra a las once.* (I'm sorry, there isn't. But I have one that overlooks the pool and the pool closes at eleven.)

Guest: *Bueno, está bien.* (Okay, that's fine.)

Clerk: *Muy bien. Llámeme cuando esté listo y le mandaré un botones para acompañarlo a la nueva habitación.* (Good. Call me when you're ready and I'll send a bellhop to take you to the new room.)

Guest: *Muy amable, gracias. Estaré listo en media hora.* (Very kind, thank you. I'll be ready in half an hour.)

Requesting Changes

TRACK 54

Now you try requesting a room change. Your room is very small and you'd like a larger one. You would prefer that it overlook the street because you like the view. Listen to the receptionist's comments first. Then listen again and respond appropriately to each. (The text is not shown here because this is meant to be a more challenging exercise.) You can find a model dialog in Appendix D.

Room Service and Housekeeping

Have you got a case of the nibbles? Do you need an extra blanket, fresh towels, or another bar of soap? It's easy to ask for these services in Spanish. Let's start with some helpful phrases and vocabulary.

Room Service

- *Quisiera ordenar/pedir . . .*
  (I'd like to order . . .)
- *¿Qué lleva . . . ?*
  (What does . . . have on it?)
- *¿Me lo puede preparar con/sin . . . ?* **(Can you make it for me with/without . . . ?)**
- *¿Cuánto tardará?*
  (How long will it take?)

Housekeeping

- *una almohada*
  (a pillow)
- *una manta/cobija*
  (a blanket)
- *unas toallas limpias*
  (clean towels)
- *una bata*
  (a robe)
- *un jabón*
  (a bar of soap)
- *papel higiénico*
  (toilet paper)

- *un secador de pelo*
  (a hair dryer)
- *un cepillo de dientes*
  (a toothbrush)
- *una máquina de afeitar*
  (a razor)
- *un peine*
  (a comb)
- *una tabla de planchar*
  (an ironing board)
- *una plancha*
  (an iron)

The verbs you are most likely to use in these contexts are *traer* (to bring), *dar* (to give), and *dejar* (to leave). When you make a special request, it is generally more appropriate to use the polite phrases you have learned rather than command forms.

Housekeeping and Room Service

Listen to each request on Track 55 as you follow along in the text. Repeat each example after you hear it.

¿Puede dejarme dos toallas más, por favor?
(Can you leave me two more towels, please?)
¿Me hace el favor de traerme otro jabón, por favor?
(Will you do me the favor of bringing me another bar of soap, please?)
Quisiera pedir un sándwich de jamón y queso. ¿Puede decirme qué más lleva?
(I'd like to order a ham and cheese sandwich. Can you tell me what else it comes with?)
¿Me lo puede preparar con mostaza, por favor?
(Can you make it for me with mustard, please?)
¿Me da otra manta, por favor?
(Will you give me another blanket, please?)

You will normally find hotel staff happy to fulfill your requests, especially if you ask politely and are patient about response time. It's pointless and often counterproductive to lose your temper, but a smile and *por favor* will go far in getting you what you want.

Place Your Order

Look at the following excerpt from a room service menu, and then play the audio to practice requesting food and beverage.

Antojitos (Appetizers)
Cóctel de camarones (Shrimp cocktail)
Plato de quesos y galletas (Cheese and cracker plate)
Gazpacho (Gazpacho)
Platos ligeros (Light dishes)
Sándwich de jamón y queso (Ham and cheese sandwich)

Omelette con tomate y pimiento (**Tomato and pepper omelette**)	
Ensalada del chef con aderezo especial (**Chef salad with special dressing**)	
***Platos fuertes* (Main courses)**	
Bistec con papas (**Steak and potatoes**)	
Pechuga de pollo a la plancha (**Grilled chicken breast**)	
Pescado fresco del día (**Fresh fish of the day**)	
Espaguetis con salsa de tomate (**Pasta and tomato sauce**)	
***Postres* (Desserts)**	
Helados variados (**Selected ice creams**)	
Pastel del día (**Cake of the day**)	
Flan (**Egg custard**)	
***Fruta* (Fruit)**	
***Bebidas* (Beverages)**	
Vino tinto o blanco, copa o botella (**Red or white wine, glass or bottle**)	
Jugos naturales variados (**Assorted fresh juices**)	
Refrescos (**Soft drinks**)	
Agua mineral (**Mineral water**)	
Café o té (**Coffee or tea**)	

TRACK 56

Place Your Order

Imagine you're in your hotel room and you decide to call room service. Listen to the questions and statements from room service on Track 56. Then listen again to place your order. You can find a model conversation in Appendix D.

Ask the Concierge: Requesting Advice

Most upscale hotels in the Spanish-speaking world have a concierge on staff to help you with everything from making sightseeing plans and getting tickets to the symphony to recommending restaurants or helping you make sense out of a train schedule. The *conserje* is almost always multilingual, and is happy to assist guests in any way possible.

TRACK 57

Ask the Concierge

Here are a few examples of questions you might have for the *conserje* in your hotel. Listen to each question on Track 57 as you follow along in the text. Repeat each example after you hear it.

¿Tiene folletos con información turística?
(Do you have any visitor information brochures?)
¿Me puede dar un plano del centro?
(Can you give me a map of downtown?)
¿Hay algún evento especial esta semana?
(Is there any special event this week?)
¿Nos puede ayudar a conseguir boletos?
(Can you help us get tickets?)
¿Qué excursiones recomienda?
(What excursions do you recommend?)
¿Me puede recomendar un restaurante tranquilo por aquí?
(Can you recommend a quiet restaurant around here?)

If you are staying somewhere without a concierge, you can ask the same questions of the desk clerk. If you'd like more information, just ask where the nearest tourist office is: *¿Dónde está la oficina de turismo?*

Rent a Vacation Home

For extended stays, you may prefer to rent a condo or vacation home. There are lots of Web sites to help you research options in the location of your choice, and you can generally use e-mail to request more detailed information. Here is some general vocabulary to get you started.

- *una casa* (**a house**)
- *un chalet* (**a country home**)
- *un piso, un apartamento* (**an apartment, condo**)
- *el balcón* (**balcony**)
- *el patio* (**patio**)
- *el jardín* (**garden, yard**)
- *un/a portero/a* (**doorman/woman, caretaker**)
- *un garaje* (**a garage**)
- *un estacionamiento* (**a parking space**)
- *en el centro* (**downtown**)
- *en las afueras* (**on the outskirts**)
- *en el campo* (**in the country**)
- *en la playa* (**on the beach**)
- *bien/mal comunicado/a* (**with good/bad transportation connections**)
- *aislado/a* (**isolated**)
- *el alquiler/la renta* (**the rent**)
- *el depósito* (**deposit**)
- *los gastos incluidos/aparte* (**utilities included/separate**)

Now let's have a look at a couple of rental ads to see what you found in the lovely coastal city of Alicante, Spain. Read over the ads and answer the questions. You can find a translation of each ad as well as answers to the questions in Appendix D.

Hermosísimo piso de dos habitaciones con cocina, sala-comedor, y cuarto de servicio. A sólo dos manzanas de la playa. Balcón con vista del mar. Portero automático, estacionamiento, todo incluido. Contrato semanal o mensual. Contáctenos por e-mail para más detalles.

¡La casa de sus sueños! Amplio chalet rústico con jardín y huerto en las afueras de Alicante. Cocina, comedor, sala, tres habitaciones y dos baños completos. Portero al lado. Bien comunicada. Media hora a la playa o el centro. Alquiler por mes. Luz, agua y gas aparte. Excríbanos para más información.

1. *¿Qué lugar es más grande?* _____
2. *¿Cuál está más cerca de la playa?* _____
3. *¿Cuál incluye los gastos?* _____
4. *¿Cuál está disponible por semana o por mes?* _____
5. *¿Cuál te interesa más y por qué?* _____

Before renting anything, be sure you understand exactly what you're getting, how much it costs, and who to call if there is a problem.

Managing Minor Inconveniences

You've already learned to request a room change in the event of a problem, but plenty of minor things might go wrong in a hotel room or rental home that can easily be fixed. For example, if your key doesn't work, the toilet is stopped up, or there isn't much water pressure in the shower, it is likely that there are simple solutions that wouldn't require a change. The simplest and most useful verb to say that something doesn't work is *no funcionar.* Here are some other helpful words and expressions to explain simple problems in your hotel room or rental.

- *no funcionar* (**not work**)
- *estar roto* (**be broken**)
- *estar fundido/a* (**be burned out**)
- *el foco, la bombilla* (**light bulb**)
- *la luz* (**light**)
- *la lámpara* (**lamp**)
- *el enchufe* (**outlet**)
- *la conexión* (**connection**)
- *el televisor* (**TV**)
- *el control remoto, el mando* (**remote control**)
- *el radio* (**radio**)
- *el despertador* (**alarm clock**)
- *el grifo* (**faucet**)
- *la ducha, la regadera* (**showerhead**)
- *el inodoro* (**toilet**)

- *el desagüe* (**drain**)
- *estar tapado/a* (**be plugged up**)
- *la presión* (**water pressure**)
- *la calefacción* (**heat**)
- *el aire acondicionado* (**air conditioning**)
- *el ventilador* (**fan, vent**)

Once you identify a problem like *la bombilla de la lámpara está fundida* (the light bulb in the lamp is burned out), the hotel staff or caretaker will usually take care of it without any further ado. If you're not sure what the problem is, you can always say: *Hay un problema con . . .* and mention the item that you're having trouble with.

Tone is all-important in problem resolution. Use polite phrases like *disculpe, perdone,* and *hay un pequeño problema* to make your request for help nonconfrontational. Avoid assigning blame. Just identify the problem discreetly, and let the staff resolve it.

Let's practice. Translate the following into Spanish. Then check your work with the models in Appendix D. Don't worry about minor differences; just compare to see if you've effectively communicated the problem.

1. Excuse me, the Internet connection doesn't work.
2. Sorry, there's a small problem with the toilet.
3. Excuse me, I think the light bulb is burned out.
4. Sorry, I can't find the remote.
5. Excuse me, can you explain to me how the heat works?
6. Sorry; I think the fan is broken.
7. There isn't much water pressure in the shower.
8. Sorry; I think the toilet is stopped up.

Now you can manage any minor inconvenience that may come up during your stay!

Chapter 14

Indirect Object Pronouns

You won't get far while you're traveling without some good meals, and the Spanish-speaking world offers plenty to dazzle your taste buds. Cuisines vary widely, influenced by geography, ethnicity, and cultural history. So, peruse those menus, ask questions about ingredients and seasonings, sample local specialties, and visit the markets. Try unusual things: guinea pig in the Andes, iguana in Mexico, fried ants in Colombia; if the locals eat it, it must be food!

Food Categories

If you want to learn the names of foods in a country, you're often better off going to the market than looking at a menu. Restaurants tend to come up with fanciful dishes and even more fanciful names for them. In the market, however, foods are labeled by their common names and generally are grouped into categories: seafood at the fish stall, fruit at the fruit stall, and so on. So, let's wander through the market and learn some food names.

Basic Foods

Las carnes y aves (Meats and poultry)

- *el bistec* (**beef**)
- *el puerco, el cerdo* (**pork**)
- *el cordero* (**lamb**)
- *el pollo* (**chicken**)
- *el pato* (**duck**)
- *el pavo* (**turkey**)
- *las costillas* (**ribs**)
- *la chuleta* (**chop**)
- *la pechuga* (**breast**)
- *los huevos* (**eggs**)
- *el hígado* (**liver**)
- *los riñones* (**kidneys**)

Los pescado y mariscos (**Fish and shellfish**)

- *el huachinango* (**red snapper, Mex.**)
- *la trucha* (**trout**)
- *el mero* (**grouper**)
- *la merluza* (**hake**)
- *los camarones* (**shrimp**)
- *el pulpo* (**octopus**)
- *los calamares* (**squid**)
- *los mejillones* (**mussels**)
- *las ostras* (**oysters**)

Las verduras (Vegetables)

- *el brócoli* (**broccoli**)
- *la patata, la papa* (**potato**)
- *el camote, la batata* (**sweet potato, yam**)
- *la calabaza* (**squash**)
- *el maíz* (**corn**)
- *la coliflor* (**cauliflower**)
- *la zanahoria* (**carrot**)
- *los frijoles* (**beans**)
- *los garbanzos* (**chickpeas**)
- *el pimiento* (**pepper**)
- *el chile* (**chili pepper**)
- *el pepino* (**cucumber**)

Las frutas (Fruits)

- *la manzana* (**apple**)
- *la naranja* (**orange**)
- *la fresa* (**strawberry**)
- *el plátano* (**banana**)
- *el melocotón, el durazno* (**peach**)
- *el limón* (**lemon**)
- *la cereza* (**cherry**)
- *el melón* (**melon**)
- *la sandía* (**watermelon**)
- *el tomate* (**tomato**)
- *las uvas* (**grapes**)
- *el pomelo, la taronja* (**grapefruit**)
- *la papaya* (**papaya**)
- *el mango* (**mango**)
- *la maracuyá* (**passion fruit**)

Keep in mind that many fruits and vegetables in particular are limited in their range and may be sold only in certain locations. Part of the fun of going to a local market is to see what foods are available and to start learning some of the local names. Meanwhile, you might take your dictionary to the supermarket to learn the names of more items.

Let's take a minute and check out the dairy and deli areas of the market, where you'll find an assortment of cheeses, sausages, and pickled items. Once again, we're just going to focus on the basics, since cheese and sausage names vary widely from one place to another.

Los productos lácteos (Dairy products)
- *la leche* (**milk**)
- *la crema* (**cream**)
- *la mantequilla* (**butter**)
- *la nata* (**whipped cream**)
- *la crema agria* (**sour cream**)
- *el yogur* (**yogurt**)
- *el requesón* (**curds, cottage cheese**)
- *el queso* (**cheese**)
- *el helado* (**ice cream**)

Los productos de charcutería (Deli products)
- *la salchicha* (**sausage**)
- *el chorizo* (**spicy sausage**)
- *la morcilla* (**blood sausage**)
- *el jamón serrano* (**salted dried ham**)
- *el fiambre* (**cold cuts**)
- *las tripas* (**tripe**)

FACT

Some very common foods like chocolate, corn, tomatoes, and potatoes are native to the Americas, and were first introduced to the rest of the world after the Spanish arrived. In turn, Spain brought other foodstuffs, including rice, to the Americas, where they have become dietary staples.

Foods are sold by particular weights and cuts and in different sizes and containers. For example, you buy most meat, fruits, and vegetables by *kilos* (kilograms) or *gramos* (grams). The same is true for cheese and deli products, though you may buy some whole (*entero*) or by the piece or chunk (*trozo*). You might specify whether you want slices (*rebanadas*) or if you would like your cheese grated (*rallado*) or meat ground (*molida*). Liquids are most often sold by liters (*litros*) though more solid dairy products are sold by grams or in containers (*envases*).

FACT

Milk is often sold in unrefrigerated cartons. It has been sterilized and doesn't need refrigeration until after opening. Some stores offer farm-fresh milk and cream that is packaged in plastic bags.

Manage the Menu: Asking for Clarification and Explanation

Knowing the names of basic food items is the first step to deciphering a menu. It's likely that the name of the dish will include some indication of its main ingredient. If it doesn't, though, you are now ready to ask your server what a dish is: *¿Qué es . . . ?* No doubt the description will name the major ingredients and might tell you how something is prepared as well. Let's take a minute to review some common ways to prepare foods:

Food Preparation
- *crudo* (**raw**)
- *natural, fresco* (**unprepared, fresh**)
- *cocido* (**cooked**)
- *hervido* (**boiled**)
- *asado* (**roasted**)
- *a la parrilla, a la plancha* (**grilled**)
- *frito* (**fried**)
- *al vapor* (**steamed**)
- *al horno* (**baked**)

You might want to inquire about the condiments included in a particular dish. The most common, of course, are salt (*sal*) and pepper (*pimienta*). Other frequently used spices include *orégano* (oregano), *perejil* (parsley), *chile* or *ají* (hot peppers), *laurel* (bay leaf), *hierba santa* or *menta* (mint), *ajo* (garlic), and *albahaca* (basil), among others. Flavors can be categorized as *picante* (spicy), *salado* (salty), *dulce* (sweet), *ácido* (sour), and *amargo* (bitter).

Let's look at a menu together and ask a few questions to find out just what we might want to order.

El Mesón del Sol
MENÚ DEL DÍA: DOS PLATOS, POSTRE O CAFÉ

Entradas frías
Crema de calabaza
Terrina de hígado de pato
Entradas calientes
Paella valenciana

Especialidades de la casa
Espárragos con almendras
Festival de mariscos
Ternera a la riojana

Crema de hongos
Judías verdes gratinadas
Tortilla de chorizo

Postres
Quesos artesanales
Crema catalana
Plato de frutas

Now, if you're adventurous, you might not care what these dishes are or how they are made. On the other hand, especially if you have any food sensitivities, you may need to know exactly what something like *Festival de mariscos* has in it. Just ask your server: *¿Qué lleva el Festival de mariscos?* If a dish name like *Suprema de lubina* completely baffles you, don't be shy about asking *¿Qué es la Suprema de lubina?* If you have food allergies, you might wish to tell your server exactly what you cannot eat and ask for a recommendation: *Tengo alergia a la cebolla. ¿Puede recomendar un plato sin cebolla?* (I'm allergic to onion. Can you recommend a dish without onion?) If you are a vegetarian and don't see anything suitable on a menu, feel free to ask your server if the chef might prepare something special for you: *Soy vegetariana. ¿Puede el chef prepararme un* *plato vegetariano?* Though vegetarianism is not particularly common in the Spanish-speaking world, chefs usually enjoy fulfilling special requests of this sort. You may have to clarify just what ingredients are off-limits, though. Lard (*grasa*) is a common cooking medium so you might request oil (*aceite*) instead, and be sure to indicate whether or not you eat eggs or fish, for example.

Types of Menus

The sample menu from the *Mesón del Sol* is a *menú del día*. This is very common, especially in Spain. For a fixed price, you can select a first and second course and dessert or coffee. These are generally very good values, and you can find a *menú del día* in restaurants of all categories. If you don't see a *menú* posted or listed in the menu, just ask. Sometimes more expensive restaurants prefer that you order *a la carte* even if they offer a *menú*. By the way, particularly in Spain, there is a difference between the words *menú* and *carta*. If you ask for the *menú* you may be ordering the fixed price meal of the day; ask for *la carta* if you want to see the menu.

Many tourist areas offer a simpler approach to eating: *el plato combinado*. There are usually several options including a chicken, fish, or meat with a vegetable or salad served on a single plate. They are typically inexpensive and, though not anything to write home about, are filling and of reasonable quality. Many restaurants that offer *platos combinados* have pictures to tell you exactly what you're getting on each one.

You may also come across restaurants that offer a *comida corriente*. This is similar to the *menú del día* in which you can choose from limited options, often listed on a board, for a fixed price. They are generally simple dishes, often local staples, designed to satisfy an appetite rather than appeal to a refined palate.

Types of Restaurants

There are many types of eateries in the Spanish-speaking world, and you are likely to find one to suit your appetite, budget, and style just about anywhere. In fact, you may come across some terrific restaurants in rather out-of-the-way places, especially in countries that have elaborate cuisines and celebrate good eating. In Spain, Mexico, Argentina, and Chile, for example, eating out can be the whole point of a day trip, and even tiny villages may be well known for a restaurant where a leisurely meal may take several hours and include outstanding local ingredients.

Restaurants are generally categorized by forks (*tenedores*), and many restaurants will proudly post their menu with the appropriate number of *tenedores* next to the entrance. That makes it easy to decide if you want to go in or not—check out the menu, look at the prices, and enter or move on without any embarrassment. Five forks is the highest rating, though one fork or no fork at all shouldn't immediately make a restaurant suspect.

Restaurant styles run the full gamut. Here are some of the possibilities:

- *Restaurante:* generally full-service with menu; all price categories.
- *Cafetería:* informal, moderately priced eatery that might be full- or self-service.
- *Mesón:* inn, generally found in villages or the countryside. Sometimes the term *mesón* is used simply to imply a cosier or more rustic type of restaurant.
- *Bar:* not a "bar" in the U.S. sense. Most will serve sandwiches, light meals, or appetizers, as well as pastries, and are suitable for all ages. You can get beer, wine, some liqueurs, sodas, coffee, and tea.
- *Bar de copas:* a bar that specializes in mixed drinks.
- *Bar de tapas:* particular to Spain, a bar that specializes in tapas (small appetizers) to accompany beer, wine, or soft drinks. Also called a tasca.
- *Croisantería-Sandwichería:* the Spanish response to fast-food restaurants—light combinations of meats, cheese, and vegetables on bread or croissants. Many are take-out style.
- *Cantina:* typically a drinking establishment in Latin America, often unwelcoming to women. Some food items may be available. However, the term is sometimes applied playfully to a normal restaurant.
- *Taquería:* informal restaurant specializing in tacos, generally ground beef or chicken with chiles and onions wrapped in a small tortilla and fried.

- ***Churrasquería:*** popular in southern cone countries, these restaurants specialize in grilled meats and fish. They often combine full service with a self-service salad bar.

Food is one of the foundations of Hispanic culture, lovingly prepared and proudly served everywhere from world class restaurants to the humblest of kitchens, so order with confidence!

Place Your Order: Indirect Object Pronouns

You've got the menu, you've learned how to ask for descriptions of dishes, and you know how to ask for recommendations and special items. You're all set to place your order. In the Spanish-speaking world, as in the United States, meals are typically ordered by course. You order the appetizer first and then the main course. Dessert and coffee are usually ordered when you finish the first two courses. The server might simply ask what you want, or he may say something like this:

> *¿Qué desea de primero?* **(What would you like for an appetizer?)**
> *¿Y de segundo?* **(And for your main course?)**
> And you might respond something like this:
> *De primero voy a tomar* . . . **(I'll have . . . as an appetizer.)**
> *Para empezar . . . y después* . . . **(To start off . . . and then . . .)**

The vocabulary of courses can be a bit confusing. In English we refer to an appetizer or starter and to a main course or entreé. In Spanish, these have different names in different places. "Appetizer" can be an *antojito*, an *entrada*, or a *primer plato*. Your main course may be the *plato principal* or *segundo plato*. The menu usually indicates the local terms.

There are really no hard-and-fast rules in ordering etiquette. The server may be terse and ask no more than *¿Qué quiere?* or *¿Qué va a tomar?*, or he may be quite eloquent, using a wide range of polite phrases and offering recommendations and commentary on the menu and your order. Complete the following dialog with appropriate phrases using the menu from *Mesón* *del Sol* to make your order selections. Then listen to the audio and respond. Check your responses with the model in Appendix D.

TRACK 58

Lunch at *El Mesón del Sol*

Buenas tardes. ¿Qué desea tomar?
Bueno, la crema de calabaza es particularmente buena, pero los espárragos y el paté también son excelentes.
Muy bien. Estoy seguro de que le gustará. ¿Qué quiere de segundo?
La suprema de lubina es una especialidad regional. Es un pescado blanco con un sabor muy rico. Lo preparamos con una salsa de vino blanco. Se lo recomiendo. ¿Y para tomar? El vino de la casa es muy bueno.
De acuerdo. Agua mineral y vino tinto. ¿Botella, media o copa?
En seguida le traigo las bebidas.

If you live in an area with Hispanic restaurants, try out your ordering skills in Spanish. You can get plenty of practice and order like a pro the next time you travel!

Indirect Object Pronouns

Indirect objects are those people or things that receive the effect of a verb secondarily. You can usually identify the indirect object by asking "for/to whom" or "for/to what" something is done. For example, you ask a waiter to recommend something to you. The direct object is the something, and you are the indirect object. The pronouns for indirect objects are identical to the direct object pronouns, except for the third person.

Indirect Object Pronouns

To or for . . .	
me	*me*
you (*tú*)	*te*
him, her, you (*usted*)	*le*
us	*nos*

Indirect Object Pronouns

To or for . . .	
you (*vosotros*)	*os*
them, you (*ustedes*)	*les*

FACT

The indirect object pronouns *le* and *les* are often used in place of the direct object pronouns *lo, la, los,* and *las* when referring to people. This is particularly common in Spain.

The placement of indirect object pronouns follows the same rule as placement for other pronouns: you can either put them in front of a conjugated verb or attach them to an infinitive or present participle. They must always be attached to affirmative commands and detached from negative commands. Look at these examples. The indirect objects are highlighted.

TRACK 59

Indirect Object Pronouns

Listen to each example on Track 59 as you follow along in the text. Repeat each one after you hear it.

> *¿Me puede recomendar alguna especialidad local?*
> **(Can you recommend a local specialty to me?)**
> *El mesero va a traernos la carta en un momento.*
> **(The waiter is going to bring us the menu in a moment.)**
> *Dígales qué es, por favor.*
> **(Tell them what it is, please.)**
> *No les haga esperar mucho.*
> **(Don't make them wait too long.)**

It's very common to include the indirect object pronoun for the third-person singular and plural even when the indirect object is mentioned. For example: *Llévale este plato al señor en la mesa número tres* (Take this dish to the man at table number three). You do the same thing with the third person and *gustar*: *Le gusta mucho el pescado a Miguel* (Miguel likes fish a lot—Fish is pleasing to Miguel). Because *le* and *les* can refer to many people, it is common to clarify them by mentioning the indirect object as well. A sentence will be correct if you leave off the indirect object pronoun, but it is much more eloquent when the pronoun is included. Let's practice a bit with indirect object pronouns. Look at the following sentences and translate them into Spanish. Then check your work against the answers in Appendix D.

1. Will you give us the menu, please?
2. Ask the waiter what the specialties are.
3. Can you bring me more water, please?
4. Will you please tell him what is in the *paella*.
5. The chef can make something vegetarian for them.

Try making up more examples using indirect object pronouns to practice ordering food in a restaurant or use any other context to practice this useful grammar structure.

There's a Fly in My Soup: Problem Solving

Things don't always go smoothly in a restaurant. While most restaurants strive to provide good service and quality meals, sometimes you have to point out minor problems. Discretion is your best tactic. Quietly get your waiter's attention, calmly explain the problem, and politely propose the solution you would like. In most cases, the problem will be resolved quickly to your complete satisfaction. Look at some examples.

Problem Solving

Listen to each example on Track 60 as you follow along in the text. Repeat each statement or request after you hear it. Pay special attention to tone.

TRACK 60

Disculpe, ¿me trae otro tenedor, por favor? (**Excuse me, will you bring me another fork, please?**)

Disculpe, me parece que hay un pequeño problema. La sopa está fría. ¿Se puede calentar, por favor? (**I'm sorry, there seems to be a small problem. The soup is cold. Can it be warmed up, please?**)

Perdone, señor. Llevo media hora esperando el primer plato. ¿Tardará mucho más? (**Excuse me, sir. I've been waiting for my appetizer for half an hour. Will it take much longer?**)

Disculpe, esta carne está muy salada. ¿Puede cambiarla, por favor? (**I'm sorry, this meat is very salty. Can you exchange it, please?**)

And, of course, if there really is a fly in your soup, you should discreetly say to the waiter, *Disculpe, hay una mosca en la sopa.* Here are a few more problems that might come up in a restaurant:

- *el vino está pasado* (**the wine is off**)
- *las verduras están crudas* (**the vegetables are raw**)
- *la ensalada está fea* (**the salad is limp, old**)
- *la carne está demasiado/poco cocida* (**the meat is overcooked/not cooked enough**)
- *este plato está sucio* (**this plate is dirty**)
- *esta copa está picada* (**this wine cup is chipped**)
- *me falta, me faltan . . .* (**I need . . . , is/are lacking**)
- *necesito . . .* (**I need . . .**)

Of course, it's much more likely that you'll want to compliment the waiter or the host on the quality of your meal. To say that everything was delicious, say *¡Todo estuvo riquísimo!*

Money Matters

In most Spanish-speaking countries, waiters don't hover about, asking you every five minutes if you want anything else. For this reason, you will need to call your waiter over to request things, including the check, which will normally only be brought when you ask for it. Catch the waiter's eye and say

La cuenta, por favor. In some places, the word *nota* is used instead of *cuenta.* You can also make your request a bit more polite using the question form you've already learned: *¿Me trae la cuenta, por favor?*

Check your bill! If you are in doubt, ask to see the menu again to check the prices of the items you have ordered. Keep in mind that the endless beverage refill is strictly a United States phenomenon. If you have ordered several soft drinks or cups of coffee, you will be charged for each one. Sometimes there is a charge for bread or extra tortillas. Many nicer restaurants will automatically add a service charge of 10 percent or so, which covers the tip. If there is a problem, simply bring it to the waiter's attention.

Money Matters

TRACK 61

Listen to each example on Track 61 as you follow along in the text. Repeat each statement after you hear it. Pay close attention to tone.

> *Disculpe, me parece que hay un pequeño error en la cuenta.*
> **(Excuse me; it seems that there is a small error in the bill.)**
> *Perdone, creo que me cobraron dos veces por la ensalada.*
> **(Excuse me; I think they charged me twice for the salad.)**
> *Disculpe, ésta no es nuestra cuenta.*
> **(Sorry, this isn't our check.)**

Once again, the rule of thumb is avoid confrontation. Try to phrase the problem neutrally rather than accuse the waiter directly. Whenever possible, simply identify the problem rather than assign blame, or use the impersonal "they" and the third-person plural of the verb as in *creo que me cobraron dos veces* (I think they charged me twice).

Chapter 15

Mastering Object Pronouns

One of the attractions of traveling is shopping for interesting things as souvenirs and gifts. Even if you're not a big spender, you'll enjoy looking at display windows, visiting markets, and wandering into unusual shops to browse. It's fun to see what's familiar and what's different from place to place. And, you'll probably find one or two treasures even if you aren't trying!

All That Glitters: Direct Object Pronouns

Jewelry may be the perfect souvenir or gift. It's easy to pack for the return trip, beautiful, often unique to a location, and available in price ranges to suit every budget. How can you go wrong with a lovely pair of earrings to remind you of your trip to Oaxaca every time you put them on? Let's take a minute to learn some basic jewelry vocabulary.

- *los aretes, los pendientes* (**earrings**)
- *el collar* (**necklace**)
- *la cadena* (**chain**)
- *el colgante, el pendiente* (**pendant**)
- *la pulsera, el brazalete* (**bracelet**)
- *el dije* (**charm**)
- *la sortija, el anillo* (**ring**)
- *el prendedor* (**pin, brooch**)
- *el reloj* (**watch**)
- *la piedra* (**stone**)
- *el oro* (**gold**)
- *la plata* (**silver**)

Jewelry terminology varies from country to country, but most terms are understood even when a different word is used locally. And, when you're shopping, it's easy to point out what you're referring to.

Be aware, however, that not everything that glitters is gold. Look for gold and silver marks on a piece of jewelry before you pay gold and silver prices. Gold-plated jewelry is *dorado* or *bañado en oro*. Silver plated is *plateado* or *bañado en plata*. There is also a silver look-alike metal common in Mexico and the Andes called *alpaca*, a nickel-based metal that looks nice but doesn't cost as much as silver. If you are shopping in out of the way places or markets, the truth-in-marketing laws don't apply. On the other hand, you can find some terrific bargains on jewelry. Much of it is handmade, often uniquely designed, and will make a wonderful souvenir or gift. In areas with rich archeological treasures, many jewelers sell reproductions of historic pieces or modern interpretations of ancient designs. In Spain, most gold jewelry is 18K, and sterling silver or *plata de ley* is marked 925. In Latin America, gold jewelry is generally made in 10K and 14K. Sterling silver is marked 925, though unmarked items may still be silver but in a lower percentage.

FACT

The word for earrings in Puerto Rico is unique in the Spanish-speaking world. They are called *pantallas*, a word that isn't understood to mean earrings anywhere else. In some countries you may learn the words *arracadas, caravanas, zarcillos,* and *aros* to refer to different types of earrings.

Let's take a moment now to review the names of some stones as well before we go on our shopping spree.

- *el diamante* **(diamond)**
- *el zafiro* **(sapphire)**
- *la esmeralda* **(emerald)**
- *el rubí* **(ruby)**
- *la perla cultivada* **(cultured pearl)**
- *la perla de agua dulce* **(freshwater pearl)**
- *la amatista* **(amethyst)**
- *la aguamarina* **(aquamarine)**
- *el citrino* **(citrine)**
- *el granate* **(garnet)**
- *el lapislázuli* **(lapiz lazuli)**
- *el peridoto* **(peridot)**
- *el ópalo* **(opal)**
- *el topacio azul* **(blue topaz)**
- *la turquesa* **(turquoise)**

Some of these stones are especially common, and good values, in certain countries. For example, fire opal (*ópalo de fuego*) comes from the Mexican state of Chiapas. Mexico is also known for the use of turquoise, lapis, jade (*jade*), and freshwater pearls, gems that were highly valued in ancient Mesoamerica. You'll see them in museum artifacts as well as in traditional and contemporary jewelry. Chile is famous for lapis lazuli, which is often inlaid into beautiful silver jewelry in contemporary designs. You can find good bargains on emeralds in Colombia, where they are mined, or Costa Rica, where they are often sent for cutting and polishing. Many lab-created stones are used in jewelry to keep the prices lower, and you can find some lovely things at very affordable prices. If you want to be sure you are buying natural stones, however, shop at a reputable jewelry store rather than a market stall.

Can I See It?

You know that the direct object in a sentence is the thing that receives the effect of the verb directly. Let's imagine a shopping situation in which you would use direct objects and direct object pronouns:

Me gusta una sortija en la vitrina. **(I like a ring in the window.)**
¿Puedo verla? **(Can I see it?)**

Remember that the direct object pronouns are gender and number specific. Watch how the examples change for different items.

Direct Object Pronouns

Listen to each example on Track 62 as you follow along in the text. Repeat each sentence or question after you hear it.

TRACK 62

Me gustan unos aretes en la vitrina.
(I like some earrings in the window.)
¿Puedo verlos?
(Can I see them?)
Me gusta un reloj en la vitrina.
(I like a watch in the window.)
¿Puedo verlo? **(Can I see it?)**
Me gustan unas pulseras en la vitrina.
(I like some bracelets in the window.)
¿Puedo verlas? **(Can I see them?)**

If you can't remember what an item is called, you can simply say you "saw something in the window and you would like to see it better": *Vi algo en la vitrina y quisiera verlo mejor.*

Complete each sentence with the appropriate direct object pronoun. Then check your answers in Appendix D.

1. *Ese collar es muy bonito. Quisiera ver _____.*
2. *Hay una sortija que me gusta en la vitrina. ¿_____ puedo ver?*
3. *Esos relojes son muy elegantes. Me gustaría ver _____.*
4. *La perla en este arete no es muy buena. Si usted _____ cambia, compraré los aretes.*
5. *Estas pulseras son perfectas para Susana. Voy a comprar _____ para ella.*

Not That One, This One

Of course, you remember the demonstratives: this, that, and those over there. Demonstrative adjectives and pronouns are as handy for shopping as direct object pronouns. As the salesperson points to various items trying to figure out which one you want to see, you can use demonstratives to help direct her to the article you mean, like this:

Shopper: *Buenos días. Busco una cadena para este dije.* (Good day. I'm looking for a chain for this charm.)

Salesperson: *Muy bien. Esta cadena es muy bonita.* (Very good. This chain is very pretty.)

Shopper: *¿Puedo verla con el dije?* (Can I see it with the charm?)

Salesperson: *Cómo no. Aquí la tiene.* (Of course. Here it is.)

Shopper: *Hmm. Ésta es muy delgada para este dije.* (Hmm. This one is very thin for this charm.)

Salesperson: *¿Le gusta ésta? Es un poco más gruesa.* (Do you like this one? It's a little heavier.)

Shopper: *No está mal pero creo que prefiero ésa.* (It's not bad but I think I prefer that one.)

Salesperson: *¿Ésta o ésa?* (This one or that one?)

Shopper: *No, no, aquélla al fondo.* (No, that one in the back.)

And that's how you get what you want with demonstratives and direct object pronouns.

Audio Practice: Shopping

Now it's your turn. Imagine that you are in a shop looking at earrings. Listen to the salesperson and complete the dialog by translating your lines from English to Spanish. You can find the complete dialog written out in Appendix D. For extra practice, listen again and repeat the sample responses.

TRACK 63

Not That One, This One

Good afternoon. There is a pendant in the window that I like.
I like that one with lapis.
Hmm. Yes, this one is pretty but I prefer that larger one.
That one over there, please.
Yes, the stone is beautiful. I like this pendant very much. I'll buy it.

ALERT!

Remember that the demonstrative adjective has no accent mark, but the demonstrative pronoun does: *esta sortija y ésa* (this ring and that one). The accent doesn't affect the pronunciation of the pronouns; it only distinguishes them from the adjective form.

Verbs Like Gustar

Clothing is another fun item to shop for while you're traveling. You can find the latest fashions in Spain a year before they get to the United States, or get fabulous deals on alpaca sweaters in Peru, Ecuador, and Bolivia. If you enjoy ethnic clothing, you're sure to find beautiful handwoven and hand-embroidered treasures in Mexico, Guatemala, and many South American countries at a fraction of the price you would pay at home. Let's start with a review of clothing vocabulary:

- *el vestido* (**dress**)
- *la falda* (**skirt**)
- *la blusa* (**blouse**)
- *el pantalón, los pantalones* (**pants**)
- *la camisa* (**shirt**)
- *la camiseta, la playera* (**T-shirt**)
- *el traje* (**suit**)
- *el chaleco* (**vest**)
- *la chaqueta* (**jacket**)
- *el suéter* (**sweater**)
- *el cinturón* (**belt**)
- *los calcetines, las medias* (**socks, stockings**)
- *el pañuelo* (**scarf**)
- *el sombrero* (**brimmed hat**)
- *la gorra* (**cap**)
- *la bufanda* (**warm scarf, muffler**)
- *los guantes* (**gloves**)
- *el abrigo* (**overcoat**)

Clothing terminology varies from country to country. A *falda* in one country may be a *pollera* in another. A *chaqueta* may be anything from a cardigan sweater to a sport or outer jacket.

Sizes (*las tallas*) also vary from place to place. Small, medium, and large will likely be *pequeño, mediano*, and *grande*, but they might be indicated by the numbers 1, 2, and 3. More specific sizes, like ladies dress sizes 6, 8, and 10, for example, will likely be indicated by the numbers 36, 38, and 40. Children's, teen's, and men's clothing each follow a unique size system. And, as in the United States, the real size of a garment depends more on the manufacturer than on any established standard.

Try It On!

The verb used in Spanish "to try on" clothing or other items worn on the body, like jewelry, is the reflexive verb *probarse*. If you want to try on dress in a store, for example, you would ask the salesclerk something like: *¿Puedo probarme este vestido, por favor?* The dressing rooms are *los probadores*.

If you're not sure where they are, ask: *¿Dónde están los probadores?* Once you try something on, you might want to know what it's made of and how to care for it. Look at the following list for fabric and care information.

Fabrics and Materials
- *el algodón* (**cotton**)
- *la seda* (**silk**)
- *la lana* (**wool**)
- *el lino* (**linen**)
- *el acrílico*(**acrylic**)
- *sintético* (**synthetic**)
- *la microfibra* (**microfiber**)
- *el nylon* (**nylon**)
- *el poliéster* (**polyester**)
- *la piel* (**fine leather, fur**)
- *el cuero* (**heavy leather**)
- *el ante, la gamuza* (**suede, chamois**)

Care
- *lavar a mano* (**hand wash**)
- *lavar a máquina* (**machine wash**)
- *lavar en seco* (**dry clean**)
- *con agua tibia* (**with warm water**)
- *con agua fría* (**with cold water**)
- *con agua caliente* (**with hot water**)
- *planchar con vapor* (**steam iron**)
- *planchar sin vapor* (**iron without steam**)
- *no planchar* (**do not iron**)

You can't know for certain how a garment will survive washing or dry cleaning. It may shrink *(encogerse)* or the colors may run or fade *(despintarse, desteñirse)*, or it might turn into a wrinkled mess *(arrugarse)* or fall apart *(deshacerse)*.

You Love It!

You've been using the verb *gustar* to say what you like. Spanish actually has a number of verbs that work just like *gustar* and will come in very handy during your shopping trip. Let's look at a few of the most useful ones for this purpose.

- *encantar* **(to delight, to love)**
- *parecer* **(to seem)**
- *interesar* **(to interest)**
- *quedar* **(to fit)**
- *molestar* **(to bother)**
- *caer bien, mal* **(to like, dislike someone)**

As you may recall, *gustar* takes indirect object pronouns to refer to the person or people to whom something is pleasing. These other verbs work exactly the same way. *Me encanta esta camisa* translates into English literally as "This shirt delights me," though the colloquial equivalent would be "I love this shirt." Other verbs are more similar to the English way of expressing the same idea, for example, *Esos pantalones me parecen muy caros* translates literally into English as "Those pants seem very expensive to me."

Keep in mind that not all of these verbs translate easily into English. For example, the verb *caer* is used in a very special way with indirect object pronouns to describe the effect a person has on you. *La dependienta me cae mal* means "I don't like the saleswoman." The literal translation "The saleswoman falls on me badly" doesn't make any sense in English. Nevertheless, this is the structure you use in most cases to talk about people you like or dislike.

To talk about how something fits, use the verb *quedar* or *andar.* In some contexts, *quedar* can also refer to how something looks on a person. Review the following examples to learn how to talk about different fit issues.

How Does It Look?

Listen to each example on Track 64 as you follow along in the text. Repeat each statement after you hear it.

TRACK 64

La blusa me queda grande.

(The blouse runs big on me.)

Esa chaqueta te queda bien.

(That jacket fits you well. That jacket looks good on you.)

Estos pantalones nos andan estrechos.

(These pants are too tight on us.)

Ese sombrero le queda horrible.

(That hat fits him terribly. That hat looks horrible on him.)

Let's summarize some fit vocabulary for convenience:

Andar o quedar. . .
- *grande* **(big)**
- *pequeño* **(small)**
- *largo* **(long)**
- *corto* **(short)**
- *estrecho* **(tight, narrow)**
- *ancho* **(loose, wide)**
- *bien/mal* **(well/badly)**
- *feo* **(unattractive)**
- *bonito* **(beautiful)**

Keep in mind that most of these terms are adjectives, so they agree in number and gender with the item described: *Esta blusa me queda estrecha, pero los pantalones me quedan anchos* (This blouse is too tight on me but the pants are too loose on me"). To say that something fits well or badly, however, you use the adverbs *bien* and *mal*: *El suéter te anda bien pero la falda te queda muy mal.*

Indirect Object Pronouns

Some countries like Spain and Argentina are famous for their gorgeous leather footwear, and one might spend more on shoes and boots than on clothing. Other places, shoes are less of a fashion statement and play a more practical role. Take a look at your footwear collection and make a list of the different types you own. Then see how many of the following items appear on your list.

- *los zapatos* **(shoes)**
- *las botas* **(boots)**
- *las sandalias* **(sandals)**
- *los tacones* **(high heels)**
- *los botines* **(short boots)**
- *las zapatillas* **(slippers, sneakers)**
- *las chanclas* **(flipflops, sandals)**
- *las pantuflas* **(fluffy slippers)**
- *los tenis* **(tennis shoes)**

The generic term for footwear in Spanish is *calzado*, but a shoe store is called a *zapatería*. However, many shoe stores use the word *calzado* to refer to their merchandise rather than the word *zapatos*.

Specialty shoes and boots are named according to the activity they are used for, for example: *zapatos de fútbol* (soccer shoes), *zapatos de golf* (golf shoes), *botas de trabajo* (work boots), and *botas de montaña* (hiking boots). And, in case you're wondering, Cinderella's glass slippers were *zapatillas de cristal*!

Using Indirect Object Pronouns

Trying on shoes will give you the opportunity to practice indirect object pronouns a little more. You use them with *gustar* and *encantar*, for example, to say that you like a pair of shoes: *Me encantan estos zapatos*. You also use indirect object pronouns with the verbs *quedar* and *andar* to talk about how shoes or boots fit: *Las botas me quedan grandes pero los tacones me andan muy bien*. You can use the verb *molestar* to say that something about a shoe bothers your foot, or the expression *hacer daño* to say that shoes hurt:

Me molestan los tacones.
(The heels bother me.)
Los zapatos elegantes siempre me hacen daño.
(Elegant shoes always hurt me.)

Use the verb *apretar (e > ie)* with indirect object pronouns to say that a shoe pinches you: *Estas botas me aprietan los dedos* (These boots pinch my toes). And use the verb *doler (o > ue)* to say your feet hurt: *Me duelen los pies.*

The Perfect Shoes

Shoe sizes are usually referred to as *números,* and the salesperson will ask you something like *¿Qué número calza?* or *¿Qué número lleva?* (What size do you wear?). If you're not sure how sizes run in the country you're in, ask the salesperson to measure your foot: *¿Puede medirme el pie, por favor?* Notice that you are using an indirect object pronoun again.

ALERT!

To refer to your size in clothing, use *talla,* but use *número* to talk about shoe size. To refer to the size of most other things, use *tamaño,* for example, . . . *el tamaño de una casa* (. . . the size of a house).

So, what do you think, *¿Qué le parece?,* asks the salesperson. If you're lucky, *te quedan perfectos y te encantan.* On the other hand, you may discover, much to your dismay, that those perfect shoes don't fit. The size is right, but they seem too wide; the toe pinches; they're too stiff; the arch is in the wrong place. The reality is that shoes are made very differently from country to country. You may be able to bring home a suitcase full of fabulous footwear bargains from your trip to Spain or Argentina, or you may end up with nothing but your worn-out sneakers.

Odds and Ends: Double-Object Pronouns

Are you an antique buff? Do you collect ceramics? What about whimsical little toys? Whatever your interests, you're sure to find fascinating odds and ends wherever you go.

- *las antigüedades* (**antiques**)
- *la cerámica* (**ceramics**)
- *los juguetes* (**toys**)
- *el cuadro* (**painting**)
- *la muñeca* (**doll**)
- *la olla* (**pot**)
- *la escultura* (**sculpture**)
- *el tapiz* (**tapestry**)
- *la canasta* (**basket**)
- *la calabaza* (**gourd**)
- *el abanico* (**fan**)
- *el bastón* (**walking stick**)

There you are, wandering the market, and you spot some terrific baskets and a great tapestry that you would love to put in your living room. So, you ask the vendor if he will please show them to you. Look at some examples:

Esas canastas son interesantes. ¿Me las deja ver, por favor?
(**Those baskets are interesting. Will you let me see them, please?**)
Nos gusta mucho ese tapiz. ¿Nos lo baja, por favor?
(**We like that tapestry a lot. Will you take it down for us, please?**)

Both of these examples use direct and indirect object pronouns together. In the first sentence, *las* refers to the direct object "the baskets" and *me* is the indirect object pronoun "me." In the second example you ask the vendor to take "it" down for you. *Lo* is the direct object pronoun for "the tapestry" and "*nos*" is the indirect object pronoun meaning "for us." Now, let's look at a couple of examples with a reflexive verb and an object pronoun. To tell your friend to try on a pair of shoes she saw in a shop, you might say:

Pruébatelos (Try them on). To ask a salesperson if you can try on a skirt, ask: *¿Me la puedo probar?* or *¿Puedo probármela?*

Placement of Double Pronouns

Whether you have one or two object pronouns, the rules of placement are the same: put them in front of a conjugated verb or negative command or attach them to an infinitive, present participle, or affirmative command. Always put the indirect object or reflexive pronoun in front of the direct object pronoun. Luckily, you won't ever have all three in the same phrase, though you may have three in the same sentence, for example: *Nos encantaría comprárnoslos* (We would love to buy them for ourselves). The first *nos* relates only to the verb *encantaría* so it stands alone. "Them for ourselves," however both relate to the verb *comprar* and follow the pronoun sequence of indirect–direct.

To remember the order of pronoun placement, remind yourself that pronouns get RID of the nouns. RID is a handy acronym for reflexive, indirect, direct.

When the use of pronouns results in combinations like *le lo, le la, les lo, les las*, change the indirect object pronoun from *le* or *les* to *se*. For example, "John likes the red shirt so I'm going to buy it for him" becomes *A John le gusta la camisa roja por eso se la voy a comprar* rather than . . . *le la voy a comprar.*

Bargaining Dos and Don'ts

Prices are not always what they appear to be in the Spanish-speaking world, but it's important to know when and how you might get a discount. Generally, there is no bargaining in shops. However, in some places, you can get a discount of 10 percent or so if you pay cash rather than use a credit card.

This 10 percent represents the surcharge the store has to pay the credit card company when you charge your purchase. On a large purchase, that 10 percent can be well worth a trip to the ATM.

In markets, however, bargaining is not only expected, it's half the fun of making a purchase. Bargaining reinforces the human relationship between buyer and seller, and in some countries is an important social exchange. Not bargaining, in fact, can be an insult to the vendor, implying that the merchandise isn't worth your time or effort or that you don't value the social interaction. On the other hand, it's equally important not to request an absurd discount for something. Reasonable discounts vary according to the value of the item. An expensive item might allow the vendor more flexibility in pricing. Inexpensive trinkets, however, might already be priced so low that you can only reasonably ask for a very small discount. If you buy multiple items, you can usually get a slightly better deal.

Bargaining Strategies

Your best strategies for bargaining are comparison shopping and being willing to walk away without the item. Vendors will usually enjoy competitive bargaining when they know you can get the same thing two stalls down, and will quickly get a sense of how serious a buyer you are. Vendors would usually rather make the sale than watch you buy from someone else. For this reason, it's best to comparison shop before you bargain for anything in a market. Then you can use the tactic of pointing out minor flaws and differences between your vendor's merchandise and the competition's. It's important, though, to have a very clear idea of what you are willing to pay for an item, and to decide beforehand whether you are willing to walk away if the vendor doesn't meet that price. Once your vendor has offered the lowest price, you should buy the item or leave rather than continue to haggle. At that point, further bargaining is inappropriate and considered rude.

Bargaining

There are a few different things you can say to test the bargaining waters. Listen to each example on Track 65 as you follow along in the text. Repeat each after you hear it.

TRACK 65

¿Puede rebajármelo un poco? **(Can you reduce it for me a little?)**
¿Me hace un pequeño descuento? **(Will you give me a little discount?)**
¿Cuál es el mejor precio? **(What is your best price?)**
¿En cuánto me lo deja? **(What will you give it to me for?)**

If the vendor replies in the negative, the asking price is probably firm. If the vendor hems and haws but lowers the price, you can probably continue to bargain a bit. Keep in mind, though, just how much of a discount you are asking for. It's easy to get caught up in bargaining and not realize that the difference you are talking about is a few cents.

A bargain is called a *ganga,* but the verb "to bargain" is *regatear.* To conclude a bargaining session, you might say *De acuerdo* or *Trato hecho* (It's a deal).

If you treat bargaining like a game and vendors like co-players, everyone will enjoy the experience much more. Bargain for fun rather than with the expectation of getting incredible deals.

Now practice your bargaining skills as you purchase a Talavera ceramic plate from a vendor in Puebla, Mexico.

TRACK 66

What a Deal!

Listen to the vendor and respond to each statement or question appropriately. (The test is not shown here because this is meant to be a more challenging exercise.) You can find a complete model dialog in Appendix D to compare with your ideas.

Chapter 16

Sightseeing: Using Superlatives

Anywhere you go, there is something special to see—something that got you interested in the destination in the first place. The Spanish-speaking world offers everything from natural to man-made wonders. Whether you are more interested in rural or urban landscapes, adventure activities or wandering city streets, sleeping under the stars or staying in a luxury resort, you're sure to find it somewhere that you can practice your Spanish.

The Superlative

The superlative singles out one item from the rest or a group of items from the rest, so it always includes the word "the." In Spanish, of course, "the" can be masculine or feminine, singular or plural, so you will use *el, la, los,* or *las.* The next thing the superlative does is refer to a characteristic, for example, the most interesting, the highest, or the least expensive. The last feature of the superlative is the comparative element. In English you use the words "most" or "least" or the superlative suffix "–est." In Spanish, you only use *más* and *menos.* An easy formula for the superlative in Spanish looks like this: *el, la, los, las + más/menos + adjectivo.* Let's look at a few examples:

> *el monumento más/menos importante*
> **(the most/least important monument)**
> *la iglesia más/menos bonita*
> **(the prettiest, most/least beautiful church)**
> *las calles más/menos interesantes*
> **(the most/least interesting streets)**
> *los edificios más/menos altos*
> **(the tallest/least tall buildings)**

To talk about the "best" and the "worst" places, you use the definite article followed by *mejor* or *peor: el mejor museo* (the best museum) or *la peor fuente* (the worst fountain). If the best and worst places are plural, you use *las* or *los + mejores* or *peores: los barrios más curiosos* (the most curious neighborhoods) or *las peores calles* (the worst streets).

Translate the following list of the top five highlights of Quito, Ecuador. Then check your answers in Appendix D.

- **the best fountains**
- **the most beautiful church**
- **the most historic neighborhood**
- **the most interesting streets**
- **the biggest museums**

If you want to warn someone about the worst of Quito, translate the next five examples and check your work in Appendix D.

- **the ugliest plaza**
- **the worst restaurant**
- **the worst places**
- **the least interesting museum**
- **the least beautiful streets**

Make Suggestions Using Vamos a + Infinitive

If you're traveling with someone else, you might need to make suggestions. You can use the obvious verbs, *recomendar* and *sugerir*, or you might want to use the very encouraging phrase: *vamos a* + infinitive. This expression, the equivalent of "let's . . ." in English, is one of the most positive ways to make a suggestion. Who could resist the enthusiasm in your voice when you say, *¡Vamos a explorar el barrio histórico!* (Let's explore the historic district!) or *¡Vamos a caminar por el centro para ver las mejores fuentes!* (Let's walk around downtown to see the best fountains!)? This expression is sometimes shortened to simply *vamos a* + place: *Vamos al museo* (Let's go to the museum), for example. In either form, this expression is a lot more encouraging than the other ways of making suggestions in Spanish.

Vamos a

TRACK 67

Listen to the comments and questions of your traveling companion and make suggestions using *vamos a*. (The text is not shown here because this is meant to be a more challenging exercise.) You can check Appendix D to see sample responses.

Asking for and Following Directions

Part of the fun of exploring a new place is getting completely turned around. When you get off track, you can often stumble upon some wonderful sights that you wouldn't otherwise have visited, or you might wander into areas that you want to get out of quickly too. In any case, even if you have a map of town, you might do well to ask directions from someone. For example:

Me he perdido. **(I'm lost.)**

No sé dónde estoy. **(I don't know where I am.)**
¿Puede decirme dónde está . . . ? **(Can you tell me where . . . is?)**
¿Puede indicarme dónde estoy en el plano?
(Can you show me where I am on the map?)
¿Cómo puedo llegar a . . . ? **(How can I get to . . . ?)**
¿Cuál es la mejor manera de ir a . . . ? **(What's the best way to go to . . . ?)**
¿Sabe dónde queda . . . ? **(Do you know where . . . is?)**
¿Por dónde voy para . . . ? **(Which way do I go for . . . ?)**

Remember to use a polite phrase like *disculpe* or *perdón* to get someone's attention so you can ask for help. Then, the trickiest part is to understand the directions. A person giving directions might use command forms, simple present, or the future with *ir*. But don't worry too much about the form of the directions. Focus on the instructional content: "go," "turn," "look for," "straight," "to the right," "around the corner," etc. Let's look at some of these key phrases:

- *seguir* **(continue, follow)**
- *doblar* **(turn)**
- *dar la vuelta* **(turn, go around)**
- *cruzar* **(cross)**
- *pasar* **(pass)**
- *buscar* **(look for)**
- *derecho, recto* **(straight)**

- *a la derecha, izquierda* (**to the right, left**)
- *a la vuelta* (**around the corner**)
- *la manzana, la cuadra* (**block**)
- *la esquina* (**corner**)
- *el cruce* (**intersection**)
- *atrás* (**back**)
- *adelante* (**ahead**)
- *al lado* (**next to**)

Lost and Found

Look at the following dialog and see if you can follow the directions. Write out an English translation and then compare your work to the translation in Appendix D.

Buenas tardes. Disculpe. Me he perdido.¿Me puede decir dónde está el Museo de Picasso?

Sí, con mucho gusto. No está muy lejos. Siga esta calle derecho por tres manzanas. En la avenida, doble a la derecha y camine dos manzanas más. Cuando llegue a una plazita con una pastelería, cruce la avenida y tome la calle Princesa. Es la ruta más interesante. Verá una entrada al Metro en la esquina. Va a llegar a otra plaza con una iglesia. Camine al lado de la iglesia hasta la calle Montcada. Entonces, doble a la izquierda. El museo de Picasso está casi al final de la calle.

Impersonal Expressions with Se

Many places in Spain and Latin America have excellent public transportation systems, *sistemas de transporte público*. Depending on the place you are visiting, you may have many or few transportation options besides a private car and your own two feet.

- *a pie* (on foot)
- *en autobús* (by bus)
- *en taxi* (by cab)
- *en metro* (by subway)
- *en tranvía* (by tram)
- *en tren* (by train)
- *en motocicleta* (by motorcycle)
- *en vespa* (by motor scooter)
- *en bicicleta* (by bicycle)
- *la parada* (bus or metro stop)
- *la entrada del metro* (metro entrance)
- *la ruta* (route)

The bus is called *el colectivo* in Argentina and *el guagua* in Puerto Rico. Mexico City, Madrid, and Barcelona have terrific *metro* systems; Buenos Aires has a wonderful *subterráneo* or *subte*, for short. Many cities have privately run minivan buses that are called by a range of names including *colectivos* or *combis*. Each van follows a particular route, and they are often less expensive, though sometimes less comfortable, than the regular bus or subway service. Some privately owned taxis operate in a similar manner, particularly to provide more frequent transportation to and from a city and the surrounding towns. There are rarely schedules for such transport; when the van or cab fills, it departs. However, service is often more frequent than the regular bus. Some cities have special train lines, *los trenes de cercanías*, to handle commuting to outlying areas that may or may not be served by other means as well.

FACT

Buses are generally either numbered or labeled with the name of the last stop of the route. Most subways systems have lines that are both numbered and colored for ease of distinguishing one from another. The Mexico City metro is famous for the pictographic symbols assigned to each line as well—for example, the Grasshopper line and the Pyramid line.

In many places you can buy packets of multiple bus or metro tickets. You may also have the option of a single pass. Some cities offer passes that are good for unlimited travel for a specified time, a week or a month, for example. Think about how much you might use any sort of public transportation to decide whether or not a pass will be worthwhile. Consider convenience as well as cost, because many transportation systems require exact change.

Getting Help on the Bus or Subway

So, you've found out that you have to take bus 32 to get to *Parque Güell.* You've never been there, and you have no idea where to get off the bus. The simplest thing to do is ask the driver to let you know what stop it is. You can also ask someone sitting or standing next to you to tell you when to get off.

TRACK 68

Asking for Help

Listen to each example on Track 68 as you follow along in the text. Repeat each one after you hear it.

¿Me puede avisar cuando lleguemos al Parque Güell, por favor?
(Can you let me know when we get to Güell Park, please?)
¿Me hace el favor de decirme cuando debo bajar para el Parque Güell?
(Will you do me the favor of telling me when I should get off for Güell Park?)
¿Me avisa dónde bajar para el Parque Güell, por favor?
(Will you let me know when to get off for Güell Park, please?)
¿Cuál es la parada para el Parque Güell? ¿Me avisa, por favor?
(Which is the stop for Güell Park? Can you let me know, please?)
¿Cuántas paradas faltan para el Parque Güell?
(How many more stops are there to Güell Park?)

Most people are happy to help out, but you might try to sit near the bus driver just so he or she remembers to let you know when you get to your stop. You might also want to ask the driver where to catch the return bus, *el autobús de regreso.*

You've learned lots of impersonal expressions, and you may hear someone use them to give you directions or make sightseeing recommendations like *Es mejor ir al museo cuando abre porque hay menos gente* (It's best to go to the museum when it opens because there are fewer people). Another common construction is the impersonal expression with *se*. You've used the pronoun *se* with reflexive verbs and to replace *le* and *les* when they are followed by third-person direct object pronouns. Well, *se* is also commonly used with verbs in the third-person singular of the present tense to say what one does or what is done. For example:

> *Aquí se habla español.*
> **(Here one speaks Spanish; or, Spanish is spoken here.)**
> *Se paga aquí.*
> **(One pays here.)**
> *Se baja por atrás.*
> **(One gets out [of the bus] in back.)**

These sorts of expressions sometimes include the verb *deber* to say what one should or should not do or *poder* to say what one can or cannot do.

> *Se debe visitar esa iglesia cuando hay un concierto.*
> **(One should visit that church when there is a concert.)**
> *No se debe andar por ese barrio de noche.*
> **(One shouldn't walk around that neighborhood at night.)**
> *¿Se puede entrar por aquí?*
> **(Can one enter this way?)**
> *No se puede pasar por allí.*
> **(One can't go that way.)**

Let's look at a few more examples that you might find useful when you're finding your way around town.

> *¿Cómo se llega a . . . ?*
> **(How does one get to . . . ?)**
> *¿Se sube por delante o por atrás?*
> **(Does one get on [the bus] in front or back?)**

¿Se come bien en este restaurante?
(Does one eat well in this restaurant? Is the food good here?)
¿Se debe hacer una reservación?
(Should one make a reservation?)

Practice: Impersonal Expressions with Se

Now you try it. Translate the following questions into Spanish using an impersonal expression with *se*. Then check your work in Appendix D.

1. How does one get into the museum?
2. Should one leave the key at reception?
3. One should see the fountain at night.
4. One can see the cathedral from the plaza.
5. One takes the number 7 bus to get to the historic district.

Keep in mind that these sorts of statements in English are usually expressed with the impersonal "you" rather than "one." The Spanish equivalents with *se* do not sound awkward, though their translation into English may.

Managing Minor Difficulties

You've already learned how to ask directions if you get lost. What about managing other minor problems that may arise? Let's imagine that there is a transportation strike; a holiday and things are closed; you lose your hotel key, tourist card, passport, purse, or wallet; or, heaven forbid, you suddenly feel ill.

Let's start with a quick review of some basic vocabulary to talk about these possibilities:

- *una huelga* **(strike)**
- *una manifestación* **(demonstration)**
- *una fiesta* **(holiday)**
- *un desfile, una procesión* **(parade, precession)**
- *la tarjeta de turista* **(tourist card)**

- *la visa* (**visa**)
- *el pasaporte* (**passport**)
- *la comisaría* (**police station**)
- *el consulado* (**consulate**)
- *la embajada* (**embassy**)
- *el hospital* (**hospital**)
- *la clínica* (**clinic**)
- *Se me perdió . . .* (**I lost . . .**)
- *Me han robado . . .* (**My . . . was snatched.**)

Many minor inconveniences, like unexpected holidays, museum closings, and the blocking of streets for demonstrations or parades, can actually turn out to be very interesting. Rather than get frustrated because shops, museums, and monuments are closed unexpectedly, find out what else might be going on in association with the event. Parades and even demonstrations are wonderful opportunities to observe the culture of the place you're visiting.

FACT

The word *cartera* can mean "wallet" or "purse," depending on the country you're in. A *billetera* is a "billfold." Another word for "purse" is *bolso*.

Health Inconveniences

Traveling can be stressful even under the best of circumstances. Don't underestimate the effect different foods, a different pace, different elevation, and different climate might have on your system. Give yourself a break and take an afternoon or day off from sightseeing. Be sure to drink plenty of water to replace fluids and try eating plain boiled rice to settle your system. If that doesn't do the trick, and if you haven't packed simple remedies, go to the nearest pharmacy. Remember that pharmacists in most Spanish-speaking countries can prescribe treatment for many conditions. If you're staying in a rural location, ask if the kitchen can prepare an herbal remedy (*reme-*

dio) or if you can be taken to the nearest town to go to a pharmacy. If your health problem requires a higher level of professional attention, ask to be directed or taken to the nearest doctor's or dentist's office, clinic, or hospital. Health care is typically much more economical in Spain and Latin America than in the States, so don't let concerns about cost lead you to ignore a potentially serious condition. Get the attention you need.

Accidental Occurrences

Spanish has a wonderful grammatical construction to talk about accidental occurrences like losing something. Use *se* followed by an indirect object pronoun to express who the event happened to, and use the preterite or the present perfect to say what happened or has happened. For example, to say that you lost your key, you can say *Se me perdió la llave* or *Se me ha perdido la llave*. If your husband lost his key, or both of you lost your keys, you would report it by saying *A mi esposo se le perdió la llave* or *Se nos perdieron las llaves*. This impersonal construction deflects blame by focusing on the event and the victim of the event rather than the perpetrator. Let's look at a few more examples:

Se me cayó/ha caído el boleto.
(I [have] dropped my ticket.)
Se nos fue/ha ido el autobús.
(The bus [has] left us behind, i.e., We [have] missed the bus.)
Se le pasó/ha pasado la hora.
(He [has] lost track of time.)
Se me mojó la visa.
(My visa got wet.)

This is the most common way to describe health issues like breaking a bone or twisting an ankle as well:

Se me rompió el brazo.
(I broke my arm.)
Se le torció el tobillo.
(He twisted his ankle.)

Another way you can explain what happened to a person is to use the indirect object pronoun and the third-person plural of the verb, for example, *Le robaron el pasaporte* (They stole his passport") or *Me quitaron la cartera* (They lifted my wallet).

Obviously, if you lose your hotel key you can simply report it and the hotel will replace it. Modern hotels use magnetic key cards that they can make quickly. If you have lost a metal key, you may have to pay for its replacement. That's a good reason to leave keys of that sort at the hotel reception desk. Some hotels make it very difficult to carry their keys around by putting them on enormous key chains.

In the event you have lost important documents, you will probably have to report to the police station or, perhaps, the nearest United States consulate or embassy. To save yourself this headache, you should only carry around photocopies of these important documents, and lock the originals in your bag or hotel safe.

Practice: Managing Difficulties

Hopefully, you'll never have a problem while you're traveling but, just in case, try translating the following into Spanish. Then compare what you wrote to the sample answers in Appendix D.

1. We were watching the parade and someone lifted our wallets.
2. I feel very sick. Can you tell me where the nearest clinic is?
3. He has to go to the embassy because he lost his passport.
4. Everything is closed today because of the holiday. Can you recommend something to us?
5. We've missed the last train. Do you know a hotel around here?

You're ready for just about anything now so get on out there and see the sights!

Chapter 17

Narrate with Preterite and Imperfect Verbs

You just had a fabulous day of sight-seeing, and you want to tell someone all about it. You need both of the past tenses: preterite for the action and imperfect for the description. This is the chapter where you're going to master narrating in the past using the preterite and imperfect tenses.

Regular Preterite Verbs

You saw all the highlights of Sevilla and are now unwinding over a delicious dinner at a riverside restaurant. Here's a list of the verbs you'll need to talk about your adventure.

- *averiguar* **(to find out)**
- *acabar* **(to finish, complete)**
- *acercarse* **(to approach)**
- *acordarse de* **(to remember)**
- *agotarse* **(to wear oneself out)**
- *buscar* **(to look for)**
- *cansarse* **(to get tired)**
- *continuar* **(to continue)**
- *charlar* **(to chat)**
- *descubrir* **(to discover)**
- *encontrar* **(to find)**
- *enseñar* **(to show, to teach)**
- *equivocarse* **(to be mistaken)**
- *escoger* **(to choose)**
- *esperar* **(to expect, hope, wait for)**
- *fijarse en* **(to take notice of)**
- *gastar* **(to spend)**
- *guiar* **(to guide, lead)**
- *indicar* **(to indicate, point out)**
- *informarse* **(to find out)**
- *invitar* **(to invite, to treat)**
- *ocurrir* **(to happen)**
- *ofrecer* **(to offer)**
- *parar* **(to stop)**
- *parecer* **(to seem)**
- *permitir* **(to permit)**
- *preocuparse por* **(to worry about)**
- *sentarse* **(to sit down)**
- *sorprenderse* **(to be surprised)**
- *subir* **(to go up)**
- *suceder* **(to take place)**
- *terminar* **(to finish)**
- *tocar* **(to touch)**
- *volver* **(to return)**

Why Sevilla?

Sevilla is one of Spain's great historic cities. Located on the banks of the Guadalquivir River, Sevilla was an important trade center from ancient times. The Romans made the settlement one of the greatest cities in the empire, and you can still visit interesting Roman remains, including segments of aqueduct, the city wall, and the toll tower that controlled trade on the river. Sevilla underwent a second major transformation during its 500 years under Moorish rule from 712 to 1248. For much of this period, the city was famous as a center of three religions and cultures: Muslim, Jewish, and Christian. The arts and sciences flourished as scholars from the three great cultures taught and learned from each other, and shared their knowledge with the rest of the known world. Great works of art, architecture, literature, philosophy, science, mathematics, astronomy, medicine, and economics owed their conception to the extraordinary cultural melting pot that was Sevilla. Returned to Christian rule, Sevilla played an important role in politics and religion during the Middle Ages and was renowned as a cultural center through Spain's Golden Age. In modern days, Sevilla endures as an important tourist destination and lively economic center where flamenco dancing and bullfighting are as much a part of the scene as politics and world trade.

Be careful with the verbs *regresar, volver,* and *devolver.* To say that you are returning to a place, use *regresar* or *volver: Regresamos (volvimos) al hotel muy tarde.* (We went back to the hotel very late). To talk about returning something, use *devolver: Devolvimos el plano al conserje* (We returned the map to the concierge).

So, what might be on your list of things to do and places to visit on a trip to Sevilla? Just take a look:

- *la Torre de Oro:* the city's iconic Roman toll tower on the banks of the Guadalquivir
- *la catedral:* one of Europe's largest, and the resting place of Christopher Columbus
- *la Giralda:* originally, the tower of Sevilla's *mezquita* (mosque), now the bell tower of the cathedral
- *el Alcázar:* the royal palace, an outstanding example of Moorish architecture and gardens, still used today by Spain's royal family
- *el Archivo de Indias:* the great archive of Spain's historic explorations of the Americas
- *el Barrio de Santa Cruz:* the former Jewish quarter, now a labyrinth of shops, restaurants, and private residences
- *los tablaos:* the flamenco clubs

- *los puentes:* magnificent bridges grace the river
- *el Parque de María Luisa:* Sevilla's most elegant park
- *la Tabacalera:* now one of the university buildings, the tobacco factory made famous in Bizet's opera *Carmen*
- *Semana Santa:* Sevilla's unique Holy Week celebration
- *Feria:* Sevilla's horse-trading fair

ALERT!

The verbs *ocurrir* and *suceder* are really only used in the third-person singular and plural conjugations. For example, *¿Qué ocurrió en Sevilla durante la época medieval?* (What happened in Sevilla during the Middle Ages?) and *Sucedieron dos eventos muy importantes* (Two very important events took place).

One Great Day

Let's see some of what our visitors did on their whirlwind tour. Complete Rosa's diary entry with the preterite of the verb indicated. Then check your work in Appendix D.

Querido diario,
Hoy Alberto y yo _____ (descubrir) las maravillas de Sevilla. Nosotros _____ (sorprenderse) de la variedad de los sitios de interés y _____ (acabar) el día muy cansados. Pero, déjame contarte, diario, todo lo que _____ (ocurrir).
Yo _____ (levantarse) a las seis de la mañana y _____ (sentarse) a leer un poco nuestra guía. También _____ (averiguar) los horarios de la catedral y el Alcázar porque me _____ (parecer) los sitios más importantes de la ciudad. Después, yo _____ (charlar) un ratito con el conserje y él me _____ (enseñar) otra guía turística de la ciudad y me _____ (indicar) los mejores sitios en el plano. Yo _____ (esperar) hasta las ocho y entonces _____ (despertar) a Alberto. A las nueve fuimos a la catedral donde _____ (admirar) sus tesoros. Entonces, nosotros _____ (subir) la torre de la Giralda

*desde donde hay una vista panorámica espléndida. Alberto _____
(cansarse) por la subida y bajada de la torre que es muy alta. Entonces, yo
_____ (acordarse) de una plaza muy tranquila cerca de la catedral.
Allí, Alberto me _____ (invitar) a un café y después de media hora
_____ (continuar, nosotros). _____ (acercarse, nosotros)
al Alcázar y _____ (buscar) la entrada. Yo la _____ (encontrar) sin dificultad mientras Alberto _____ (parar) un momento para
comprar una guía en la librería. ¡Qué increíble es el Alcázar con su arquitectura extraordinaria y hermosos jardines! Nuestra guía nos _____
(informar) de muchos detalles interesantes. Después de más de dos horas,
nosotros _____ (salir). Teníamos mucha hambre así fuimos al Barrio
de Santa Cruz para buscar donde comer.*

Irregular Preterite Verbs

Before we go any further, let's review some more verbs that have irregular
conjugations in the preterite. You already learned a number of completely
irregular preterite verbs in Chapter 9: *ir, ser, ver, estar, tener,* and *hacer.* You
also learned that a few verbs have minor stem changes in the third-person of
the preterite: *dormir > durmió, durmieron* and *vestir > vistió, vistieron.* Here
are a few more verbs that change their stem vowel in the preterite:

e > i
- *divertirse* **(to enjoy oneself):** *se divirtió, se divirtieron*
- *pedir* **(to request, ask for):** *pidió, pidieron*
- *preferir* **(to prefer):** *prefirió, prefirieron*
- *impedir* **(to prevent):** *impidió, impidieron*
- *seguir* **(to follow):** *siguió, siguieron*
- *conseguir* **(to get, acquire, achieve):** *consiguió, consiguieron*
- *sugerir* **(to suggest):** *sugirió, sugirieron*

Irregular Preterite 1

Now, let's practice a bit. Listen to the questions with irregular e > i preterite verbs on Track 69. Answer each question using the same verb. You can
find the transcript and sample answers in Appendix D.

Additionally, *–er* and *–ir* verbs whose stems end in a vowel like *caer, leer,* and *oír* have slight spelling changes in the third person preterite conjugations to maintain the correct pronunciation of their vowel sounds. These verbs substitute a *y* for the *i* in the third-person preterite endings.

- *caer, caerse* **(to fall, fall down):** *(se) cayó, (se) cayeron*
- *leer* **(to read):** *leyó, leyeron*
- *oír* **(to hear):** *oyó, oyeron*

Remember that this change only occurs in verbs that end in *–er* and *–ir,* so *guiar* doesn't.

Remember that there are shifts in meaning with the verbs *poder, querer,* and *saber* in the preterite. *Pude ver toda la ciudad* means "I was able (managed) to see the entire city." *Quise ir a la Feria pero no conseguí boletos* means "I wanted [tried] to go to the fair but couldn't get tickets." *Supe que el museo estaba cerrado el domingo* means "I found out/learned that the museum was closed on Sunday."

Other verbs present significantly more irregular changes. You saw in Chapter 9 that the stem of *hacer* changes to *hic–* in the preterite. The stem vowels of *querer* and *venir* also change to *i* in the preterite, and these verbs have the same irregular unstressed first- and third-person singular endings as *hacer*:

- *querer: quise, quisiste, quiso, quisimos, quisistéis, quisieron*
- *venir: vine, viniste, vino, vinimos, vinistéis, vinieron*

You also remember that *estar* and *tener* acquire a *u* in the preterite: *estuv–* and *tuv–*. The verbs *poder, poner,* and *saber* also change to *u. Poner* and *saber* have an additional spelling change, and all three verbs have unstressed first- and third-person singular endings.

- *poder: pude, pudiste, pudo, pudimos, pudistéis, pudieron*
- *poner: puse, pusiste, puso, pusimos, pusistéis, pusieron*
- *saber: supe, supiste, supo, supimos, supistéis, supieron*

Irregular Preterite 2

TRACK 70

Answer the questions on Track 70 using irregular preterite verbs. Then check your work in Appendix D where you'll find a complete transcript as well as sample answers.

Another category of irregular verbs in the preterite is formed by *decir*, *traer*, and all verbs ending in *–ducir* like *conducir* and *traducir*. Look at the changes these verbs undergo:

decir **(to say):** *dije, dijiste, dijo, dijimos, dijistéis, dijeron*
traer **(to bring):** *traje, trajiste, trajo, trajimos, trajistéis, trajeron*
conducir **(to drive, conduct, lead):** *conduje, condujiste, condujimos, condujistéis, condujeron*

ALERT!

Remember that, unlike regular verbs in the preterite, irregular verbs in the preterite are not stressed—and do not have an accent—on the last syllable of the first- and third-person singular conjugations.

Practice with Irregular Preterite

Let's practice the irregular preterite by translating the following sentences into Spanish. You can check your work with the model answers in Appendix D.

1. Juan asked me for the car keys and drove to Granada.
2. Marta and Elena didn't hear the explanation, but they read their guidebook.

3. I don't know where I put my purse.
4. The concierge suggested a flamenco club and the friends got tickets for that night.
5. I didn't bring a dress, but your friend gave me a pretty skirt.

Practice makes perfect, and that is certainly the key to mastering the regular and irregular preterite verb conjugations. Keep a running list of what you and your friends and family did during each day for about a week and you'll internalize many of these forms.

Regular and Irregular Preterite Verbs

Rosa wasn't always able to write lengthy diary entries because she was so busy in Sevilla. However, she jotted down notes. Help her complete the following notes with the preterite of the verb in parentheses. This time, the regular verbs are mixed in with the irregulars, so you'll really have to pay attention. Remember that the first- and third-person singular conjugations (*yo* and *él, ella, usted*) of regular verbs always have an accent on the last vowel: *visité* and *visitó*, for example. An outstanding feature of the irregular verbs is that these conjugations are not stressed on the final vowel: *dije* and *dijo*, for example. Double-check your work and then compare your answers to the answer key in Appendix D.

1. *Yo _____ (buscar) el museo de arqueología pero no lo _____ (encontrar).*
2. *Un niño muy simpático nos _____ (guiar) por el Barrio de Santa Cruz.*
3. *Yo _____ (equivocarse) de autobús y nosotros _____ (tener) que volver al centro y esperar a otro.*
4. *Alberto _____ (decidir) comprarme un pañuelo de regalo y él mismo lo _____ (escoger) en una tienda muy cara.*
5. *Otro día Alberto me _____ (traer) una olla de cerámica muy bonita.*
6. *Yo _____ (querer) tocar una escultura en el museo, pero el guardián no me lo _____ (permitir).*

Did you remember to change the spelling of *busqué* and *me equivoqué*? Though these are regular verbs, remember that you have to make the *c > qu* spelling change to preserve the pronunciation of the /k/ sound of the infinitive. Any verb with a hard *–c* before the infinitive ending has the same spelling change in the first person of the preterite, for example, *acercarse*, *comunicar*, and *tocar*: *me acerqué, comuniqué*, and *toqué*.

Postcards: Preterite and Imperfect

Remember that there are two past tenses in Spanish: the preterite and the imperfect. You can think of the preterite as the snapshot of an event, for example, *Vimos un tablao* (We saw a flamenco show) and *Fui al Parque María Luisa* (I went to the *María Luisa Park*). The imperfect describes what was going on at the time, and fills in the background of the story like this: *Estábamos muy cansados, pero fuimos a ver un tablao* (We were very tired, but we went to see a flamenco show) and *Era una tarde muy bonita y fui al Parque María Luisa* (It was a beautiful afternoon, and I went to the María Luisa Park). Think of the two parts of a postcard: the image, and the note on the back. The photo is like a preterite statement; it captures a moment or illustrates a destination. The note you write on the back, however, probably includes preterite and imperfect to say where you went, what you did, and what it was like. Read what Rosa wrote on the back of a postcard and jot down which verbs are in the preterite and which are in the imperfect.

Anoche fui a un tablao con Mariana. Empezó muy tarde, pero ¡valió la pena! Las mujeres llevaban vestidos muy bonitos y los hombres eran muy elegantes. Mientras uno tocaba la guitarra y otro cantaba, las mujeres bailaban. ¡Yo quería bailar también, pero no se pudo! Volvimos al hotel a las cuatro de la mañana y no nos levantamos hasta las once.

Did you write down the preterite verbs *fui, empezó, valió, pudo, volvimos,* and *nos levantamos* and the imperfect verbs *llevaban, eran, tocaba, cantaba,* and *bailaban?* If so, you're right on track. Let's look at each and talk a bit about why Rosa used preterite or imperfect to describe each aspect of her outing.

Preterite examples:
- *fui:* **"I went"** describes the outing as a completed past action.
- *empezó:* **"It began"** describes a precise moment in the past—the instant that the show started. Remember that beginnings and endings in the past are most commonly expressed in the preterite.
- *valió:* **"It was worth it"** refers to the outing as a completed past event.
- *no se pudo:* **"It couldn't be done"** describes the fact that Rosa had no opportunity to dance during the show. It wasn't allowed, for example.
- *volvimos:* **"We returned"** describes the completed action of returning to the hotel.
- *nos levantamos:* **"We got up"** describes the completed action of getting up.

Imperfect examples:
- *llevaban:* **"They were wearing"** describes a state of being in the past.
- *eran:* **"They were"** describes a state of being in the past.
- *tocaba:* **"One played"** describes an ongoing action in the past.
- *cantaba:* **"One sang"** describes an ongoing activity in the past.
- *bailaban:* **"They danced"** describes an ongoing activity in the past.

Now write your own post card from Sevilla. The photo shows a scene of people dressed in flamenco clothes by the door of the cathedral. The *Giralda* is on the right of the entrance and you can see people taking pictures through the windows. Translate the following into Spanish to write on the back of the card. Then check your work in Appendix D.

Semana Santa began yesterday, and a lot of people were wearing flamenco dresses and suits in front of the cathedral. While they were waiting for the procession, some of them sang and danced. I went up the Giralda and took pictures. There were a lot of people watching from the windows. It was beautiful.

Preterite Versus Imperfect

It's not always easy to decide whether to use the preterite or imperfect in a narration. In fact, sometimes you can use either one, and your choice will change the meaning slightly or dramatically. You've already learned that some verbs, like *querer, conocer, and saber,* significantly change their meaning from one tense to another. In other cases, the difference is more subtle. Look at the following examples and explanations:

- *Fue un viaje maravilloso.* The use of the preterite indicates that the speaker conceives of the trip as being over and done with.
- *Era un viaje maravilloso.* The use of the imperfect, in a sense, takes the speaker back to the trip to remember how marvelous it was while it was going on.
- *Juan se preocupó cuando yo no encontré mi cartera.* The preterite is used to relate two specific cause and effect events: "I couldn't find my wallet" (at a particular moment) and "Juan got worried" (a reaction to the lost wallet, a change of emotional state).
- *Juan se preocupaba cuando yo no encontraba mi cartera.* The use of the imperfect highlights the repeated nature of these events: "Every time I couldn't find my wallet, Juan would get worried."
- *Cuando los músicos empezaban a tocar el público todavía charlaba.* The imperfect describes two ongoing events in the past: "When the musicians were beginning to play (tuning their instruments, trying a few chords) the audience was still chatting."

- *Cuando los músicos empezaron a tocar el público todavía charlaba.*
  The preterite in the first phrase describes the moment that the music began, while the imperfect in the second phrase highlights the background conversation of the audience, still chatting even though the music had begun.

Read the following sentences and then write an equivalent in Spanish using preterite or imperfect to communicate the same sense as the English. Check your choices with the answers in Appendix D.

1. We had to (were obliged) wait an hour to go up the *Giralda*.
2. While we waited, I noticed that there were a lot of people in the plaza.
3. Raúl was telling me something about what he did last night.
4. Raúl told me that he went to a flamenco club.
5. We wanted to go to the *Alcázar* in the afternoon, but we found out that it was closed.

Chapter 18

From Mountains to Seashore: Prepositions

18

Whether you climb up, hike down, swim around, or paddle out to that island offshore, you need prepositions to do it. Prepositions' primary function is to tell us where things are located and what direction the action is moving. Prepositions are so flexible, though, that when they are used in combination with certain verbs and in idiomatic expressions, their meanings can change dramatically. So read through this chapter carefully and check out what prepositions can do for you.

Prepositions: Part 1

Whatever draws you to the mountains, in whatever season, prepositions will help you get to your destination and make sure you have a good time while you're there. Let's start with some basic vocabulary to talk about the things you might do on a visit to the mountains.

- *la colina* (**hill**)
- *la montaña* (**mountain**)
- *la cima* (**mountain top, peak**)
- *la falda* (**mountain side**)
- *la cuesta, el pendiente* (**sloping ground**)
- *el sendero* (**path**)
- *el prado* (**meadow**)
- *el arroyo* (**stream**)
- *el cañón* (**canyon**)
- *el precipicio* (**cliff**)
- *el panorama* (**view**)
- *escalar* (**to climb**)
- *hacer, practicar el senderismo* (**to hike**)
- *la mochila* (**backpack**)
- *los prismáticos, los binoculares* (**binoculars**)

You already know some other vocabulary pertinent to a mountain visit: *las botas de montaña* are perfect for the rugged outdoors, and *un sombrero* will protect you from the sun. You've also already learned the verbs *caminar* and *andar*, which are often used to refer to hiking instead of the more cumbersome *hacer* or *practicar el senderismo*. To talk about going (hiking, climbing) up or down a mountain, use *subir* and *bajar*.

FACT

Mountaineering or mountain climbing is generally referred to as *el alpinismo* in Spain and *el andinismo* in South America. The Alps give their name to the sport in Europe, while the Andes inspire the term in South America.

Expand your list with verbs like *cargar* (to carry) for your *mochila*, *atravesar* (cut across) for that *arroyo* or *cañón*, and *apreciar* (to enjoy, appreciate) for that mountain *panorama*.

In the Mountains

TRACK 71

Listen to each example on Track 71 as you follow along in the text. Repeat each sentence after you hear it.

> *No me gusta cargar una mochila muy pesada.*
> **(I don't like to carry a very heavy backpack.)**
> *Atravesamos el arroyo con mucho cuidado.*
> **(We crossed over the stream very carefully.)**
> *Cuando llegaron a la cima de la montaña, los caminantes descansaron media hora para apreciar el panorama.*
> **(When they got to the top of the mountain, the hikers rested for half an hour to enjoy the view.)**

If you go up to the mountains in the winter, it's likely that you're headed to a ski resort or to some trails for cross-country skiing. The sport of skiing is referred to as *el esquí*, and cross-country skiing is called *el esquí nórdico*. Let's have a look at some more of the specialized vocabulary you'll need.

- *la estación de esquí* **(ski resort)**
- *esquiar* **(to ski)**
- *los esquís* **(skis)**
- *los palos* **(ski poles)**
- *la pista* **(ski slope)**
- *el teleférico* **(gondola)**
- *sufrir un accidente* **(to have an accident)**
- *chocar con* **(to crash into)**
- *rescatar* **(to rescue)**

You've already learned a number of reflexive verbs that you can use while you're at the ski resort: *ponerse*, *caerse*, and *romperse*, for example.

By changing *subir* and *bajar* to reflexives, *subirse* and *bajarse*, you can use them to talk about "hopping onto" or "off" something like the ski lift.

> *Me puse los esquís y luego me subí al teleférico.*
> **(I put on my skis and then I hopped on the ski lift.)**
> *Elizabeth se cayó cuando esquiaba y se rompió el brazo.*
> **(Elizabeth fell while she was skiing and broke her arm.)**

ALERT!

The verbs *subir* and *bajar* can be used in several ways. They mean to get on, into, off, or out of a vehicle, as well as to climb or hike up or down a mountain. As reflexives, they make any of these actions more emphatic, rather like "zip" up or down or "hop" on or off in English.

Vacation in the Mountains

Before we go any further, let's talk a little bit about your last vacation in the mountains. Translate the following sentences to say what you and your friends did. Then check your work with the model answers in Appendix D.

1. My friends and I skied in the Sierra Nevada at a beautiful ski resort.
2. Rafael had an accident and ran into a tree on the slope.
3. You took a backpack with some food and water when you went hiking through the canyon, didn't you?
4. Juan and Marta preferred the gondola, but María hiked up on foot.
5. There are many paths to reach the meadow at the top of the mountain.

So, where might you go to enjoy the mountains or a ski resort in the Spanish-speaking world? Spain's highest and longest mountain range is the Pyrenees (*los Pirineos*), where you can find many ski resorts. There are also great places to ski in the *Sierra Nevada* in southern Spain, near Granada. Both of these mountain ranges host tourism year-round, from summer hiking and adventure activities of all sorts to skiing and related snow sports in the winter. Mexico and Central America boast plenty of mountainous areas for hiking and climbing, though none has enough snow for skiing. Nearly every country in South America features some segment of the Andes where adventure sports of all kinds are practiced. The major South American ski resorts are in Chile and Argentina, and world-class mountaineering is available all along the Andean range, which has some of the world's highest peaks and most challenging climbs.

Basic Prepositions

Now you've got some basic mountain and ski vocabulary under your belt. Let's move on to the prepositions that make all these activities possible. Notice that many of these prepositions have multiple equivalents in English.

- *a* (**to, at, by, on**)
- *hacia* (**toward, about**)
- *en* (**in, on, at, by**)
- *de* (**from, of, about**)
- *hasta* (**until, to, as far as, up to**)
- *desde* (**from, since**)
- *sobre* (**on, upon, above, over, about**)
- *bajo* (**under**)
- *entre* (**between, among**)
- *con* (**with**)
- *sin* (**without**)
- *contra* (**against**)

Many of these prepositions fall into three basic categories: prepositions of place, of direction, and of time. Look at the following chart to review some of the contexts in which these prepositions can be used.

Prepositions

Of Place	Of Direction	Of Time
	a	*a*
	hacia	*hacia*
en		*en*

Of Place	Of Direction	Of Time
de	de	de
	hasta	hasta
desde	desde	desde
sobre		sobre
bajo		
entre		entre
contra	contra	

This may seem like a lot of flexibility, but you'll quickly realize that these multiple functions of prepositions aren't as confusing as you thought. Look over the following examples and you'll see:

Fuimos a casa a las ocho.
(We went home at eight. – direction and time)
Estaremos en tu casa en cinco minutos.
(We'll be at your house in five minutes. – place, time)
Hoy sólo esquiamos hasta el arroyo. Mañana seguiremos hasta la tarde.
(Today we only skied to the stream. Tomorrow we'll continue until afternoon. – direction and time)
El avión pasará sobre el volcán sobre las once.
(The plane will fly over the volcano around eleven. – place and time)

It's important to keep in mind that these prepositions can have other meanings as well, and their meanings may shift in translation. Sentences that use particular prepositions in English may use a different preposition in Spanish or none at all, and vice versa. For example, you say "I'm going home" in English, but the same sentence in Spanish requires the directional preposition *a*: *Voy a casa.* Similarly, you can say something is *sobre la mesa* in Spanish, and use the same preposition to express about what time you might arrive somewhere: *sobre las ocho.* These two ideas are expressed using two different prepositions in English: "on the table" and "around eight." The same thing happens with idiomatic expressions. For example, in English you hike up that mountain slope "on foot" but in Spanish you do it *a pie.*

Your best approach is to simply accept the differences and focus on the way Spanish prepositions are used rather than try to translate from English.

You have already learned the many meanings of the prepositions *por* and *para*. To summarize them briefly, *por* can mean "for, by, through, along, by means of, because of, and for the sake of." The meanings of *para* include "for, to, by, and toward," among others.

TRACK 72

Basic Prepositions

Listen to each sentence in Spanish and write down an English equivalent. (The text is not included here because this is meant to be a more challenging exercise.) Remember that English might use a different preposition than Spanish, and there may also be more than one correct way to express the sentence in English. Refer to Appendix D to see a transcript of the audio and check yours translations against the sample answers provided.

Verb and Preposition Partnerships

English and Spanish both use many verb + preposition combinations. To get an idea of how common this is, look up the verb "get" in your English/Spanish dictionary and marvel at all the prepositions that "get" can be paired with and all the different meanings those combinations generate. Then look at how many ways "get" can be translated into Spanish. If you had any doubts, you'll finally "get" the idea that translation isn't simple word substitution.

In many cases, the literal meanings of prepositions are lost in the verb + preposition partnerships. Remember that English and Spanish verb-preposition combinations may be completely different, and some combinations in English are expressed with a single verb in Spanish, and vice versa. For example, in English you "look for" the trail on a hike; in Spanish, *buscas el sendero*, with no preposition. Similarly, in English you "look at" the view from the ski lift, but in Spanish, *miras el panorama*. Of course, the reverse also occurs. Many Spanish verb + preposition combinations are expressed with a single verb in English, for example, *disfrutar de* (to enjoy), *fijarse en* (to notice), and *jugar a* (to play a sport). Let's take a moment to look at some more Spanish verb + preposition combinations that will help you out on your trip to the mountains.

- *asistir a* **(to attend a class, lecture, etc.)**
- *echarse a* **(to set out, to start)**
- *invitar a* **(to invite to)**
- *ponerse a* **(to begin to)**
- *acabar con* **(to finish off)**
- *encontrarse con* **(to run into someone by chance)**
- *acabar de* **(to have just . . .)**
- *acordarse de* **(to recall, remember)**
- *cansarse de* **(to get tired of)**
- *tratar de* **(to try to)**
- *pensar en* **(to think about, consider)**
- *tardar en* **(to delay, to be late in doing something)**

TRACK 73

Verb and Preposition Partnerships

Now let's see some of these combinations in action. Listen to each example on Track 73 as you follow along in the text. Repeat each after you hear it.

Asistí a una clase de esquí cuando llegué a la estación.
(I attended a ski class when I arrived at the ski resort.)
Acabamos de bajar la montaña por una cuesta muy empinada.
(We have just come down the mountain by way of a very steep slope.)
¿No te acordaste de traer los esquís?
(Didn't you remember to bring your skis?)
Melina no tardó mucho en llegar.
(Melina wasn't very late in arriving.)

Practice some more with these verb and preposition combinations as you play around with the new vocabulary from this lesson. Make up a story about a trip you took, and say what everyone did using as many prepositions and verb + preposition combinations as you can.

Prepositions: Part 2

There are plenty of world-class beaches in the Spanish-speaking world too, where you can practice your language skills while enjoying the sun and surf. In fact, the only Spanish-speaking countries with no coastline are Paraguay and Bolivia, in South America. Let's take a moment to learn some new vocabulary to talk about fun and games by the seaside.

Basic Beach Vocabulary

- *la playa* (**beach**)
- *la arena* (**sand**)
- *las olas* (**waves**)
- *la orilla* (**seashore**)
- *la marea* (**tide**)
- *las palmeras* (**palm trees**)
- *las conchas* (**shells**)
- *los peces* (**fish**)
- *el traje de baño, el bañador* (**swimsuit**)
- *el bronceador* (**suntan lotion**)
- *el protector solar* (**sunscreen**)
- *las gafas/los lentes de sol* (**sunglasses**)
- *el barco de vela* (**sailboat**)
- *el barco de remo* (**rowboat**)
- *el yate* (**yacht**)
- *la tabla de surf* (**surfboard**)
- *la caña de pescar* (**fishing pole**)
- *el equipo de buceo* (**skin, scuba-diving equipment**)
- *el puerto* (**port**)
- *el muelle* (**dock**)
- *el arrecife* (**reef**)

Activities

- *nadar* (**swim**)
- *tomar el sol* (**sunbathe**)
- *correr las olas* (**surf, body-surf**)
- *pescar* (**fish**)
- *navegar* (**sail, boat**)
- *bucear* (**skin- or scuba-dive**)
- *mirar la puesta del sol* (**watch the sunset**)
- *ver el amanecer* (**see the sunrise**)
- *observar las estrellas* (**look at the stars**)

There are plenty of other beach activities, like parasailing and windsurfing, that are generally referred to by their names in English. If you want to ask about availability of these, you can ask something like *¿Dónde puedo practicar/hacer parasailing?*

In the event you'd rather get away from it all, leave the resort crowd, and camp out on some secluded little cove, you're going to need some other things.

- *acampar* (**camp**)
- *hacer una fogata* (**make a campfire**)
- *relajarse en una hamaca* (**relax in a hammock**)
- *montar* (**set up**)
- *la tienda de campaña* (**tent**)
- *el saco de dormir* (**sleeping bag**)
- *el mosquitero* (**mosquito net**)
- *la estufa* (**stove**)
- *las ollas* (**pots and pans**)
- *la linterna* (**flashlight**)
- *el fuego* (**fire**)
- *los fósforos* (**matches**)

FACT

Camping is a very popular activity in Spain, especially among young people and budget-minded adults. Camping is less common in Latin America. Nevertheless, throughout the Spanish-speaking world, many people enjoy the outdoors camp.

Practice: By the Water

So, how do prepositions come into play along the seashore? Well, let's take a look. You can *hacer castillos de arena* (make sandcastles), *tirarse al agua* (dive into the water), *bucear sobre el arrecife* (snorkel over the reef), *meterse en / dentro del saco de dormir* and *dormir bajo las estrellas* (sleep under the stars), for example. Practice a bit more by translating these ideas into Spanish using prepositions and your new vocabulary. You can find sample answers in Appendix D.

1. We relaxed in a hammock between two palm trees.
2. María set up a mosquito net over her sleeping bag.
3. Silvia sunbathed from eight until ten.
4. You found some shells under the dock, didn't you?
5. I went fishing on the sailboat.

So, you can see how important prepositions are for expressing where and when you do things.

Compound Prepositions

Just as verbs and prepositions sometimes get together, sometimes prepositions join forces with each other to make new meanings. Here are a number of important compound prepositions:

- *enfrente de* (**in front of**)
- *detrás de* (**behind, in back of**)
- *antes de* (**before**)
- *después de* (**after**)
- *cerca de* (**near**)
- *lejos de* (**far from**)
- *dentro de* (**inside, within**)
- *fuera de* (**outside of**)
- *debajo de* (**underneath**)
- *al lado de* (**next to**)
- *alrededor de* (**around**)
- *además de* (**in addition to**)

Many of these phrases function as adverbs as well as prepositions, but you may not even be aware of that grammatical difference. You'll find them supremely useful any way they are used.

Compound Prepositions

TRACK 74

Listen to each example on Track 74 as you follow along in the text. Repeat each sentence after you hear it.

Debes dejar tus botas fuera de la tienda de campaña, pero lejos del fuego.
(You should leave your boots outside of the tent but far from the fire.)
Colgué mi hamaca cerca de la orilla para escuchar las olas.
(I hung up my hammock near the water's edge to listen to the waves.)
Antes de hacer una fogata es importante limpiar la zona alrededor del fuego.
(Before making a bonfire, it's important to clean up the area around the fire.)

More Verb and Preposition Partnerships

The camping vocabulary list includes some additional verb + preposition combinations: *tirarse al agua* (to dive into the water) and *meterse en* or *meterse dentro del saco de dormir* (to get into your sleeping bag). Let's add to that list with some other common verb and preposition combinations in Spanish.

- *acostumbrarse a* **(to get used to)**
- *aprender a* **(to learn to)**
- *atreverse a* **(to dare to)**
- *comenzar a* **(to begin to)**
- *contentarse con* **(to be content with)**
- *contar con* **(to count on)**
- *aprovecharse de* **(to take advantage of)**
- *cuidar de* **(to take care that)**
- *gozar de* **(to enjoy)**
- *enterarse de* **(to find out)**
- *preocuparse de* **(to worry about)**
- *reírse de* **(to laugh at)**

To practice a bit, complete Mario's story about a camping trip he took with friends. Then check your work in Appendix D.

Todo comenzó cuando yo _____ (learned to) bucear. Jaime decidió que teníamos que hacer un viaje a la playa para _____ (camp) y _____ (enjoy) mar. Yo no _____ (didn't dare to) decir que no aunque no me gusta dormir _____ (outside). Entonces, yo

_____ (counted on) *Jaime para traer todo el equipo necesario y yo* _____ (worried about) *la comida. Pues, cuando llegamos a la playa y Jaime* _____ (began to) *organizar sus cosas, yo* _____ (found out) *que Jaime no* _____ (did not bring) *una tienda de campaña, mosquetero, ollas, o fósforos. Por suerte nosotros* _____ (were able to) *conseguir algunas cosas esenciales de otras personas. Al final nosotros* _____ (laughed at) *nuestra aventura porque* _____ (enjoyed) *todo lo que hicimos ese fin de semana.*

Talking about the Weather with Hay, Hacer, and Estar

Contrary to English, only a few weather conditions are described using the verb "to be" in Spanish. The present continuous with *estar* is used to describe a weather event in process, for example, *está lloviendo* (it's raining) and *está nevando* (it's snowing). You can also use *estar* to say that it's cloudy or clear: *está nublado* and *está despejado*. That's about it. Most weather conditions in Spanish are expressed using the verb *hacer* + a noun. A few are expressed using only a verb. Look at the following examples:

¿Qué tiempo hace? **(What's the weather like?)**
Hace buen tiempo. **(The weather is nice.)**
Hace mal tiempo. **(The weather is bad.)**
Hace frío. **(It's cold.)**
Hace calor. **(It's hot.)**
Hace sol. **(It's sunny.)**
Hace viento. **(It's windy.)**
llover, o > ue **(to rain)**
nevar, e > ie **(to snow)**
Llueve. **(It's raining.)**
Nieva. **(It's snowing.)**
la lluvia **(the rain)**
la nieve **(the snow)**
lloviznar **(to drizzle)**
la llovizna **(drizzle)**

granizar **(to hail)**
el granizo **(hail)**
las nubes **(the clouds)**
el viento **(the wind)**

When the weather is very nice, you can say: *Hace muy buen tiempo.* To say it's very or not very cold or hot, for example, use *mucho* or *poco*: *Hace mucho frío. Hace poco calor.* Remember that to say you are hot or cold or you feel hot or cold, you must use the verb *tener*: *Tengo calor; tengo frío.* To say it's raining hard or snowing a little, say *Llueve mucho* and *Nieva poco.* Of course, to express the negative of any of these ideas, just put *no* in front of the verb:

No hace buen tiempo.
No hace sol.
No nieva mucho.

If you're really feeling negative about the weather, use *nunca*, for example, *Nunca hace sol aquí* (It's never sunny here).

To talk about foggy conditions, you can say *Hay neblina.* You can also use *hay* to talk about the existence of a weather condition like *Hay mucha nieve* (There is a lot of snow) or *Hay mucho viento* (There is a lot of wind).

Practice talking about the weather by describing the current weather conditions using as many of these expressions as possible.

Prepositions in Weather Expressions

You've had a little break from prepositions, but let's get back to them because they turn up in many Spanish weather expressions. Look at these examples:

Está por llover. **(It's about to start raining.)**
Está a punto de llover. **(It's about to start raining.)**
Llueve a cántaros. **(It's pouring. lit.: It's raining jugs full.)**
Empezó a nevar. **(It started to snow.)**
Por fin, dejó de / cesó de soplar el viento. **(Finally, the wind stopped blowing.)**

To talk about the weather at a particular time of day, use the prepositions *en* or *por*: *Generalmente llueve en/por la tarde.* And, when you're sick and tired of the weather, remember that *Después de la tormenta viene la calma.*

Weather Prediction

How often do you listen to the weather prediction? There are many online resources that you can use to practice weather expressions. On a Spanish newspaper site, for example, look for words like *el pronóstico* (weather prediction) and *el clima* (climate) or *el tiempo* (weather) to identify the weather link. The following audio activity will help you test your skills as you listen to two weather predictions.

Weather Prediction 1

TRACK 75

Listen to the weather report on Track 75 and answer the questions that follow. You can find a transcript of the audio and sample answers to the questions in Appendix D.

1. *¿Qué tiempo va a hacer hoy?*
2. *¿Hará mucho o poco sol?*
3. *¿Cuándo va a llover?*

Weather Prediction 2

TRACK 76

Listen to the weather report on Track 76 and answer the questions that follow. You can find a transcript of the audio and sample answers to the questions in Appendix D.

1. *¿Será un buen fin de semana para acampar en la playa?*

2. *¿Qué tiempo va a hacer en las montañas?*
3. *¿Para cuándo podrás esquiar?*

Months and Seasons

You probably already know the names of the months in Spanish, but let's review them just in case.

- *enero* (**January**)
- *febrero* (**February**)
- *marzo* (**March**)
- *abril* (**April**)
- *mayo* (**May**)
- *junio* (**June**)
- *julio* (**July**)
- *agosto* (**August**)
- *septiembre* (**September**)
- *octubre* (**October**)
- *noviembre* (**November**)
- *diciembre* (**December**)

FACT

Remember that the months of the year, like the days of the week, are not normally capitalized in Spanish. The names of the seasons aren't capitalized either.

To express a date, use the following formula: *el* + date + *de* + month. For example, to say "April fifteenth," you would say: *el quince de abril.* Ordinal numbers are only used for the first of the month: *el primero de julio.* To refer to what happens "in" a month, use the preposition *en: Llueve mucho en octubre.*

Take a few minutes to write down the weather, events, and activities you associate with each month.

TRACK 77

The Months

Listen to each example on Track 77 as you follow along in the text. Repeat each after you hear it.

Donde yo vivo hace más frío en enero que en los otros meses.
Comienza a hacer buen tiempo en febrero y trabajo mucho en mi jardín.
En abril y mayo puede hacer muy buen tiempo, pero a veces hay tormentas fuertes.
En noviembre celebramos el Día de Acción de Gracias; es la fiesta que más me gusta.

Take a few minutes to answer the following questions orally or in writing:

¿Qué tiempo te gusta más y por qué?
¿Qué mes te gusta más y por qué?

There are some interesting idiomatic expressions and sayings in Spanish that mention certain months. Look at the following examples:

Luna de enero, cielo sereno.
(January moon, calm sky.)
Febrerillo loco, un día peor que otro.
(Crazy little February, one day is worse than another.)
Marzo ventoso, abril lluvioso.
(Windy March, rainy April.)
tener . . . abriles **(to be . . . old):** *Mi abuelo tiene noventa abriles.*
(My grandfather is ninety years old.)
Cuando caen las lluvias de abril, crecen las flores de mayo.
(When the April rains fall, the flowers of May grow.)
En abril, aguas mil.
(In April, a thousand showers.)
Hasta el cuatro de mayo no te quites el sayo.
(Until the fourth of May, don't take off your smock.)

hacer / sacar su agosto **(to make a bundle, a financial killing):** *Tu hermano hizo su agosto cuando invirtió en esa estación de esquí.*
(Your brother made a bundle when he invested in that ski resort.)

The names of the four seasons in Spanish are: *primavera* (spring), *verano* (summer), *otoño* (fall), and *invierno* (winter). Of course, there are idiomatic expressions that use the seasons, too, for example:

Está en la primavera (el otoño) de la vida.
(He's in the spring / fall of his life)
Una golondrina no hace verano.
(One swallow doesn't make it summer.)

Keep in mind that not every Spanish-speaking country has four seasons, and the weather features of any season may be different from what you experience where you live.

In many places, seasons are referred to as *temporadas.* Some countries divide the year into the dry and rainy season, for example: *la temporada seca* and *la temporada de lluvias.* This same word describes such things as "seasonal activities" *actividades de temporada* and "seasonal clothing" *ropa de temporada.* Many tourist destinations have high and low seasons, *temporada alta* and *temporada baja,* which is usually reflected in the number of tourists and the cost and availability of lodging. If you travel *fuera de temporada* (off-season), you can get some great deals but be sure the off-season climate suits your plans.

Chapter 19

Helping Hands: Spanish for Volunteers

A little bit of Spanish can make a big difference in helping you help Spanish speakers in your community. Whether you volunteer with an organization like Welcome Wagon, a social service provider, a hospital, or a school, your knowledge of Spanish will be a valuable asset. This chapter covers some vocabulary and constructions that will serve you well as a volunteer.

Introducing Your Community Services

Moving to a new community can be a daunting experience at the best of times. Imagine what it is like for people who don't speak the language of their new home well and don't know where to begin exploring the community and learning how to get things done. As a welcome committee representative (*representante del comité de bienvenida*) for your community, your knowledge of Spanish will be invaluable in helping new Spanish-speaking residents.

ALERT!

Find out what sort of community the newcomers are from: a small town, a large city, a rural area. Explain the way your community is organized. Provide maps, bilingual informational fliers, etc., to help the newcomers get oriented.

Getting Around Town

Newcomers will appreciate a tour of places and services in their new community. Start with the following, and add as many more destinations as you think are appropriate:

- *el centro* (**downtown**)
- *la calle Mayor* (**Main Street**)
- *la carretera* (**highway**)
- *el centro de recreo* (**recreation center**)
- *el parque de recreo* (**playground**)
- *el centro comercial* (**commercial center, mall**)
- *el supermercado* (**supermarket**)
- *la farmacia* (**pharmacy**)
- *la tienda, la boutique* (**store, boutique**)
- *la ferretería* (**hardware store**)
- *el garaje* (**garage**)
- *la gasolinera* (**gas station**)

- *la lavandería* (**laundromat**)
- *el correos* (**post office**)
- *el banco* (**bank**)
- *el ayuntamiento, el municipio* (**city hall**)
- *la comisaría* (**police station**)
- *la biblioteca* (**library**)
- *el centro cultural* (**cultural center**)
- *el teatro* (**theater**)
- *el cine* (**cinema**)
- *el hospital* (**hospital**)
- *la sala de emergencias* (**emergency room**)
- *la clínica* (**clinic**)
- *la iglesia* (**church**)
- *la guardería* (**daycare center**)
- *la escuela* (**school**)

As an ambassador for your community, you are the bridge between two cultures. Ask questions about the newcomers' home community, and find out what places and services they frequented. Ask about their children and make suggestions for them that are age-appropriate. Keep in mind that the newcomers may be accustomed to places and services that aren't available in your community. Your community may offer services that the newcomers have never had access to. Be sure to include pertinent information about each place, as appropriate. Track 80 includes some examples.

TRACK 78

Getting Around Town

Listen to each example on Track 78 as you follow along in the text. Repeat each one after you hear it.

Puedes pagar las cuentas de agua aquí en el ayuntamiento.
(**You can pay your water bill here at city hall.**)
Las lavanderías son de autoservicio y las máquinas usan monedas de 25 centavos.
(**The laundromats are self service and the machines use twenty-five cent coins.**)

El Centro Cultural ofrece muchos programas gratis, generalmente los domingos.

(The Cultural Center offers a lot of free programs, generally on Sundays.)

El uso de la biblioteca es gratis y hay muchos programas especiales para niños y adultos.

(The library is free and there are many special programs for children and adults.)

Try to be as comprehensive as you can. Make no assumptions other than that the newcomers want to learn as much as possible about their new community. By asking questions and taking them to different places around town, you'll quickly get a sense of what they need to know.

What's Done Where and How?

If possible, conduct your tour over several days so you have time to visit a wide variety of community locations and can explain to the newcomers what's done where, when, and how. For example, show them how to pay the city water bill, how to set up phone service, or how to fill out a request for a library card and check out books. Take the newcomers grocery shopping to help them find different items on their lists, and teach them how to ask for things they can't find. Go with them to the hardware store to pick up odds and ends that they need to organize their new household.

You can make an enormous difference in how newcomers adapt to their new surroundings. In addition to helping them with basic needs, buy them house plants, take them out for coffee at your favorite cafe, or attend a performance at one of the local cultural venues together. Be a friend! It's much easier for a newcomer to overcome barriers of language and culture when they know someone in their new community cares about them as individuals.

At the Library

The public library may be an entirely unfamiliar entity to newcomers from areas where such things don't exist. Take your new friends on a tour of the library, showing them how the library is organized, how to use the card catalog, and whom to ask for help locating materials. Tell them about the inter-library loan system, and explain how to request materials that might not be available locally. Explain procedures for checking out books, and help them apply for a library card. Review library policies relevant to usage of the computers, printers, and photocopiers. Ask the librarian for a brochure containing rules and regulations and newsletters of monthly events. Point out materials and programs of particular interest, for example, adult film series, musical events, lectures and classes, story time for children, and book sales.

FACT

You can probably arrange for a librarian to conduct an informal tour of the facilities and materials while you act as interpreter for a Spanish-speaking new arrivals.

Review the following vocabulary to help you explain library services:

- *las horas de apertura* **(hours)**
- *el mostrador* **(check-out counter)**
- *el catálogo, el índice* **(card catalog)**
- *referencia* **(reference)**
- *los estantes* **(shelves)**
- *la sala de periódicos y revistas* **(periodicals room)**
- *la sala de lectura* **(reading room)**
- *la sala de computadoras* **(computer room)**
- *los materiales para niños* **(children's materials)**
- *los materiales para adolescentes* **(young-adult materials)**
- *el/la bibliotecario/a* **(librarian)**
- *el carnet, la tarjeta de biblioteca* **(library card)**
- *la fecha límite* **(due date)**
- *la multa* **(fine)**
- *el título* **(title)**
- *el tema* **(topic)**

And here's a list of helpful verbs to talk about what you do in the library:

- *sacar* **(to take out, check out)**
- *pedir* **(to request)**
- *reservar* **(to reserve)**
- *devolver* **(to return)**
- *renovar* **(to renew)**
- *buscar* **(to look up, as in the card catalog)**
- *pagar una multa* **(to pay a fine)**
- *usar, utilizar* **(to use)**

TRACK 79

At the Library

Look at the following examples of how you might use some of this new vocabulary and listen to each on Track 79. Repeat each one after you hear it.

Buscas materiales por título o tema en el catálogo.
(You look up materials by title or topic in the card catalog.)
Puedes sacar hasta cinco libros por dos semanas.
(You can check out up to five books for two weeks.)
Puedes renovar materiales por una semana.
(You can renew materials for one week.)
Hay un sistema de préstamos entre bibliotecas. Puedes pedir un libro y lo mandan de otra biblioteca. Sólo pagas el franqueo.
(There is a lending system between libraries. You can request a book and they send it from another library. You only pay postage.)
Si devuelves materiales después de la fecha límite, pagas una multa de diez centavos por día.
(If you return materials after the due date, you pay a fine of ten cents per day.)

Your library may not have cataloguing information available in Spanish. If not, offer to translate this information for librarians to use when helping a Spanish speaker find materials. The librarian can simply show the patron the list and the patron can indicate what type of information he or she is seeking.

Explain how your library organizes materials and how the card catalog lists them. Show the newcomer how to find different sorts of items, ranging from periodicals to fiction to reference to children's books.

The way books are shelved in a library can be very confusing. Be sure to explain the differences thoroughly. For example:

Las novelas están organizadas en orden alfabético por el apellido del autor.
(Novels are organized in alphabetical order by the author's last name.)
Los materiales de no ficción están organizados por número y las tres primeras letras del apellido del autor.
(Nonfiction materials are organized by number and the three first letters of the author's last name.)
Los libros nuevos están en esta sección.
(The new books are in this section.)

Someone who has never used a library may be shy about becoming a regular patron because it's rather overwhelming. Your Spanish-language tour can make it more manageable.

Social Services

If you volunteer at a social service agency in your community, it is likely that you will use Spanish more for meeting critical needs than social ones. Nevertheless, don't underestimate the importance of a friendly greeting and general chit-chat as you help clients. Your knowledge of Spanish will enable you to be even more effective in understanding and resolving problems of Spanish-speaking applicants for social services.

As a Spanish speaker, you can make a significant difference in evaluating and meeting the needs of Hispanic clients for social services.

One of the primary resources you might wish to have in Spanish is a comprehensive list of emergency numbers as well as contact information for all your community services. You can adapt the following as you make up your own list of resources:

- *emergencias: 911* **(911 emergency)**
- *la policía* **(police)**
- *los bomberos* **(fire department)**
- *el refugio* **(shelter)**
- *el centro de ancianos* **(senior center)**
- *el centro juvenil* **(youth center)**
- *el centro de beneficencia* **(charity center)**
- *el comedor de beneficencia* **(charity kitchen)**
- *el centro de apoyo económico* **(economic aid)**
- *el centro de apoyo familiar* **(family aid)**

You can also list a variety of services under the heading *Agencia*, for example:

- *La Agencia de Servicios Legales* **(Legal Aid)**
- *La Agencia para Vivienda Asequible* **(Affordable Housing)**
- *La Agencia para Servicios Infantiles* **(Child Services)**
- *La Agencia de Salud Pública* **(Public Health)**
- *La Agencia de Salud Mental* **(Mental Health)**
- *La Agencia para Planificación Familiar* **(Family Planning)**

It's important that you investigate and practice explaining in Spanish where each agency is located, its hours, what services are available, what documents are required, and what limitations there may be so you can direct your clients to the organization most suited to their specific needs.

ALERT!

Keep in mind that undocumented residents, in particular, may be very reluctant to take advantage of services designed to help them. Ease their fears by explaining that their residency status will not be questioned when they apply for many of these social services.

Another problematic area for newcomers is managing money. You might start by explaining the various names for bills (*billetes*) and coins *(monedas)*, which can be quite confusing. For example:

- *un centavo*: **one cent, a penny**
- *cinco centavos*: **five cents, a nickle**
- *diez centavos*: **ten cents, a dime**
- *veinticinco centavos*: **twenty-five cents, a quarter**
- *cincuenta centavos*: **fifty cents, a half dollar**
- *un dólar*: **a dollar, a buck**
- *cinco dólares*: **five dollars, five bucks, a fiver**
- *diez dólares*: **ten dollars, ten bucks, a ten**
- *veinte dólares*: **twenty dollars, twenty bucks, a twenty**
- *cincuenta dólares*: **fifty dollars, fifty bucks, a fifty**
- *cien dólares*: **a hundred dollars, one hundred dollars, a hundred bucks, a hundred**

Role-play with newcomers how prices are written and stated so when they hear something like "That's a buck twenty," they will understand that it means: *un dólar y veinte centavos*. Additionally, someone accustomed to a cash economy might be overwhelmed by the payment options available in the United States For example, you can pay:

- *en efectivo* **(by cash)**
- *con tarjeta de crédito* **(with a credit card)**

- *con tarjeta de débito* (**with a debit card**)
- *con cheque personal* (**with a personal check**)
- *con un cheque certificado* (**with a certified, cashier's check**)
- *con giro postal* (**with a postal money order**)
- *en línea, electrónicamente* (**online, electronically**)

You'll want to investigate and practice explaining the details for each form of payment, including information about additional costs (*costos adicionales*), special fees (*cargos especiales*), and scheduling and recording payments. You might also want to provide information about loans (*préstamos*) and how to get them, especially if your organization offers emergency loans (*préstamos de emergencia*).

Help at the Hospital

Spanish-speaking volunteers can lend a hand in a variety of nonmedical situations at their local hospital. For example, you can help decipher the admissions documents and explain to patients how names, addresses, dates, etc., are written on English forms. You can escort patients to various places in the hospital, easing their fears with friendly conversation. You can also distract children who have accompanied adults on a visit to a family member by playing with them in the lounge, giving the adults some private time. Let's take a look at some of the language you will need for each task.

Filling Out Forms

Forms are tricky documents for a non-English speaker to figure out, especially when they contain abbreviations or require that squares be checked off or circles filled in. Names and last names must be separated, and dates must be expressed in a particular order of month, day, and year, sometimes spelled out, and sometimes expressed with numbers. Remember that information is normally expected in block or print letters (*letra de imprenta* or *letra de molde*).

Every form is different, so if you volunteer at the admissions desk at the hospital, take some time to become very familiar with their forms, and practice explaining how to fill them out in Spanish. It's also a good idea to ask if patients need help—by asking *¿Puedo ayudarlo/la con el formulario?* (Can I help you with the form?)—before assuming that they will.

Hospital Escort

Some hospitals use volunteers to take people to the various labs and testing areas. The reception desk might also appreciate a Spanish-speaking volunteer to escort visitors to the patient's room, lounge areas, cafeteria, and gift shop or to deliver gifts and flowers. Look over the following vocabulary, and expand this list with words and expressions specific to your duties at the hospital where you volunteer:

- *Administración* (**Administration**)
- *Ingresos, Admisiones* (**Admission**)
- *la cafetería* (**cafeteria**)
- *la tienda de regalos* (**gift shop**)
- *la sala de espera* (**waiting room or lounge**)
- *la sala de cuidados intensivos* (**intensive care**)
- *la maternidad* (**maternity**)
- *la sala de partos* (**delivery room**)
- *la sala de recién nacidos* **or** *guardería* (**nursery**)
- *la pediatría* (**pediatrics**)
- *el centro de donación de sangre* (**blood donation center**)
- *el centro de diálisis* (**dialysis center**)
- *el laboratorio* (**laboratory**)
- *la radiología* (**radiology**)
- *la capilla* (**chapel**)
- *el consejero, la consejera* (**counselor**)
- *los ascensores* (**elevators**)
- *las escaleras* (**stairs**)
- *la silla de ruedas* (**wheelchair**)
- *la camilla* (**gurney**)

If you are going to accompany someone to a particular location in the hospital, introduce yourself as a *voluntario* or *voluntaria*, and explain where you are going to take the visitor or patient. Track 82 includes some examples.

ALERT!

The floors of large buildings like hospitals are called *plantas* in Spanish. The ground or main floor is generally called the *planta baja* or *planta principal.*

TRACK 80

Hospital Escort

Listen to each example on Track 80 as you follow along in the text. Repeat each one after you hear it.

Buenos días (buenas tardes, buenas noches). Me llamo Alberta y soy voluntaria aquí en el hospital.
(Good morning, afternoon, evening. My name is Alberta and I'm a volunteer here at the hospital.)
Voy a indicarle dónde está la sala de espera.
(I'm going to show you where the waiting room is.)
Voy a acompañarlo/la al laboratorio.
(I'm going to accompany you to the lab.)
Vamos a pediatría. Está en la planta seis.
(We're going to Pediatrics. It's on the sixth floor.)

School Volunteers

Schools always need volunteers. Your Spanish skills might be used during registration to explain the forms and procedures, you might serve as a liaison between the school and parents, and you could tutor in a variety of content areas in English, using your Spanish to set your students at ease or give instructions.

Registration

One of the most valuable tasks you can volunteer for is that of helping parents negotiate the complexities of registration forms. Earlier in this chapter you learned about some of the primary features of forms; let's look at some additional vocabulary specific to school registration.

- *la hoja de matrícula* **(registration form)**
- *matricular* **or** *inscribir* **(to register)**
- *la edad* **(age)**
- *el grado* **(grade)**
- *la lengua materna* **(first language)**
- *el distrito escolar* **(school district)**
- *el lugar de residencia* **(place of residence)**
- *el lugar de empleo* **(place of employment)**

The registration form for the school where you volunteer may also include questions about special classes or programs, for example:

- *La Educación Especial* **(Special Education)**
- *La Terapia del Habla* **(Speech Therapy)**
- *El Inglés Como Segunda Lengua* **(English as a Second Language)**
- *La Educación Bilingüe* **(Bilingual Education)**
- *Programa para Estudiantes Dotados o Talentosos* **(Gifted and Talented Program)**
- *El Tutorio, Las Clases Individualizadas* **(Tutoring)**
- *El Programa de Comidas* **(Meal Plan)**

During the registration process, parents will probably have to provide the following:

- *el certificado, el acta de nacimiento* **(birth certificate)**
- *el récord de inmunizaciones y vacunas* **(immunization and vaccination records)**
- *el carnet de la seguridad social* **(Social Security card)**
- *prueba de residencia* **(proof of residency)**

At the same time that parents are registering their child, you might want to explain the general course of study (*el programa de estudios*) for their child's grade level, the school schedule and calendar (*el horario escolar, el calendario escolar*), the specifications of the uniform (*el uniforme*), and the norms regarding drop-off and pick-up (*las normas para dejar y recoger a los niños*), or the school bus schedule (*el horario del bus escolar*).

Tutoring

Unless you are a high-level speaker of Spanish, it is most likely that your tutoring will be conducted in English. Nevertheless, even a little Spanish will come in very handy for getting to know your students and setting them at ease as well as giving simple instructions. Before you begin, be sure to review all the materials that you have received from the teacher, and ask any questions you may have. In addition to preparing the content for each tutoring session, think about and practice what you might need to communicate in Spanish to your students. Track 81 includes some examples.

TRACK 81

Tutoring

Listen to each example on Track 81 as you follow along in the text. Repeat each one after you hear it.

> *Hoy vamos a practicar la multiplicación.*
> **(Today we're going to practice multiplication.)**
> *Vamos a repasar el cuento que leíste en clase ayer.*
> **(We're going to review the story you read in class yesterday.)**
> *Por favor, saca tu libro de ciencias.*
> **(Take out your science book, please.)**
> *Esta noche debes completar las hojas de práctica y traerlas mañana.*
> **(This evening, you should complete the practice sheets and bring them tomorrow.)**

Chapter 20
Strategies for Lifetime Learning

If you've come this far and still want more Spanish, you've just joined the club of "Lifetime Learners!" Now you're wondering where you go from here, aren't you? Don't worry; there's always more learning to do and new aspects of language and culture to discover. Read on for some helpful guidelines to continuing your Spanish journey.

Building on What You Know

You've got a good foundation; the next step is to build on what you've learned. One of the best ways to start out is to take a chapter theme from this book, or any other materials that you have, and expand on that theme. Let's use Chapter 15's topic of shopping as an example of what you can do with any theme you select. After reviewing the vocabulary that you've learned, use your dictionary to expand your list. Go through your closet and dresser and list every item of clothing you own. Practice describing each item in as much detail as possible. Say what you like about it, remind yourself of how you acquired it, how much it cost, etc. Do the same thing for every type of item you might shop for and you will expand your vocabulary enormously!

FACT

You can never learn too many words! Make a game of expanding your vocabulary in different categories that you find interesting. Set goals to learn a certain number of words each week.

Practice Vocabulary and Grammar in Context

Using the theme you have reviewed as a context, practice conversational interactions in as many ways as you can think of by writing out dialogs, role-playing with a friend, or simply talking to yourself. Little by little, make your practice more complex. For example, ask the salesperson more questions; shop for more items; practice talking about problems with an item you want to buy or have bought and are returning. For themes that you are less expert with, use your imagination to create likely scenarios. Repetition is the key to internalizing vocabulary and becoming comfortable with multiple possibilities in any given situation. Let's take a minute to summarize:

- Review what you know.
- Expand on what you know thematically.
- Use a dictionary and other resources to increase your vocabulary thematically.

- Invent thematic scenarios to practice vocabulary and grammar points in context. Practice saying the same thing in a variety of ways.

When you feel like you have exhausted the possibilities for one theme, move on to another one your find particularly interesting. You will never run out of topics to pursue and, with the Internet, it's very easy to access information about them in Spanish.

Learn about Your Hobbies

Another way to spice up your learning is to explore some of your hobbies in the context of the Hispanic world. Learn all the vocabulary related to one of your hobbies, and find out where and how it is practiced in Spain and Latin America. Practice talking about your hobby in Spanish. Say how long you have been interested in it, how you got started, and why you like it. Follow your favorite sports online; learn about athletes and entertainers that you are interested in. Investigate the history, art, music, literature of a country that you might like to visit.

Use the Spanish Around You

Without a doubt, the ideal environment in which to learn another language is total immersion—spending an extended period of time in a country where that language is spoken. There are plenty of wonderful places to live and learn in the Spanish-speaking world, but doing so may not suit your lifestyle, schedule, or budget. The next best option is to take advantage of every possible medium of Spanish input available to you where you live, such as classes, private tutoring, conversation partners, printed matter of all sorts, films, TV, and radio. Seek out opportunities to practice what you're learning at home, at work, and in your community.

Take advantage of any opportunity that presents itself. Even simple errands can be learning experiences. For example, if your hardware store has bilingual labels, take a little time to learn the Spanish words for and related to the items you are buying. You could shop for groceries at a Hispanic supermarket. If you are sitting in the dentist's office and there is a Spanish-language magazine available, read it instead of one in English.

Evaluate Your Language Models

Be aware, however, that there are reliable and unreliable models of Spanish out there, just as there are in English or any other language. If you ask the impish little boy next door how to say something in Spanish, he may find it funny to mislead you by teaching you an embarrassing phrase. On the other hand, children often display infinite patience with students of their language because they are suddenly the experts and you, the adult, are learning from them. Spending time as a volunteer among Hispanic students at a local school may prove to be as enriching a linguistic experience for you as for the children you tutor.

No matter how isolated you may be, you can still have access to materials in Spanish through your computer and the Internet. Use the Spanish-language search engines, available through most Internet portals, and you'll find countless sites on every topic imaginable.

Use Resources by and for Spanish Speakers

When using materials from the Internet to practice your Spanish, focus on sites written by native speakers for native speakers. Be selective, choosing resources like newspapers, tourist information, and cultural pages that are likely to have been written in standard Spanish with a greater attention to accuracy and eloquence than a blog or a personal Web page.

Vocabulary and Grammar Development

Reading in Spanish is a terrific way to increase your vocabulary, practice grammar, and become more comfortable with the way Spanish is used in many contexts. You might start by choosing one or two topics you are interested in that you are likely to find articles about in English- and Spanish-language newspapers. If you focus on current events, it will be easy to find articles in Spanish and English about the same event. Many newspapers are available online, so you won't have a problem finding Spanish-language resources for this exercise. Each time you find an article about one of your topics in English, read it carefully. Then read an article about the same topic in Spanish. That way, you'll learn a lot of new vocabulary from context clues because you are already familiar with the news item in English.

FACT

If you read news articles about the same event in English and then Spanish, you will be able to understand more new vocabulary and turns of phrase in the Spanish article from context. The more you read, the easier it will get.

Read Actively

Print out the article in Spanish and underline a manageable number of new vocabulary words or phrases. Check the meaning of new vocabulary in a dictionary, and then use each word in a sentence to help you remember its meaning.

Another good technique for making the most of newspaper articles is to underline examples of particular grammar points in context. Since you are already familiar with the content of the news story in English, you'll likely be able to follow along fairly easily in Spanish. Don't be afraid to make intelligent guesses at meaning.

Practice What You Learn

After you've made a list of new vocabulary, and you've underlined important grammar structures, the next step is to summarize the article using as much of the new vocabulary and as many of the grammar models as you can. If you do this regularly, you will increase your vocabulary and refine your use of grammar considerably.

You can do the same thing by reading stories or novels in English and Spanish. If you have a favorite author, start there. Otherwise, you might choose one of the internationally known authors from Spain or Latin America whose work is readily available in translation. Fiction can be a bit more complex since language is often used figuratively, and narrative style can present challenges that straightforward journalistic writing does not. Nevertheless, you will learn a great deal by reading fiction in the same way, identifying new vocabulary and particular examples of grammar. You should break the narrative down into small chunks for summarizing. When you're done, use your notes to retell the story to a friend.

Poetry is probably the most challenging of the written forms. However, if you are a fan of poetry, don't let the challenge keep you from trying out this technique.

Collect Synonyms and Antonyms

For each new word you collect, try to learn at least one synonym and antonym for it as well, whenever appropriate. A good dictionary of Spanish synonyms and antonyms will be very helpful for this task. In addition to expanding your vocabulary, synonyms can help you avoid repetition, and you will sound much more eloquent when you use a word with a more precise meaning for what you want to express.

Circumlocution: Explain What You Mean

What if, for some inexplicable reason, you completely forget a word and all its synonyms? To avoid this potentially frustrating scenario, another very effective approach to vocabulary development is to learn the definitions of words in Spanish, and to practice explaining what you mean without using the exact word. This may sound like beating around the bush, but it's actually a well-documented communicative strategy called "circumlocution."

Imagine, for example, that you have just gotten to your hotel room in Santiago, Chile. You're absolutely exhausted from the flight and want to take a restorative shower and nap before you unpack and hit the street. Unfortunately, you discover that there is no soap in the bathroom and no pillow upon which to rest your weary head. You're so frazzled that you can't remember how to say "soap" and "pillow" in Spanish, and your dictionary is buried somewhere in your luggage. Nevertheless, you bravely pick up the phone, call housekeeping, and say something like: *Necesito algo con que lavarme y esa cosa en la cama para poner la cabeza* (I need something to wash myself with and that thing on the bed to put my head on). It isn't elegant, but it's completely effective.

Listen Carefully

There are lots of ways you can practice listening comprehension in Spanish without traveling abroad. If you have access to Spanish-language TV or radio programming in your area, take full advantage of it! TV is usually easier to follow than radio because you have images associated with what you hear. Additionally, TV actors and program hosts tend to speak more slowly than radio announcers do. Getting caught up in a Spanish serial program is a great way to practice listening in on conversations, and there is generally enough repetition that it is fairly easy to follow a story line. Watching the news in Spanish is also an excellent way to practice since much news reporting is based on visual images. Rent feature films in Spanish. You can always turn on the subtitles for a little extra help though you should be aware that they might prove to be more of a distraction than an aid. If they are available, turn on the subtitles in Spanish instead of English.

FACT

Practice listening to Spanish with TV, radio, and Spanish-language films. Using the subtitles for films in Spanish or English can help you manage vocabulary and grammar you haven't learned yet.

Listen Attentively

You may have to train yourself to do this. Listen to Spanish with an ear to how vocabulary and grammar are used, especially when they are used in ways that are new to you. Listen with a notebook handy so you can jot down interesting new words, phrases, and examples of grammatical usage that you want to examine further. Then follow up on your notes. Consult dictionaries, grammar references, phrase books, and Spanish speakers to help you decipher new material, especially when examples seem to vary from the usages that you know. Sometimes, you can get language questions answered in chat rooms dedicated to Spanish usage. Once you have understood the new material, practice it frequently to internalize it.

Push the Envelope: Overcome the "Fear" Factor

Let's face it: learning a new language can be intimidating. Even the most confident individual can be overwhelmed by the enormity of the task of learning Spanish or embarrassed into silence by a casual misstatement. When thoughts like these start to get in the way of your learning, remind yourself of the following:

- Everyone makes embarrassing mistakes, even native speakers.
- Everyone forgets words and occasionally stumbles over sentences, even native speakers.
- Everyone goes absolutely blank periodically, even native speakers.
- Everyone has an accent; even native speakers will find some accents in Spanish more difficult to understand than others. Have you ever turned on the subtitles to understand a film in English? It's the same thing.
- Most people are more interested in understanding what you are saying than worried about how you are saying it, even native speakers!

Don't let your fears get in the way of practicing Spanish. No doubt you are gracious with less-than-perfect speakers of English; and most Spanish speakers are equally patient with learners of their language. You can safely assume that the majority of people just want to understand you. It's nice if the grammar is perfect and the vocabulary precise, but it isn't really a requirement for effective communication. The best way to improve your skills in Spanish is to continue listening, learning, and practicing.

Appendix A:

Spanish-to-English Glossary

abierto/a	open	el andén	train, bus platform	avanzar	advance, scroll down, go forward
el/la abogado/a	lawyer	el anillo	ring	averiguar	find out
el abono	fertilizer	el año	year	el avión	plane
el abrigo	overcoat	antes de	before	avisar	let know, warn
abrir	open	el antibiótico	antibiotic	ayudar	help
absolutamente	absolutely	anualmente	annually	el ayuntamiento	city hall
los abuelos	grandparents	apretar	press	bajar un documento	download a document
aburrido	boring, bored	aprobar	pass		
acabar	finish, complete	la aptitud	aptitude	el balcón	balcony
acampar	camp	el árbol	tree	bañarse	take a bath
las acciones	stock	el arbusto	bush	el banco	bank, bench
acercarse	approach	archivar	file	barrer	sweep
aconsejar	advise	el/la archivero/a	file clerk	el barrio	neighborhood
acordarse de	remember	el archivo, archivero	file cabinet	el barro	mud, clay
acostar	put to bed	la arena	sand	básico/a	basic
acostarse	go to bed	el arete	earring	bastante	a lot, enough
adelantar	get ahead	el/la arquitecto/a	architect	la bata	robe
la administración	administration	arreglar	fix	los beneficios	benefits
el aeropuerto	airport	arreglarse	get ready	la biblioteca	library
afeitarse	shave oneself	el arroyo	stream	el/la bibliotecario/a	librarian
afortunadamente	fortunately	el/la artista	artist, performer	bien	well
agotarse	wear oneself out	artísticamente	artistically	el/la biólogo/a	biologist
el/la ahijado/a	godson, goddaughter	artístico	artistic	los bisabuelos	great-grandparents
		asado/a	roasted		
alegrarse	get happy	ascender	move up	la blusa	blouse
la alergia	allergy	asegurar	make sure, insure	la boca	mouth
la alfombra	rug, carpet	el asiento	seat	el boleto	ticket
la almohada	pillow	el/la asistente	assistant	la bombilla	light bulb
alquilar	rent	la aspiradora	vacuum cleaner	bordar	embroider
amable	friendly, kind	atender	attend to	borrar	erase, delete
el amanecer	sunrise	atentamente	attentively	el bosque	forest
el análisis	analysis	atlético/a	athletic	el botón	button
ancho	loose, wide				
andar	walk, go about				

el brazo	arm	el chaleco	vest
bucear	scuba-dive, snorkel	el champú	shampoo
la bufanda	warm scarf, muffler	la chaqueta	jacket
		charlar	chat
el buscador	browser	el chiste	joke
la cabeza	head	la(s) ciencia(s)	science
el cable	cable	las ciencias sociales	social science
cada	each	la cima	peak
la cadena	chain	el cine	cinema
la cadera	hip	la cintura	waist
la cafetera	coffeemaker	el cinturón	belt
los calcetines	socks	la ciudad	city
la calefacción	heat	el coche	car
las calificaciones	scores	cocido/a	cooked
calladamente	quietly	la cocina	kitchen
callado/a	quiet	cocinar	cook
el calor	heat	colaborar	collaborate
cambiar	change, exchange	coleccionar	collect
cambiarse	change oneself, change clothes	el/la colega	colleague
		colgar	hang, hang up
la camioneta	van	la colina	hill
la camisa	shirt	el collar	necklace
la camiseta	T-shirt	comenzar	begin, start
el campo	countryside, field	cómico/a	funny, comical
el cañón	canyon	la comida	food, meal
cansado/a	tiresome, tired	la comisaría	police station
cansarse	get tired	como	as
la capilla	chapel	la cómoda	dresser
cargar	carry, charge	el/la compañero/a	partner, buddy
el carnet	identification card, library card, license	la compañía	company
		compartir	share
la carpeta	folder	el comportamiento	behavior
el/la carpintero/a	carpenter	comportarse	behave
la carretera	highway	la comprensión	comprehension
la carretilla	wheelbarrow	comprensivo/a	understanding
el carro	car	la computadora	computer
la carta	letter	la concha	shell
las cartas	playing cards	conducir	drive, lead
el castellano	Spanish	la conexión	connection
el centro	downtown	confirmar	confirm
el centro de recreo	recreation center	confundirse	get confused
cepillarse los dientes	brush one's teeth	conocer	know, meet
el cepillo de dientes	toothbrush	el conocimiento	knowledge
el cerebro	brain, mind	conservador/a	conservative
cerrado/a	closed	considerar	consider
el césped	lawn, grass	la contabilidad	accounting
		el/la contable	accountant
		el/la contador/a	accountant
		contratar	hire

el control de calidad	quality control
convencer	convince
conversar	talk over
coordinar	coordinate
la copa	goblet
la copiadora	copier
copiar	copy
el corazón	heart
el correo electrónico	email
el correos	post office
correr	run
cortar	cut, mow
corto	short
coser	sew
la costa	coast
la costilla	rib
crudo/a	raw
cruzar	cross
el cuaderno	notebook
cubrir	cover
el cuello	neck
la cuenta	bill, check
el cuerpo	body
el cuidado	care
cuidadosamente	carefully
el/la cuñado/a	brother-in-law, sister-in-law
dar un paseo	go for a stroll
de vez en cuando	once in a while
deber	should
el dedo	finger, toe
dejar	leave, allow, stop
delicado/a	delicate
el deporte	sport
el desagüe	drain
descansar	rest
descubrir	discover
el desfile	parade
el desierto	desert
desordenado/a	messy
despedir	fire, lay off
despedir(se)	say goodbye
el despertador	alarm clock
despertar	wake someone up
despertarse	wake up
después de	after
destrozado/a	destroyed
los detalles	details

devolver	return something	la escoba	broom	el fuego	fire
dibujar	draw	escoger	choose	la fuente	fountain
el diente	tooth	la escritura	writing	funcionar	work, function
el/la director/a	director	escuchar	listen to	fundamental	essential
dirigir	direct, oversee	el espejo	mirror	furiosamente	furiously
la disciplina	discipline	esperar	expect, hope,	furioso/a	furious
discutir	argue		wait for	las galletas	cookies, crackers
el diseño	design	el/la esposo/a	spouse	las ganancias	earnings
divertirse	enjoy oneself,	esquiar	ski	ganar	earn
	have a good time	la esquina	corner	la garganta	throat
doblar	turn, fold	la estación	season, train	la gasolinera	gas station
documentar	document		station	gastar	spend
doler	pain, hurt	el estacionamiento	parking space	generalmente	generally
dormir	sleep, put	el estado	state, condition	gentil	accomodating
	to sleep	la estampilla	postage stamp	la geografía	geography
dormirse	fall asleep	el estante	shelf	el/la geólogo/a	geologist
dormitorio	bedroom	el estómago	stomach	la gerencia	management
la ducha	shower	estrecho	tight, narrow	el/la gerente	manager
ducharse	take a shower	la estrella	star	el giro postal	postal money
el/la dueño/a	owner	el estudio	study		order
duro	hard	la estufa	stove	la gorra	cap
edad	age	excéntrico/a	eccentric	el grifo	faucet
egoísta	selfish	el expediente	file, dossier	los guantes	gloves
el ejercicio	exercise	explicar	explain	guardar	put away
el/la electricista	electrician	fabricar	make	la guardería	daycare center
embarazada	pregnant	la falda	skirt	el/la guía	guide, guidebook
emocionalmente	emotionally	el fax	fax	guiar	guide, lead
empezar	begin, start	la fecha límite	due date	el gusto	pleasure, taste
la empresa	company	felizmente	happily	la habilidad	ability
el/la empresario/a	entrepreneur	la ferretería	hardware store	hacer clic	click on, select
encargarse de	be responsible	el ferry	ferry	hacer	do, make, be
	for	la fiebre	fever	hasta	until
el enchufe	outlet	fijarse en	take notice of	el/la hermanastro/a	stepbrother,
encontrar	find	la finanza	finance		stepsister
energético/a	energetic	la firma	signature	la herramienta	tool
el/la enfermero/a	nurse	flojo/a	weak, lazy, loose	hervido/a	boiled
enfermo/a	ill, sick	la flor	flower	la hierba	grass
enfocarse	focus	el foco	light bulb	el/la hijastro/a	stepson/
el enfoque	focus	la fogata	campfire		stepdaughter
enojado/a	angry	la forma	shape	la hoja	leaf
enojarse	get angry	los fósforos	matches	el hombro	shoulder
entender	understand	la foto	photo	la hora	hour, time
entregar	turn in	el franqueo	postage	el horario	schedule
el entusiasmo	enthusiasm	frecuentemente	frequently	las horas de apertura	hours of business
equivocarse	be mistaken	el fregadero	kitchen or	la huelga	strike
escalar	rock, mountain		utility sink	el hueso	bone
	climb	fregar	scrub, mop	el humano	human
las escaleras	stairs	la frente	forehead	la iglesia	church
el escáner	scanner	frito/a	fried	igualmente	likewise

imprescindible	imperative	levantarse	get up	metódicamente	methodically
la impresora	printer	libre	free	metódico/a	methodical
imprimir	print	libremente	freely	mirarse	look at oneself
el inalámbrico	wireless	la librería	bookcase,	la mochila	backpack
indicar	indicate,		bookstore	mojado/a	wet
	point out	limpiar	clean	molestar	bother, annoy
el índice	index, card	limpio/a	clean	molesto/a	annoying
	catalog	el/la lingüista	linguist	la montaña	mountain
informarse	find out	la linterna	flashlight	montar	ride, set up
la informática	information	el llano	plain	morir	die
	technology	la llegada	arrival	el mostrador	counter
infrecuentemente	infrequently	llevarse con	get along with	mover	move
el/la ingeniero/a	engineer	la lluvia	rain	los muebles	furniture
el inodoro	toilet	locamente	crazily	el muelle	dock
la insecticida	insecticide	loco/a	crazy	la multa	fine
insignificante	insignificant	el lugar	place	el municipio	city hall,
instalar	install	la maceta	flowerpot		municipality
inteligentemente	intelligently	la madera	wood	el músculo	muscle
interesado/a	interested	la madrastra	stepmother	la nalga	buttock
interesar	interest	la madrina	godmother	la nariz	nose
inventar	invent	el/la maestro/a	teacher	el/la nieto/a	grandchild
la inversión	investment	mal	badly	la nieve	snow
invertir	invest	la maleta	suitcase	el/la novio/a	boy/girlfriend
la investigación	research	la mañana	morning,	la nuera	daughter-in-law
investigar	research		tomorrow	nunca	never
el invierno	winter	mandar	order, send	observar	observe, watch
invitar	invite, treat	manejar	manage, drive	obtener	obtain
la inyección	injection	la manguera	hose	ocurrir	happen
el jabón	soap	la mano	hand	ofrecer	offer
el jardín	garden, yard	la manta	blanket	el oído	inner ear, hearing
el/la joyero/a	jeweler	la manufactura	manufacturing	el ojo	eye
jubilarse	retire	maquillarse	put on makeup	la ola	wave
el/la juez	judge	la máquina de	razor	el olfato	sense of smell
jugar	play a game	afeitar		la olla	pot, pan
el labio	lip	el marcador	marker	olvidar, olvidarse (de)	forget
el lago	lake	la marea	tide	ordenado/a	neat
el lapicero	marker	el mareo	dizziness	ordenar	put things
el laptop	laptop computer	el marketing	marketing		in order
largo/a	long	más	more	la oreja	outer ear
el lavabo	wash basin	las matemáticas	math	la orilla	seashore
la lavadora	washing machine	la matrícula	registration	el oro	gold
la lavandería	laundromat	mayor	elderly, older,	la ortografía	spelling
el lavaplatos	dishwasher		greater	el otoño	autumn
lavarse	wash oneself	las medias	stockings	el padrastro	stepfather
la lectura	reading	la mejilla	cheek	el padrino	godfather
legal	legal	mejor	better	la página de entrada	home page
la lengua	tongue	menos	less	la página web	Web page
lentamente	slowly	mensualmente	monthly	el pájaro	bird
levantar	raise	el mes	month	la pala	shovel

la pantalla	screen, monitor
los pantalones	pants
el pañuelo	handkerchief, scarf
el papel higiénico	toilet paper
el paquete	package
la parada	stop
parar	stop
parecer	seem
la pareja	couple, partner
el parentesco	kinship, family relationship
el parque	park
el parque de recreo	playground
pasar	pass
pasarlo bien	have a good time
pasear	stroll, go about
el pasillo	aisle
el pastel	cake
el pecho	chest, breast
el pedazo	piece
pedir	request, ask for, order
peinarse	comb one's hair
el peine	comb
la película	movie, film
el pendiente	pendant, earring
pensar	think
perder	lose, miss
perderse	get lost
las pérdidas	losses
perezoso/a	lazy
periódicamente	periodically
el periódico	newspaper
permitir	permit
personal	personnel
el pez	fish
pescar	fish
el pie	foot
la piedra	stone
la piel	skin, fur
la pierna	leg
el/la piloto/a	pilot
pintar	paint
el piso	floor
el placer	pleasure
la plancha	iron
planchar	iron
la planta	plant, floor

la plata	silver
la playa	beach
la playera	T-shirt
el/la plomero/a	plumber
poco	a little, not often
la podadora	pruning tool
podar	prune
poner	put
ponerse	put on
el portátil	laptop computer
el postre	dessert
el prado	meadow
el precipicio	cliff
preocuparse	worry
presentar	introduce, present
la presión	pressure
el préstamo	loan
la primavera	spring
el/la primo/a	cousin
probar	taste, try
probarse	try on
la producción	development, production
progresar	progress
el proyector	projector
la prueba	test
el/la psicólogo/a	psychologist
el pueblo	town
la puerta	gate, door
el puerto	port
la puesta del sol	sunset
el pulmón	lung
la pulsera	bracelet
quedar, quedarse	remain, stay
quejarse	complain
quitarse	take off
el/la radiólogo/a	radiologist
rama	branch
rápidamente	quickly
raramente	rarely
el rastrillo	rake
el ratón	mouse
recoger	gather, pick up
recomendable	recommended
recortar	trim
los recursos humanos	human resources
la red	Web, Internet

la referencia	reference
la regadera	watering can, hose
regar	water
reírse	laugh
la relación	relationship
relajarse	relax
religioso/a	religious
el reloj	watch, clock
renovar	renew
repasar	review
reservado/a	reserved
reservar	reserve
respetar	respect
la retención	retention
retener	retain
retirarse	retire
retroceder	go back
reunirse	get together
revisar	review, audit
el río	river
la rodilla	knee
romper	break, tear
roto/a	broken
ruidoso/a	noisy
saber	know, find out
sacar	to take out, check out
sacudir	dust
la sala	living room
la salida	departure
salir	go out
saludar	greet
la sangre	blood
el secador de pelo	hair dryer
la secadora	dryer
secarse	dry oneself off
seguir	continue, follow
el seguro	insurance
seleccionar	click on, select
el sello	stamp, seal
la selva	jungle
semanalmente	weekly
sembrar	sow
la semilla	seed
el sendero	path
sentado/a	seated
sentarse	seat oneself
el sentido	sense, meaning

sentir	feel	el tacto	touch, tact
el servidor	server	la talla	size
siempre	always	tan	as
la sierra	saw, mountain range	tanto	as much
el sillón	easy chair	la taquilla	ticket booth
el sitio web	Web site	la tarea	task, homework
el sobre	envelope	la tarjeta	card
el/la sobrino/a	nephew, niece	la tarjeta postal	postcard
el/la socio/a	associate, employee	la taza	cup
el/la sociólogo/a	sociologist	el teclado	keyboard
el sombrero	brimmed hat	tejer	knit or weave
sorprenderse	be surprised	el tema	topic
la sortija	ring	la temporada	season
sostener	sustain	la terminal	bus station, ferry terminal
el/la sub-director/a	sub-director	el tiempo	time
el/la subgerente	assistant manager	la tierra	soil, land
subir	go up	el timbre	postage stamp
subirse	get on	tímido/a	shy
suceder	take place	tirar	throw away
el/la suegro/a	father-in-law, mother-in-law	la toalla	towel
el sueldo	salary	el tobillo	ankle
el suéter	sweater	tocar	play a musical instrument, touch, strike
el tablero	message board or whiteboard	todo/a	all
		tomar	take
		el torso	torso

trabajador/a	hardworking
el/la traductor/a	translator
traer	bring
el traje	suit
tranquilamente	calmly
tranquilo/a	calm, easygoing
transferir	transfer
el tranvía	tram
trasbordar	transfer
el tren	train
el tronco	trunk, stem
utilizar	use
el vagón	train car
la vecindad	neighborhood
el/la vecino/a	neighbor
la vena	vein
la ventana	window
el ventilador	fan, vent
el verano	summer
el vestido	dress
vestir	dress
vestirse	get dressed
volverse	become, turn into
el yerno	son-in-law
el zoológico	zoo

Appendix B

English-to-Spanish Glossary

ability	*la habilidad*
absolutely	*absolutamente*
accomodating	*gentil*
accountant	*el/la contador/a*
accounting	*la contabilidad*
administration	*la administración*
advance	*avanzar*
advise	*aconsejar*
after	*después (de)*
age	*la edad*
airport	*el aeropuerto*
aisle	*el pasillo*
alarm clock	*el despertador*
all	*todo/a*
allergy	*la alergia*
allow	*dejar, permitir*
always	*siempre*
analysis	*el análisis*
angry	*enojado/a*
ankle	*el tobillo*
annoy	*molestar*
annoying	*molesto/a*
annually	*anualmente*
antibiotic	*el antibiótico*
approach	*acercarse*
aptitude	*la aptitud*
architect	*el/la arquitecto/a*
argue	*discutir*
arm	*el brazo*
arrival	*la llegada*
artist	*el/la artista*
artistic	*artístico*
artistically	*artísticamente*
as much	*tanto*
as	*como, tan*
ask for	*pedir*
assistant	*el/la asistente*
assistant manager	*el/la subgerente*

associate	*el/la socio/a*
athletic	*atlético/a*
attend to	*atender*
attentively	*atentamente*
audit	*revisar*
autumn	*el otoño*
backpack	*la mochila*
badly	*mal*
balcony	*el balcón*
bank	*el banco*
basic	*básico/a*
be	*ser, estar, hacer, tener*
be mistaken	*equivocarse*
be responsible for	*encargarse de*
be surprised	*sorprenderse*
beach	*la playa*
become	*volverse*
bedroom	*el dormitorio*
before	*antes (de)*
begin	*comenzar, empezar*
behave	*comportarse*
behavior	*el comportamiento*
belt	*el cinturón*
bench	*el banco*
benefits	*los beneficios*
better	*mejor*
bill	*la cuenta*
biologist	*el/la biólogo/a*
bird	*el pájaro*
blanket	*la manta*
blood	*la sangre*
blouse	*la blusa*
body	*el cuerpo*
boiled	*hervido/a*
bone	*el hueso*

bookcase	*la librería, el estante*
bored	*aburrido/a*
boring	*aburrido/a*
bother	*molestar*
boyfriend	*el novio*
bracelet	*la pulsera*
brain	*el cerebro*
branch	*la rama*
break	*romper*
breast	*el pecho*
brimmed hat	*el sombrero*
bring	*traer*
broken	*roto/a*
broom	*la escoba*
brother-in-law	*el cuñado*
browser	*el buscador*
brush one's teeth	*cepillarse los dientes*
buddy	*el/la compañero/a*
bus station	*la terminal*
bush	*el arbusto*
business hours	*las horas de apertura*
buttock	*la nalga*
button	*el botón*
cable	*el cable*
cake	*el pastel*
calm	*tranquilo/a*
calmly	*tranquilamente*
camp	*acampar*
campfire	*la fogata*
canyon	*el cañón*
cap	*la gorra*
car	*el auto, el coche, el carro, el vagón*
card	*la tarjeta*
card catalog	*el índice*

care	el cuidado	convince	convencer	draw	dibujar
carefully	cuidadosamente	cook	cocinar, el/la	dress	el vestido, vestir
carpenter	el/la carpintero/a		cocinero/a	dresser	la cómoda
carry	cargar, llevar	cooked	cocido/a	drive	conducir, manejar
chain	la cadena	cookies	las galletas	dry oneself off	secarse
change	cambiar	coordinate	coordinar	dryer	la secadora
change clothes	cambiarse	copier	la copiadora	due date	la fecha límite
chapel	la capilla	copy	la copia, copiar	dust	el polvo, sacudir,
charge	cargar, pagar	corner	la esquina		quitar el polvo
	con tarjeta	counter	el mostrador	each	cada
chat	charlar	countryside	el campo	ear	el oído (inner
check	la cuenta	couple	la pareja		ear), la oreja
check out	sacar	cousin	el/la primo/a		(outer ear)
cheek	la mejilla	cover	cubrir	earn	ganar
chest	el pecho	crackers	las galletas	earnings	las ganancias
choose	escoger		(saladas)	earring	el arete
church	la iglesia	crazily	locamente	easy chair	el sillón
cinema	el cine	crazy	loco/a	easygoing	tranquilo/a
city	la ciudad	cross	cruzar	eccentric	excéntrico/a
city hall	el ayuntamiento,	cup	la taza	elderly	mayor
	el municipio	cut	cortar	electrician	el/la electricista
clay	el barro	daughter-in-law	la nuera	e-mail	el correo
clean	limpiar, limpio/a	daycare center	la guardería		electrónico
click on	hacer clic,	delete	borrar	embroider	bordar
	seleccionar	delicate	delicado/a	emotionally	emocionalmente
cliff	el precipicio	departure	la salida	employee	el/la empleado/a,
clock	el reloj	desert	el desierto		el/la socio/a
closed	cerrado/a	design	el diseño	energetic	energético/a
coast	la costa	dessert	el postre	engineer	el/la ingeniero/a
coffeemaker	la cafetera	destroyed	destrozado/a	enjoy oneself	divertirse,
collaborate	colaborar	details	los detalles		pasarlo bien
colleague	el/la colega	development	el desarrollo, la	enough	bastante
collect	coleccionar,		producción	enthusiasm	el entusiasmo
	recoger	die	morir	entrepreneur	el/la empresario/a
comb	el peine, peinarse	direct	dirigir	envelope	el sobre
	(one's hair)	director	el/la director/a	erase	borrar
comical	cómico/a	discipline	la disciplina	essential	fundamental
company	la compañía,	discover	descubrir	exchange	cambiar
	la empresa	dishwasher	el/la lavaplatos	exercise	el ejercicio
complain	quejarse	dizziness	el mareo	expect	esperar
comprehension	la comprensión	do	hacer	explain	explicar
computer	la computadora	dock	el muelle	eye	el ojo
condition	el estado, la	document	documentar, el	fall asleep	dormirse
	condición		documento	fan	el abanico, el
confirm	confirmar	door	la puerta		ventilador
connection	la conexión	download a	bajar un	father-in-law	el suegro
conservative	conservador/a	document	documento	faucet	el grifo
consider	considerar	downtown	el centro	fax	el fax
continue	continuar, seguir	drain	el desagüe	feel	sentir

ferry	el ferry	funny	cómico/a	handkerchief	el pañuelo
ferry terminal	la terminal	furious	furioso/a	hang, hang up	colgar
fertilizer	el abono	furiously	furiosamente	happen	ocurrir, suceder
fever	la fiebre	furniture	los muebles	happily	felizmente
field	el campo	garden	el jardín	hard	duro, difícil
file	archivar; el	gas station	la gasolinera	hardware store	la ferretería
	archivo, el	gate	la puerta	hardworking	trabajador/a
	expediente	gather	recoger	have a good time	divertirse,
file cabinet	el archivo, el	generally	generalmente		pasarlo bien
	archivero	geography	la geografía	head	la cabeza
file clerk	el/la archivero/a	geologist	el/la geólogo/a	hearing	el oído
film	la película	get ahead	adelantar,	heart	el corazón
finance	la finanza		avanzar	heat	la calefacción,
find	encontrar	get along with	llevarse con		el calor
find out	averiguar,	get angry	enojarse	help	la ayuda, ayudar
	descubrir,	get confused	confundirse	highway	la carretera
	informarse,	get dressed	vestirse	hill	la colina
	saber (pret.)	get happy	alegrarse	hip	la cadera
fine	la multa	get lost	perderse	hire	contratar
finger	el dedo	get on	subir, subirse	home page	la página de
finish	acabar, terminar	get ready	arreglarse,		entrada
fire	despedir, el fuego		prepararse	homework	la tarea
fish	el pez, pescar	get tired	cansarse	hope	esperar
fix	arreglar	get together	reunirse	hose	la manguera
flashlight	la linterna	get up	levantarse	hour	la hora
floor	el piso, la planta	girlfriend	la novia	human	el humano
flower	la flor	gloves	los guantes	human resources	los recursos
focus	enfocarse, el	go back	regresar,		humanos
	enfoque		retroceder, volver	hurt	doler
fold	doblar	go out	salir	identification card	el carnet
folder	la carpeta, el	go to bed	acostarse	ill	enfermo/a
	expediente,	go up	subir	imperative	imprescindible
	el folder	goblet	la copa	index	el índice
follow	seguir	godfather	el padrino	indicate	indicar
food	la comida	godmother	la madrina	information	la informática
foot	el pie	goddaughter	la ahijada	technology	
forehead	la frente	godson	el ahijado	infrequently	infrecuentemente
forest	el bosque	gold	el oro	injection	la inyección
forget	olvidar,	grandchild	el/la nieto/a	insecticide	la insecticida
	olvidarse de	grandparents	los abuelos	insignificant	insignificante
fortunately	afortunadamente	grass	el césped, la	install	instalar
fountain	la fuente		hierba, la yerba	insurance	el seguro
free	libre	great-grandparents	los bisabuelos	insure	asegurar
freely	libremente	greater	mayor	intelligently	inteligentemente
frequently	frecuentemente	greet	saludar	interest	interesar, el interés
fried	frito/a	guide	el/la guía, guiar	interested	interesado/a
friendly	amable,	guidebook	la guía	Internet	el Internet, la red
	simpático/a	hair dryer	el secador de pelo	introduce	presentar
function	funcionar	hand	la mano	invent	inventar

invest	*invertir*	living room	*la sala*	mud	*el barro*
investment	*la inversión*	loan	*el préstamo*	municipality	*el municipio*
invite	*invitar*	long	*largo/a*	muscle	*el músculo*
iron	*la plancha,*	look at oneself	*mirarse*	narrow	*estrecho*
	planchar	loose	*ancho, flojo/a*	neat	*ordenado/a*
jacket	*la chaqueta*	lose	*perder*	neck	*el cuello*
jeweler	*el/la joyero/a*	losses	*las pérdidas*	necklace	*el collar*
joke	*el chiste*	lung	*el pulmón*	neighbor	*el/la vecino/a*
judge	*el/la juez*	make sure	*asegurar*	neighborhood	*el barrio, la*
jungle	*la selva*	make	*fabricar, hacer*		*vecindad*
keyboard	*el teclado*	manage	*manejar*	nephew	*el sobrino*
kind	*amable*	management	*la gerencia*	never	*nunca*
kinship	*el parentesco*	manager	*el/la gerente*	newspaper	*el periódico*
kitchen	*la cocina*	manufacturing	*la manufactura*	niece	*la sobrina*
kitchen sink	*el fregadero*	marker	*el lapicero, el*	noisy	*ruidoso/a*
knee	*la rodilla*		*marcador*	nose	*la nariz*
knit	*tejer*	marketing	*el marketing*	notebook	*el cuaderno*
know	*conocer, saber*	matches	*el fósforo*	nurse	*el/la enfermero/a*
knowledge	*el conocimiento*	math	*las matemáticas*	observe	*observar*
lake	*el lago*	meadow	*el prado*	obtain	*obtener*
land	*la tierra*	meal	*la comida*	offer	*ofrecer*
laptop computer	*el laptop, el*	meaning	*el sentido*	older	*mayor*
	portátil	meet	*conocer,*	once in a while	*de vez en cuando*
laugh	*reírse*		*encontrar, reunirse*	open	*abierto/a, abrir*
laundromat	*la lavandería*	message board	*el tablero*	order	*mandar,*
lawn	*el césped, el pasto*	messy	*desordenado/a*		*ordenar, pedir*
lawyer	*el/la abogado/a*	methodical	*metódico/a*	outlet	*el enchufe*
lay off	*despedir*	methodically	*metódicamente*	overcoat	*el abrigo*
lazy	*flojo/a, perezoso/a*	mind	*el cerebro,*	oversee	*dirigir*
leaf	*la hoja*		*la mente*	owner	*el/la dueño/a*
leave	*dejar, salir*	mirror	*el espejo*	package	*el paquete*
leg	*la pierna*	miss	*perder*	pain	*doler; el dolor*
legal	*legal*	monitor	*el monitor, la*	paint	*la pintura, pintar*
less	*menos*		*pantalla*	pan	*la olla*
let know	*avisar*	month	*el mes*	pants	*el pantalón, los*
letter	*la carta*	monthly	*mensualmente*		*pantalones*
librarian	*el/la*	mop	*fregar*	parade	*el desfile*
	bibliotecario/a	more	*más*	park	*el parque*
library	*la biblioteca*	morning	*la mañana*	parking space	*el*
library card	*el carnet, la tarjeta*	mother-in-law	*la suegra*		*estacionamiento*
	de la biblioteca	mountain	*la montaña*	partner	*el/la pareja, el/la*
license	*el carnet, la*	mountain climb	*escalar*		*compañero/a,*
	licencia	mountain range	*la sierra*		*el/la socio/a*
light bulb	*bombilla, foco*	mouse	*el ratón*	pass	*aprobar, pasar*
likewise	*igualmente*	mouth	*la boca*	path	*el sendero*
linguist	*el/la lingüista*	move	*mover*	peak	*la cima*
lip	*el labio*	move up	*ascender, subir*	pendant	*el pendiente*
listen to	*escuchar*	movie	*la película*	performer	*el/la artista*
little	*poco, pequeño/a*	mow	*cortar*	periodically	*periódicamente*

permit	permitir	put on	ponerse	river	el río
personnel	el personal	put on makeup	maquillarse	roasted	asado/a
photo	la foto	put things in order	ordenar	robe	la bata
pick up	recoger	put to bed	acostar	rock climb	escalar
piece	el pedazo	quality control	el control de	rug	la alfombra
pillow	la almohada		calidad	run	correr
pilot	el/la piloto/a	quickly	rápidamente	salary	el sueldo
place	el lugar, poner	quiet	callado/a	sand	la arena
plain	el llano	quietly	calladamente	saw	la sierra
plane	el avión	radiologist	el/la radiólogo/a	say goodbye	despedir(se)
plant	la planta, plantar	rain	la lluvia, llover	scanner	el escáner
platform	el andén (bus	raise	levantar	scarf	la bufanda
	or train)	rake	el rastrillo		(muffler), el
play	jugar (a game),	rarely	raramente		pañuelo
	tocar (an	raw	crudo/a	schedule	el horario
	instrument)	razor	la máquina	science	la(s) ciencia(s)
playground	el parque		de afeitar	scores	las calificaciones
	de recreo	reading	la lectura	screen	la pantalla
playing cards	las cartas	recommended	recomendable	scroll down	avanzar
pleasure	el gusto,	recreation center	el centro de recreo	scrub	fregar
	el placer	reference	la referencia	scuba-dive	bucear
plumber	el/la plomero/a	registration	la matrícula	seashore	la orilla
point out	indicar , mostrar	relationship	el parentesco	season	la estación, la
police station	la comisaría		(family), la		temporada
port	el puerto		relación	seat	el asiento
postcard	la tarjeta postal	relax	relajarse	seat oneself	sentarse
post office	el correos	religious	religioso/a	seated	sentado/a
postage stamp	la estampilla, el	remain	quedar	seed	la semilla
	sello, el timbre	remember	acordarse de,	seem	parecer
postage	el franqueo		recordar	select	hacer clic, escoger,
postal money order	el giro postal	renew	renovar		seleccionar
pot	la maceta	rent	alquilar	selfish	egoísta
	(flowerpot), la	request	pedir	send	enviar, mandar
	olla (cooking pot)	research	la investigación,	sense of smell	el olfato
pregnant	embarazada		investigar	sense	el sentido
present	presentar	reserve	reservar	server	el servidor
press	apretar	reserved	reservado/a	set up	montar
pressure	la presión	respect	respetar	sew	coser
print	imprimir	rest	descansar	shampoo	el champú
printer	la impresora	retain	retener	shape	la forma
production	la producción	retention	la retención	share	compartir
progress	progresar, el	retire	jubilarse, retirarse	shave oneself	afeitarse
	progreso	return	devolver	shelf	el estante
projector	el proyector		(something),	shell	la concha
prune	podar		volver	shirt	la camisa
pruning tool	la podadora	review	repasar, revisar	short	bajo/a (height),
psychologist	el/la psicólogo/a	rib	la costilla		corto/a (length)
put	poner	ride	montar	should	deber
put away	guardar	ring	el anillo, la sortija	shoulder	el hombro

shovel	la pala	stop	dejar, la parada, parar	toothbrush	el cepillo de dientes
shower	la ducha				
shy	tímido/a	stove	la estufa	topic	el tema
sick	enfermo/a	stream	el arroyo	torso	el torso
signature	la firma	strike	la huelga, tocar	touch	el tacto, tocar
silver	la plata	stroll	dar un paseo, pasear	towel	la toalla
sister-in-law	la cuñada			town	el pueblo
size	la talla	study	estudiar, el estudio	train	el tren
ski	esquiar	sub-director	el/la sub-director/a	train car	el vagón
skin	la piel			tram	el tranvía
skirt	la falda	suit	el traje	transfer	transferir, trasbordar (bus to metro, for example)
sleep	dormir	suitcase	la maleta		
slowly	lentamente	summer	el verano		
snorkel	bucear	sunrise	el amanecer		
snow	la nieve	sunset	la puesta del sol	translator	el/la traductor/a
soap	el jabón	sustain	sostener	treat	invitar
social science	las ciencias sociales	sweater	el suéter	tree	el árbol
		sweep	barrer	trim	recortar
sociologist	el/la sociólogo/a	take	tomar	trunk	el tronco
socks	los calcetines	take a bath	bañarse	try	probar
soil	la tierra	take a shower	ducharse	try on	probarse
son-in-law	el yerno	take notice of	fijarse en	T-shirt	la camiseta, la playera
sow	sembrar	take off	quitarse		
Spanish	el castellano, el español	take out	sacar	turn	doblar
		take place	ocurrir, suceder	turn in	entregar
spelling	la ortografía	talk over	conversar	turn into	volverse
spend	gastar	task	la tarea	understand	comprender, entender
sport	el deporte	taste	el gusto, probar		
spouse	el/la esposo/a	teacher	el/la maestro/a	understanding	comprensivo/a
spring	la primavera	tear	romper	until	hasta
stairs	las escaleras	test	la prueba	use	utilizar
stamp	la estampilla, el sello, el timbre	think	pensar	utility sink	el fregadero
		throat	la garganta	vacuum cleaner	la aspiradora
star	la estrella	throw away	tirar	van	la camioneta
start	comenzar, empezar	ticket	el boleto	vein	la vena
		ticket booth	la taquilla	vent	el ventilador
state	el estado	tide	la marea	vest	el chaleco
station	la estación	tight	apretado, estrecho	waist	la cintura
stay	quedarse	time	la hora, el tiempo	wait for	esperar
stepbrother, stepsister	el/la hermanastro/a	tired	cansado/a	wake up	despertar (someone), despertarse (oneself)
		tiresome	cansado/a		
stepfather	el padrastro	toe	el dedo		
stepmother	la madrastra	toilet	el inodoro		
stepson/ stepdaughter	el/la hijastro/a	toilet paper	el papel higiénico	walk	andar
		tomorrow	mañana	warn	avisar
stock	las acciones	tongue	la lengua	wash basin	el lavabo
stockings	las medias	tool	la herramienta	wash oneself	lavarse
stomach	el estómago	tooth	el diente	washing machine	la lavadora
stone	la piedra				

watch	*observar, mirar, el reloj*	Web site	*el sitio web*	winter	*el invierno*
water	*regar*	weekly	*semanalmente*	wireless	*el inalámbrico*
watering can	*la regadera*	well	*bien*	wood	*la madera*
wave	*la ola*	wet	*mojado/a*	work	*funcionar, trabajar*
weak	*flojo/a*	wheelbarrow	*la carretilla*		
wear oneself out	*agotarse*	whiteboard	*el tablero*	worry	*preocuparse*
weave	*tejer*	wide	*ancho*	writing	*la escritura*
Web	*el Internet, la red*	window	*la ventana, la ventanilla* (in a vehicle)	yard	*el jardín*
Web page	*la página web*			year	*el año*
				zoo	*el zoológico*

Appendix C

Idiomatic Expressions and Refrains

Spanish is rich in idiomatic expressions and pithy sayings. This selection is organized thematically to tie into each chapter and make it easier for you to try them out. Each expression is accompanied by an explanation in English, an English equivalent when there is one, and a sentence example in Spanish to model how the expression can be used.

Chapter 1: *Paso a paso se va lejos:* Step by step one goes far.

estar a dos pasos: to be nearby (lit. to be two steps away)

Estás a dos pasos de alcanzar tu reto.: You're near to reaching your goal.

meter la pata: to put your foot in it

Metí la pata cuando me confundí de palabras.: I really put my foot in it when I mixed up my words!

a ver: let's see

A ver cuánto sabes ya.: Let's see how much you already know.

Chapter 2: *¡Así es!*: That's it!

no entender ni jota: to not understand a thing (lit. to not understand even the letter 'j')

Usted no entiende ni jota de la explicación ¿verdad?: You don't understand a bit of the explanation, do you?

estar tan claro como el agua: to be as clear as day (lit. "to be as clear as water)

Sí, entiendo. Está tan clara como el agua.: Sure I understand. It's as clear as day.

no tener pelos en la lengua: to say what's what (lit. to have no hairs on the tongue)

Pablo siempre dice la verdad. No tiene pelos en la lengua.: Pablo always tells the truth. He calls a spade a spade.

Chapter 3: *Estar a punto*: To be ready

estar como una cabra: to be as crazy as a goat

Ana está como una cabra. Está bailando y cantando como loca.: Ana is as crazy as a goat. She's dancing and singing like mad.

ser una lata: to be a mess, a problem
Mi familia es muy grande y a veces es una lata, porque todos queremos hablar.: My family is very large and sometimes it's a problem because we all want to talk.
llevarse con: to get along with
Yo me llevo bien con mi hermana mayor pero me llevo muy mal con mi hermano.: I get along very well with my older sister, but I don't get along at all with my brother.

Chapter 4: *¡Pregunte no más!*: Just ask!

andar con preguntas: to be full of questions (lit. to walk around with questions)
Emilio anda con mil preguntas.: Emilio has a lot of questions.
decir que sí / no: to say yes / no
Tú nunca dices que sí, pero tampoco dices que no.: You never say yes, but you don't say no either.
querer decir: to mean (lit. to want to say)
¿Qué quiere decir eso?: What does that mean?

Chapter 5: *Cada oveja con su pareja*: Birds of a feather flock together. (lit. Each sheep has its mate.)

dar la mano: to shake hands
Cuando dos personas se conocen por primera vez, se dan la mano.: When two people meet for the first time, they shake hands.
contar con: to count on
Yo siempre cuento con mi hermana en situaciones difíciles.: I always count on my sister in difficult situations.
tener don de gentes: to get along with everyone (lit. to have the gift of people)

Mi tío se lleva bien con todo el mundo; tiene don de gentes.: My uncle gets along with everyone; he's got the gift of people.

Chapter 6: *El que ríe último, ríe major.*: He who laughs last, laughs best.

a la hora: punctually
Tú siempre llegas a la hora; eres muy puntual.: You always arrive on time; you're very punctual.
de cuando en cuando: occasionally
De cuando en cuando vamos al cine.: Occasionally, we go to the movies.
en menos que canta un gallo: in a flash, in a jiffy (lit. in less time than it takes a rooster to crow)
Voy a estar lista en menos que canta un gallo.: I'll be ready in a flash.

Chapter 7: *día tras día*: day after day

ganarse la vida: to earn a living
¿Cómo vas a ganarte la vida?: How are you going to earn a living?
hacerse cargo de: to take charge of
Yo me hago cargo de la correspondencia para la oficina.: I take charge of the office correspondence.
hacer horas extras: to work overtime
A veces todos tenemos que hacer horas extras.: Sometimes we all have to work overtime.

Chapter 8: *Pájaro en mano vale cien volando.*: A bird in the hand is worth two in the bush. (lit. A bird in hand is worth a hundred flying.)

entrar por un oído y salir por el otro: to go in one ear and out the other

Lo que le digo a mi hijo le entra por un oído y le sale por el otro.: What I tell my son goes in one ear and out the other.

valer / costar un ojo de la cara: to be worth / to cost a fortune

Ser miembro del gimnasio cuesta un ojo de la cara, ¿verdad?: Being a member of the gym costs a fortune, doesn't it?

a corto / largo plazo: in the short / long term

Mi intención a largo plazo es mantener un buen peso.: My long-term intention is to maintain a good weight.

Chapter 9: *Dicho y hecho*: Said and done

contar cuentos: to tell tales

Mi abuelo siempre contaba cuentos de su juventud.: My grandfather always told tales about his youth.

de la noche a la mañana: suddenly, overnight

Marisa decidió buscar otro trabajo de la noche a la mañana.: Marisa suddenly decided to look for another job.

desde hace: since . . . ago

Ellos han vivido aquí desde hace un mes.: They have been living here since a month ago.

Chapter 10: *A pedir de boca*: Just by asking

pedirle peras al olmo: to ask the impossible (lit. to ask for pears from an elm tree)

No es posible hacer todo eso; estás pidiendo peras al olmo.: It's not possible to do all that; you're asking the impossible.

dejar para: to put off

Es mejor no dejar para mañana lo que puedes hacer hoy: It's best not to put off until tomorrow what you can do today.

estar en casa: to be at home

¿Puede venir el jueves? Mañana no estoy en casa.: Can you come on Thursday? Tomorrow I'm not at home.

Chapter 11: *¡Así se hace!*: That's how it's done!

poner a uno al día: to bring someone up to date

Juan estuvo enfermo una semana y ahora tenemos que ponerle al día.: Juan was sick for a week and now we have to bring him up to date.

ahogarse en un vaso de agua: to get all worked up about nothing (lit. to drown in a glass of water)

Efraín es un hombre nervioso; a veces se ahoga en un vaso de agua.: Efraín is a nervous man; sometimes he gets all worked up about nothing.

dar en el clavo: to hit the nail on the head

Julia dio al clavo cuando descubrió la solución al problema.: Julia hit the nail on the head when she figured out the solution to the problem.

Chapter 12: *Todos a bordo.*: All on board.

ida y vuelta: round-trip

Es más económico comprar boletos de ida y vuelta.: It's more economic to buy round-trip tickets.

hacer el equipaje (las maletas): to pack your luggage (bags)

Es mejor hacer el equipaje con tiempo en vez de hacerlo al último momento.: It's better to pack your bags in plenty of time than to pack them at the last minute.

de un modo u otro: one way or another

Tenemos que llegar a Salamanca esta noche de un modo u otro.: We've got to get to Salamanca tonight one way or another.

Chapter 13: *¡Qué sueñes con los angelitos!*: Sweet dreams!

ni en sueños: in your dreams
Yo no voy a quedarme en esa pensión tan fea. ¡Ni en sueños!: I'm not going to stay in that nasty *pensión*. In your dreams!

soñar con: to dream about
Soñé con mi abuelita anoche.: I dreamed about my grandmother last night.

dormir como un tronco: to sleep like a log
Estaba tan cansado que dormí como un tronco.: I was so tired that I slept like a log.

Chapter 14: *Panza llena, corazón contento*: A full belly makes for a happy heart.

no entender ni papa: to not understand a thing (lit. to not understand even a potato)
No entiendo ni papa de lo que pone en la carta.: I don't understand a thing that's on on the menu.

estar en su salsa: to be in your element (lit. to be in your sauce)
A Elena le gusta probar comidas nuevas. Está en su salsa aquí.: Elena likes to try new foods. She's in her element here.

estar para chuparse los dedos: to be finger-licking good
Esta comida está riquísima. Está para chuparse los dedos.: This meal is delicious. It's finger-licking good.

Chapter 15: *No es oro todo lo que reluce*: All that glitters is not gold.

valer / costar un Potosí: to be worth / cost a fortune (lit. to be worth / cost a silver mine from Potosí, Bolivia)

Ese collar cuesta un Potosí; es carísimo.: This necklace costs a fortune; it's terribly expensive.

darle igual a uno: to be all the same to someone
No importa si compramos la olla o el plato; me da igual.: I don't care if we buy the pot or the plate; it's all the same to me.

como anillo al dedo: to fit like a glove (lit. like a ring to the finger)
Ese vestido te queda como anillo al dedo.: That dress fits you like a glove.

Chapter 16: *Lo mejor de lo mejor*: The best of the best

llamarle la atención: to catch someone's eye, to get someone's attention
Vimos una fuente magnífica que me llamó la atención por su estilo.: We saw a magnificent fountain that caught my eye because of its style.

valer la pena: to be worth it
Pasé tres horas en el museo de arte moderno, pero no valió la pena.: I spent three hours in the modern art museum, but it wasn't worth it.

tratar de: to try to
¿Vas a tratar de ver todas las plazas del centro histórico?: Are you going to try to see all the plazas in the historic district?

Chapter 17: *¡Vaya día que tuve!*: What a day I had!

estar rendido, estar frito: to be worn out, to be fried
No paré en todo el día; estoy rendido.: I didn't stop all day; I'm worn out.

al amanecer, al anochecer: at daybreak, at nightfall
El avión salió al amanecer.: The plane left at daybreak.

de arriba abajo: from top to bottom
Visitamos la ciudad de arriba abajo.: We visited the city from top to bottom.

Chapter 18: *El sol sale para todos.*: The sun shines for all.

llover a cántaros: to rain cats and dogs (lit. to rain jugs full)
Ayer llovió a cántaros y todos nos empapamos.: Yesterday it rained cats and dogs and we all got soaked.
tomar el fresco: to get some fresh air
Después de la comida, salimos a tomar el fresco.: After lunch, we went out for a breath of fresh air.
nadar entre dos aguas: to sit on the fence (lit. to swim between two waters)
Decídete; ¡no sigas nadando entre dos aguas!: Make up your mind; quit sitting on the fence.

Chapter 19: *Una mano lava la otra.*: Do unto others… (lit. One hand washes the other.)

echar una mano: to lend a hand, to help out
Vamos a echar una mano en el centro de voluntarios.: Let's lend a hand at the volunteer center.
en buenas manos: in good hands
No se preocupe; ya está en buenas manos.: Don't worry; you're in good hands now.
volar con sus propias alas: to stand on one's own two feet (lit. to fly with one's own wings)
Dentro de poco tiempo usted va a volar con sus propias alas.: In a short time you'll be standing on your own two feet.

Chapter 20: *Poco a poco se va lejos*: Little by little one goes far.

La práctica hace la perfección.: Practice makes perfect.
No te desanimes; la práctica hace la perfección.: Don't get discouraged; practice makes perfect.
estar como pez en el agua: to be in one's element (lit. like a fish in water)
Con un poco de práctica, vas a estar como pez en el agua.: With a bit of practice, you'll be like a fish in water.
a la larga: in the long run
Es difícil medir el progreso cada día pero a la larga vas a aprender mucho.: It's hard to measure the daily progress, but in the long run, you'll learn a lot.

Appendix D

Answer Key

Chapter 2

Track 11. Written Accent or Not?

1. *mamá*
2. *miércoles*
3. *árbol*
4. *vivir*
5. *revista*
6. *periódico*
7. *simpática*
8. *México*
9. *estudian*
10. *Rodríguez*

Track 12: Where Do the Accents Go?

Un día, Esteban, un joven de Panamá, pregunta a su amiga Úrsula: ¿Qué quieres hacer este fin de semana que es fiesta? Úrsula, quien recuerda que la fiesta comienza el miércoles, responde que deben hacer una excursión al campo. Primero, los jóvenes van al supermercado y compran los artículos necesarios. Después, visitan la frutería para llevar plátanos y naranjas. Finalmente paran en la droguería y compran protector solar y protección contra los mosquitos y otros insectos. El martes por la tarde ya tienen todo preparado y saben donde van a pasar la fiesta. El miércoles en la madrugada salen. ¡Cómo se van a divertir!

Translation: One day, Esteban, a young man from Panama, asks his friend, Ursula: "What do you want to do this weekend, which is a holiday?" Ursula, who remembers that the holiday begins on Wednesday, responds that they should take a trip to the country. First, the young people go to the supermarket and buy all the necessary items. Then, they visit the fruit stand to take bananas and oranges. Finally, they stop in the drugstore and buy sun screen and protection from mosquitoes and other insects. Tuesday afternoon they already have everything ready and they know where they are going to spend the holiday. Early Wednesday morning they leave. What a good time they are going to have!

Chapter 3

¿Hay, Ser, or Estar?

1. *Yo estoy en Caracas, Venezuela.*
2. *Tú eres mexicano, ¿verdad?*
3. *No hay muchas personas en el restaurante.*
4. *¿Qué hora es?*
5. *El museo está en el centro de la ciudad.*
6. *Elena está enferma; va al doctor esta tarde.*

7. *Ellos son interesantes.*
8. *Nosotros no estamos contentos.*
9. *Hay un libro bueno en la mesa.*
10. *Yo soy alta.*

¿Ser, Estar, Hacer, or Tener?

1. *Alberto es de Ecuador.*
2. *Hace calor en Quito hoy.*
3. *Tengo calor.*
4. *Julia tiene sed.*
5. *Estamos cansados.*
6. *El café está frío.*
7. *Ustedes no están contentos.*
8. *No hace sol en Santiago.*
9. *¿Tienes sed?*
10. *Ellos son personas simpáticas.*

Describing People, Places, and Things

1. *El pueblo de mi madre es pequeño.*
2. *El niño está sentado en el banco.*
3. *Las películas internacionales son interesantes.*
4. *Las calles de nuestra vecindad son limpias en general.*
5. *Eliana es hondureña y es muy trabajadora.*
6. *La Ciudad de México es ruidosa y grande.*
7. *Mi amigo está enojado, porque no hay bancos en el parque.*
8. *La taquilla del cine está abierta ahora.*
9. *Víctor es aburrido; no es interesante.*
10. *Tu casa está tranquila, porque los niños están en el parque.*

Nouns and Adjectives

1. *Las costumbres en España son interesantes.*
2. *Quito es una ciudad internacional.*
3. *La doctora es chilena.*
4. *Las calles de nuestro pueblo son tranquilas.*
5. *Tu problema es difícil.*
6. *Los mapas son bonitos.*
7. *El origen del autor es cubano.*
8. *El novio de Marisa es trabajador.*
9. *Mi mano está rota.*
10. *La ciudad es bonita.*

Simple Present of Regular Verbs

1. *Tú hablas con tus amigos todos los días.*
2. *Yo no como carne. Soy vegetariana.*
3. *Ustedes viven en Montevideo, ¿verdad?*
4. *Susana y yo estudiamos español en la universidad.*
5. *¿Quién visita este fin de semana?*
6. *Tú aprendes muy rápido.*
7. *Melisa no depende de sus padres.*
8. *¿Subscribe usted al periódico de su pueblo?*

Track 13: The Present Continuous

Es la una y cuarto de la tarde. Luis está comiendo. (It's one fifteen in the afternoon. Luis is eating.)

Son las dos. Luis y su esposa están saliendo del apartamento. (It's two o'clock in the afternoon. Luis and his wife are leaving the apartment.)

Son las dos y veinticinco de la tarde. Luis está sacando dinero del cajero automático. (It's two twenty-five in the afternoon. Luis is making a withdrawal from the ATM.)

Son las tres y cinco de la tarde. La esposa de Luis está entrando a la farmacia. (It's five after three in the afternoon. Luis's wife is entering the pharmacy.)

Son las tres y seis de la tarde. Luis está hablando por teléfono. (It's six past three in the afternoon. Luis is talking on the phone.)

Son las tres y cuarto de la tarde. Luis está subiendo al coche de un amigo. (It's three fifteen in the afternoon. Luis is getting into a friend's car.)

Son las tres y veinte de la tarde. La esposa de Luis está caminando hacia el parque. (It's twenty past three in the afternoon. Luis's wife is walking toward the park.)

Son las tres y veintisiete de la tarde. Luis y su amigo están recogiendo a su esposa. (It's three twenty-seven in the afternoon. Luis and his friend are picking up his wife.)

Son las tres y veintiocho de la tarde. Los tres están escapando. (It's three twenty-eight in the afternoon. The three are escaping.)

Son las once y diez de la noche. Luis y su esposa están volviendo a casa. (It's eleven ten in the evening. Luis and his wife are returning home.)

Simple Present and Present Continuous
1. *Mi abuela es una persona simpática.*
2. *Nuestro pueblo está en Chile.*
3. *Los niños salen mañana.*
4. *Como mucho pero no soy gordo.*
5. *Tus amigos están jugando fútbol ahora.*
6. *José prepara la cena esta noche.*
7. *Raquel está llamando a su madre.*
8. *Yo no vivo en Miami, pero mi hermana vive allí.*

Chapter 4

Yes or No Question Formation
1. *¿Es delgada Marta?*
2. *¿Hablan ellos con su abuela?*
3. *¿Está La Paz en Bolivia?* or *¿La Paz está en Bolivia?*
4. *¿Soy yo bonita?*
5. *¿Comes tú mucho?* or *¿Tú comes mucho?*
6. *¿Trabajamos nosotros el día de fiesta?*
7. *¿Viven tus amigos en Cusco?*
8. *¿Regresa Javier el lunes?*
9. *¿Ven los niños mucha televisión?*
10. *¿Voy yo a Paraguay en marzo?*

Track 16: Answering Yes-or-No Questions
¿Hablas español bien? (Do you speak Spanish well?)
Sí, hablo bien. No, no (lo) hablo bien.

¿Vive usted en Latinoamérica? (Do you live in Latin America?)
Sí, vivo en Latinoamérica. No, no vivo en Latinoamérica.

¿Trabajas todos los días? (Do you work every day?)
Sí, trabajo todos los días. No, no trabajo todos los días.

¿Hablo muy rápido? (Do I speak very quickly?)
Sí, habla(s) muy rápido. No, no habla(s) muy rápido.

¿Es su ciudad más interesante que Madrid? (Is your city more interesting than Madrid?)
Sí, mi ciudad es más interesante que Madrid. No, mi ciudad no es más interesante que Madrid.

¿Hace buen tiempo hoy? (Is the weather nice today?)
Sí, hace buen tiempo hoy. No, no hace buen tiempo hoy.

¿Visitas muchos países? (Do you visit a lot of countries?)
Sí, visito muchos países. No, no visito muchos países.

¿Estudia tu hermano en la universidad? (Is your brother studying in the university?)
Sí, mi hermano estudia en la universidad. No, mi hermano no estudia en la universidad.

¿Están los museos en el centro? (Are the museums downtown?)
Sí, los museos están en el centro. No, los museos no están en el centro.

¿Necesitamos reservaciones para el restaurante? (Do we need reservations for the restaurant?)
Sí, ustedes necesitan reservaciones para el restaurante. No, ustedes no necesitan reservaciones para el restaurante.

Track 18: Answering "Or" Questions
My brother is very athletic. He plays tennis and baseball. He is a very strong guy, but he isn't very big. He's thin and short. My brother is also very nice and goes out a lot with his friends. They go to the movies or to a restarurant to eat and talk. I am not as active as my brother. I am calmer, but I also go out with my friends.

¿Es atlético o tranquilo tu hermano?
Mi hermano es atlético.

¿Juega tu hermano al fútbol o al baloncesto?
Mi hermano juega al tenis y al béisbol.

¿Es tu hermano grande o delgado?
Mi hermano no es muy grande; es delgado.

¿Es tu hermano simpático o antipático?
Mi hermano es muy simpático.

¿Eres activa o tranquila?
Yo soy tranquila.

Tag Questions

1. *Tu hermana toca la guitarra, ¿no es cierto?*
2. *Las tiendas abren a las diez, ¿verdad?*
3. *Eduardo y Pedro trabajan en la mañana, ¿no?*
4. *Los conciertos en la plaza son buenos, ¿no crees?*
5. *Tú puedes comer en el restaurante mexicano, ¿de acuerdo?*

Track 20: Answering Tag Questions

Ustedes no comen en la cafetería, ¿verdad? (You don't eat in the cafeteria, right?)
No, nosotros no comemos en la cafetería.

Podemos visitar el museo de arte, ¿no es cierto? (We can visit the art museum, can't we?)
Sí, podemos visitar el museo de arte.

Olivia es muy bonita, ¿no crees? (Olivia is very pretty, don't you think?)
Sí, Olivia es muy bonita.

Tú necesitas estudiar más, ¿no? (You need to study more, don't you?)
Sí, necesito estudiar más.

Esa película no es muy interesante, ¿verdad? (That film isn't very interesting, is it?)
No, esa película no es muy interesante.

Vamos al restaurante argentino mañana, ¿de acuerdo? (We're going to the Argentine restaurant tomorrow, aren't we?)
Sí, vamos al restaurante argentino mañana.

Tus hermanos hacen mucho ejercicio, ¿sí? (Your brothers do a lot of exercise, right?)
Sí, mis hermanos hacen mucho ejercicio.

Hace buen tiempo hoy, ¿no crees? (The weather is nice today, don't you think?)
Sí, hace buen tiempo hoy.

México es más grande que Venezuela, ¿no es cierto? (Mexico is bigger than Venezuela, isn't that right?)
Sí, México es un país muy grande.

Tú llevas los sándwiches para el picnic, ¿de acuerdo? (You're bringing the sandwiches for the picnic, okay?)
Sí, yo llevo los sándwiches para el picnic.

Ask Questions

1. *¿Dónde viven Juan y Martín?*
2. *¿Quién trabaja en la galería Indigo?*
3. *¿Qué necesitas para preparar flan?, ¿Cuáles son los ingredientes para flan?*
4. *¿Cómo están ustedes?, ¿Cómo estáis vosotros?*
5. *¿Por qué enseña español la señora Martínez?*
6. *¿Cuándo van tus amigos al Uruguay?*
7. *¿Cuál es más interesante, el cine o el teatro?*
8. *¿A qué hora comienza la película?, ¿Cuándo comienza la película?*
9. *¿De quién es tu regalo?*
10. *¿Cómo aprendes una lengua nueva?, ¿Qué es importante para aprender una lengua nueva?*
11. *¿Cuánto café toma tu mamá?*
12. *¿Cuántas personas hay en la clase?*

Track 21: Answering Questions

¿De dónde eres? (Where are you from?)
Soy de (los) Estados Unidos. (I'm from the United States.)

¿Cómo es tu país? (What's your country like?)
Mi país es muy variado y muy interesante. (My country is very varied and very interesting.)

¿Qué haces en tu país? (What do you do in your country?)
Trabajo en una agencia de viajes. (I work in a travel agency.)

¿Por qué estás en Paraguay? (Why are you in Paraguay?)
Estoy en Paraguay porque pocas personas visitan este país. (I'm in Paraguay because few people visit this country.)

¿Qué vas a visitar en Paraguay? (What are you going to visit in Paraguay?)
Voy a visitar los museos, los parques, los centros culturales y los pueblos históricos. (I'm going to visit the museums, the parks, the cultural centers, and the historic towns.)

¿Por qué vas a visitar esos lugares? (Why are you going to visit those places?)
Voy a visitar los museos para aprender más sobre el arte y la cultura de Paraguay . . . (I'm going to visit the museums to learn more about the art and culture of Paraguay . . .)

¿Cuánto tiempo vas a pasar aquí? (How much time are you going to spend here?)
Voy a pasar tres semanas aquí. (I'm going to spend three weeks here.)

¿Cuántas personas hay en tu familia? (How many people are there in your family?)
Hay tres personas en mi familia: yo, mi esposo y mi hija. (There are three people in my family: me, my husband, and my daughter.)

¿En qué hotel estás? (What hotel are you in?)
Estoy en un hotel pequeño cerca de la plaza. (I'm in a little hotel near the square.)

¿Cuándo sales para Asunción? (When do you leave for Asunción?)
Salgo para Asunción el jueves. (I leave for Asunción on Thursday.)

Write Embedded Questions

1. *¿Saben ustedes dónde están los libros?* (Do you know where the books are?)
2. *¿Entiendes tú por qué el restaurante está cerrado?* (Do you understand why the restaurant is closed?)
3. *¿Puede usted explicar cómo llego a la estación de tren?* (Can you explain to me how I get to the train station?)
4. *¿Puede Jaime decirme quién trabaja allí?* (Can Jaime tell me who works there?)
5. *¿Podéis vosotros descubrir qué hay en el jardín?* (Can you discover what is in the garden?)
6. *¿Saben ellos adónde va Milagros?* (Do they know where Milagros is going?)
7. *¿Sabe usted a qué hora comienza el programa?* (Do you know what time the program begins?)
8. *¿Puede Marisa explicarme cómo preparar el flan?* (Can Marisa explain to me how to make flan?)

Interrogatives and Relatives

1. *¿Quieres saber dónde / con quién / por qué / cómo trabaja Mario?* (Do you want to know where / with whom / why / how Mario works?)
2. *No importa cuánto cuesta, voy a comprar esa chaqueta.* (It doesn't matter how much it costs, I'm going to buy that jacket.)
3. *Necesito aprender cómo preparar la paella.* (I need to learn how to make paella.)
4. *Juan es el chileno que / quien vive en mi calle.* (Juan is the Chilean who / that lives on my street.)
5. *El museo de arte está en la zona cultural donde están los otros museos.* (The art museum is in the cultural district where the other museums are.)

6. *¿Pueden ustedes decirnos cuándo / a qué hora cierran las tiendas?* (Can you tell us when / at what time the stores close?)
7. *Necesitamos comprar un regalo porque es el cumpleaños de Sara.* (We need to buy a gift because it's Sara's birthday.)
8. *Sara es la chica con / de quien yo tomo clases de español.* (Sara is the girl with / from whom I take Spanish classes.)
9. *No entiendo por qué no podemos visitar Buenos Aires.* (I don't understand why we can't visit Buenos Aires.)
10. *¿Quién sabe hasta cuándo / qué hora está abierta el correos?* (Who knows until when / what time the post office is open?)

Chapter 5

Practice: Possessives

1. *Mi libro es interesante.*
2. *Tus zapatos son bonitos.*
3. *Su novio es puertorriqueño.*
4. *Sus ideas son muy buenas.*
5. *Vuestros hermanos están trabajando ahora, ¿verdad?*
6. *Sus gafas (lentes) están en la mesa.*
7. *Nuestras profesoras (maestras) son inteligentes.*
8. *Su dinero está en el banco.*
9. *Nuestra abuela es (está) vieja.*
10. *Vuestro amigo es activo.*

Track 23: Possession with *De*

1. *Las maletas de Susana son verdes.*
2. *La puerta del cuarto está rota.*
3. *El nuevo amigo de mi hermano es mexicano.*
4. *La Paz es la ciudad más alta de Bolivia.*
5. *Las clases de los estudiantes son interesantes.*
6. *Las fotos de Alberto y Mario están en la computadora de Alberto.*

Track 24: Meeting and Greeting

Quiero presentarte a mi novio, Ramón. (I want to introduce you to my boyfriend, Ramón.)
Mucho gusto, Ramón.

Déjeme presentarle a la profesora Ortega. (Let me introduce you to professor Ortega.)
Es un placer conocerla, profesora.

Doña Catalina, el señor Suárez. (Ms. Catalina, Mr. Suárez.)
Mucho gusto, señor.

Cara, te presento a Julio. (Cara, this is Julio.)
Hola, ¿cómo estás?

Profesora, quiero presentarle a mis padres, los señores Ramírez. (Professor, I'd like to introduce you to my parents, Mr. and Mrs. Ramírez.)
Es un gusto conocerlos, señores.

Track 25: Questions about Family and Friends

¿Cuántas personas hay en tu familia? (How many people are there in your family?)
Somos ocho: mis padres, tres hermanos, dos hermanas y yo. (There are eight of us: my parents, three brothers, two sisters, and I.)

¿Cómo son? (What are they like?)
Mis padres son muy abiertos y activos. Mis hermanos son muy simpáticos. (My parents are very open and active. My brothers and sisters are very nice.)

¿Viven tus abuelos? (Are your grandparents alive?)
Sí, mis abuelos paternos tienen setenta y setenta y uno y viven en California. Mi abuelo materno está muerto, pero mi abuela materna vive en nuestro pueblo. (Yes, my paternal grandparents are seventy and seventy-one and live in California. My maternal grandfather is dead, but my maternal grandmother lives in our town.)

¿Qué relación tienes con tus hermanos y hermanas?

Somos muy amigos aunque todos somos muy diferentes. (We are good friends although we are all very different.)

¿Cómo es tu mejor amigo? (What's your best friend like?)
Mi mejor amiga es una colega en el trabajo. Es muy tranquila pero muy alegre también. Salimos mucho. (My best friend is a colleague at work. She is very calm but very lively as well. We go out a lot.)

Equal and Unequal Comparisons
1. *Jaime es más alto que Abuelita.*
2. *Abuelita es más callada que Jaime.*
3. *Jaime es tan perezoso como Abuelita.*
4. *Abuelita es más reservada que Jaime.*
5. *Jaime es más pesado que Abuelita.*
6. *Abuelita es más comprensiva que Jaime.*
7. *Jaime es más abierto que Abuelita.*
8. *Abuelita es más callada que Jaime.*

Impersonal Expressions with Infinitives
1. *Es importante compartir las cosas con tus hermanos y hermanas.* (It's important to share things with your brothers and sisters.)
2. *Es una buena idea ayudar a los suegros cuando lo necesitan.* (It's a good idea to help your in-laws when they need it.)
3. *Es imprescindible escuchar las ideas de todos antes de tomar una decisión.* (It's imperative to listen to everyone's ideas before making a decision.)
4. *Es necesario conversar tranquilamente sobre los problemas para resolverlos.* (It's necessary to talk over problems calmly in order to solve them.)
5. *Es mejor pensar antes de hablar.* (It's better to think before speaking.)
6. *Es fundamental respetar a los compañeros.* (It's essential to respect your companions.)
7. *No es bueno discutir con los abuelos.* (It's not good to argue with your grandparents.)

8. *Es recomendable comprender que las personas tienen ideas diferentes.* (It's advisable to understand that people have different ideas.)

Chapter 6
Who Does What?
1. *Yo colecciono sellos.* (I collect stamps.)
2. *Tía Susana pinta paisajes.* (Aunt Susana paints landscapes.)
3. *Mis abuelos observan pájaros.* (My grandparents bird-watch.)
4. *Tu prima y yo charlamos en el café.* (Your cousin and I chat in the cafe.)
5. *La madrina de Eva teje.* (Eva's godmother knits/weaves.)
6. *Tú cocinas comidas muy ricas.* (You cook delicious meals.)
7. *Jorgito anda en bicicleta.* (Jorgito rides around on his bike.)
8. *Mi cuñada pasea con su perro.* (My sister-in-law walks her dog.)
9. *Vosotros escucháis música.* (You listen to music.)
10. *Ustedes inventan juegos.* (You invent games.)

Track 31: What Do You Like to Do?

¿Te gusta andar en bicicleta? (Do you like to ride a bike?)
Sí, me gusta andar en bicicleta. or *No, no me gusta andar en bicicleta.*

¿A tu hermano le gusta cocinar? (Does your brother like to cook?)
Sí, le gusta cocinar.

¿A quiénes les gusta tomar fotos? (Who likes to take pictures?)
A mi amiga y a mí nos gusta tomar fotos.

¿Dónde te gusta pasear? (Where do you like to stroll?)
Me gusta pasear por el centro.

¿Qué les gusta leer a ti y a tus amigos? (What do you and your friends like to read?)
Nos gusta leer novelas y el periódico.

Compare Activities

1. *Olivia saca fotos más que Pilar. Pilar saca fotos menos que Olivia. Pilar no saca fotos tanto como Olivia.*
2. *Olivia cocina más que Pilar. Pilar cocina menos que Olivia. Pilar no cocina tanto como Olivia.*
3. *Olivia monta en bicicleta más que Pilar. Olivia monta en bicicleta menos que Pilar. Olivia monta en bicicleta tanto como Pilar.*
4. *Olivia monta a caballo menos que Pilar. Pilar monta a caballo más que Olivia. Olivia no monta a caballo tanto como Pilar.*
5. *Olivia fabrica cosas más que Pilar. Pilar fabrica cosas menos que Olivia. Pilar no fabrica cosas tanto como Olivia.*

How Often?

1. *Nuestros tíos salen al cine todos los sábados.* or *Todos los sábados, nuestros tíos salen al cine.*
2. *Mi sobrina nunca teje.* or *Mi sobrina no teje nunca.*
3. *Tus nietos no visitan mucho.*
4. *Mi esposo trabaja con madera de vez en cuando.* or *De vez en cuando, mi esposo trabaja con madera.*
5. *La abuela toma su medicina cada hora.* or *Cada hora, la abuela toma su medicina.*
6. *Los niños ven televisión casi todos los días.* or *Casi todos los días, los niños ven televisión.*
7. *La novia de Alejandro llama por teléfono cada noche.* or *Cada noche, la novia de Alejandro llama por teléfono.*
8. *Mi madrina pinta todos los fines de semana.* or *Todos los fines de semana, mi madrina pinta.*

Adjective to Adverb

1. *artísticamente*
2. *calladamente*
3. *furiosamente*
4. *metódicamente*
5. *delicadamente*
6. *cómicamente*
7. *libremente*
8. *básicamente*
9. *generalmente*
10. *religiosamente*

Compare with Adverbs

1. *¿Quién trabaja menos rápidamente?* (Who works less quickly?)
   Sonia trabaja menos rápidamente que Alán.
2. *¿Cuál de los dos trabaja más cuidadosamente?* (Which of the two works more carefully?)
   Sonia trabaja más cuidadosamente que Alán.
3. *¿Quién colabora mejor con los demás?* (Who collaborates better with others?)
   Sonia colabora con los demás mejor que Alán.
4. *¿Quién comunica mejor?* (Who communicates better?)
   Alán comunica tan bien como Sonia.
5. *¿Quién llega más puntualmente?* (Who arrives more punctually?)
   Alán llega más puntualmente que Sonia.

Track 32: Adverbs Make the Difference

Yo leo tanto como mi hermano. (I read as much as my brother.)

Mis padres ven televisión menos que mis abuelos. (My parents watch less television than my grandparents.)

Yo cocino menos que mi pareja. (I cook less than my spouse.)

Mi sobrino anda en bicicleta más que mi hermano. (My nephew rides his bike more than my brother.)

Nosotros usamos la computadora tanto como nuestros hijos. (We use the computer as much as our children.)

Chapter 7

Reflexive Verb Conjugations

1. *Carmen generalmente se despierta muy temprano.* (Carmen generally wakes up early.)
2. *Me baño y me lavo el pelo cada mañana.* (I take a bath and wash my hair every morning.)
3. *Anita se maquilla cuidadosamente y después se viste.* (Anita makes herself up carefully and then gets dressed.)
4. *Mi hermano y yo nos afeitamos todos los días.* (My brother and I shave every day.)
5. *¿Te lavas los dientes después de desayunar?* (Do you brush your teeth after eating breakfast?)
6. *Adán siempre se viste elegantemente.* (Adam always dresses elegantly.)
7. *¿Se quitan ustedes los lentes de contacto antes de ducharse?* (Do you take out your contacts before taking a shower?)
8. *Los niños se ponen ropa cómoda para jugar.* (The kids put on comfortable clothing to play.)
9. *Yo me siento en el medio cuando voy al cine.* (I sit in the middle when I go to the movies.)
10. *Ellos normalmente se acuestan temprano.* (They normally go to bed early.)

Track 34: *Por or Para?*

1. *¿Por qué te levantas temprano?* (Why do you get up early?)
   Me levanto temprano para salir a caminar antes del trabajo. (I get up early to go out for a walk before work.)
2. *¿Para quién trabajas?* (Who do you work for?)

Trabajo para una compañía que fabrica muebles. (I work for a company that makes furniture.)

3. *Pasas por el parque cuando vas al centro, ¿verdad?* (You go by the park when you go downtown, don't you?
   Sí paso por el parque cuando voy al centro. (Yes, I go by the park when I go downtown.)
4. *¿Por qué te gusta ese coche?* (Why do you like that car?)
   Me gusta ese coche por el color. (I like that car because of its color.)
5. *Cuando Olga está de vacaciones, ¿quién trabaja por ella?* (When Ogla is on vacation, who works for her?)
   Cuando Olga está de vacaciones, María trabaja por ella. (When Olga's on vacation, María works for her.)
6. *¿Para quién es ese paquete?* (Who is that package for?)
   Es para el jefe. (It's for the boss.)
7. *¿Por qué vas al restaurante italiano?* (Why do you go to the Italian restaurant?)
   Voy al restaurante italiano para comer pasta. (I go to the Italian restaurant to eat pasta.)
8. *¿Adónde va tu tía?* (Where is your aunt heading?)
   Mi tía va para la casa de su amiga. (My aunt is heading to her friend's house.)

Por and *Para*

1. *No me gusta este libro; voy a cambiarlo por otro.* (I don't like this book; I'm going to exchange it for another.)
2. *¿Tienes hambre? ¿Vamos por un sándwich?* (Are you hungry? Shall we go for a sandwich?)
3. *Javier siempre se acuesta temprano para levantarse temprano.* (Javier always goes to bed early in order to wake up early.)

4. *Tu propuesta es muy interesante. Para mí es mejor que las otras.* (Your proposal is very interesting. In my opinion, it's better than the others.)

5. *Necesitamos por lo menos tres personas por equipo.* (We need at least three people per team.)

Transitive or Reflexive?

1. *José usualmente pone sus libros en la mesa.*
2. *María se pone ropa buena para ir a un restaurante.*
3. *No me gusta bañarme; me ducho.*
4. *A veces bañamos el perro.*
5. *Tú lavas tus ventanas mucho para disfrutar de la vista.*
6. *Te lavas las manos antes de comer, ¿verdad?*
7. *Generalmente, nos quitamos los zapatos cuando entramos a la casa.*
8. *Mis abuelos quitan las cosas de la silla y me siento.*

Track 35: Transitives and Reflexives

1. *Necesito cambiar cien dólares por pesos mexicanos.*
   I need to exchange one hundred dollars for Mexican pesos.

2. *La abuela canta para dormir a su nieto.*
   The grandmother sings to put her grandson to sleep.

3. *Casi siempre me pierdo el tren y por eso llego tarde al trabajo.*
   I almost always miss the train and that's why I arrive at work late.

4. *Carlos se vuelve difícil cuando está cansado.*
   Carlos becomes difficult when he is tired.

5. *Nos quedamos en hoteles buenos cuando viajamos.*
   We stay in good hotels when we travel.

Chapter 8
Parts of the Body

1. *manos, El corazón es un músculo que mueve la sangre.*
2. *costillas, Comemos con la boca y los dientes y la comida va al estómago.*
3. *cerebro, Los pulmones y las costillas están en el pecho.*
4. *dientes, Las manos y los pies tienen dedos.*
5. *rodillas, Procesamos información con los ojos, los oídos y la lengua.*

Talk about the Future with Ir

1. *Yo voy a correr tres veces por semana.* (I'm going to run three times a week.)
2. *Nos vamos a reunir regularmente con amigos para jugar al tenis.* (We're going to get together regularly with friends to play tennis.)
3. *Tú vas a descansar después del trabajo.* (You're going to rest after work.)
4. *Mi tía va a ponerse en forma; va a ir al gimnasio.* (My aunt is going to get in shape; she's going to go to the gym.)
5. *Raquel va a consultar con el doctor para saber qué le pasa.* (Raquel is going to consult with the doctor to find out what's wrong with her.)
6. *Vosotros os vais a tomar las vitaminas todos los días.* (You are going to take vitamins every day.)
7. *Los niños van a lavarse los dientes después de cada comida.* (The kids are going to brush their teeth after every meal.)
8. *Mi amiga y yo vamos a preocuparnos menos por el peso y pensar más en alimentarnos mejor.* (My friend and I are going to worry less about our weight and think more about eating better.)

Track 38: What Interests You?

¿Te interesan los deportes? (Do sports interest you?)
Me interesan mucho el béisbol y el fútbol, pero no me interesa la natación. (Baseball and football interest me a lot but swimming doesn't interest me.)

¿Prefieren ustedes practicar el ciclismo o la tabla de vela? (Do you prefer cycling or sailboarding?)
Preferimos practicar el ciclismo. (We prefer cycling.)

¿Qué te gusta hacer para estar en forma? (What do you like to do to stay in shape?)
Me gusta mucho caminar. También practico yoga. (I like to walk very much. I also practice yoga.)

¿Qué hacen tus amigos para bajar de peso? (What do your friends do to lose weight?)
Mis amigos practican deportes y se alimentan bien. (My friends practice sports and eat well.)

¿Dónde y cuándo vas a jugar al béisbol? (Where and when are you going to play baseball?)
Voy a jugar al béisbol en el parque mañana por la tarde. (I'm going to play baseball tomorrow afternoon.)

What Will the Future Bring?

1. *Si tú nos invitas, nosotros iremos a tu casa la semana que viene.* (If you invite us, we'll go to your house next week.)
2. *Juan hace mucho ejercicio; estará en muy buena forma.* (Juan exercises a lot; he must be in great shape.)
3. *Mañana yo empezaré a correr cada día con Ramón.* (Tomorrow I'll start running every day with Ramón.)
4. *Tú tienes mucha fiebre; ¿llamarás al doctor?* (You've got a high fever; will you call the doctor?)
5. *¿Qué harán Maro y Estéban si dejan de jugar al fútbol?* (What will Maro and Estéban do if they stop playing soccer?)

Chapter 9
The Imperfect

1. *Mi hermano era muy divertido cuando era niño.*
2. *Susana y yo éramos buenas amigas.*
3. *Cuando tú tenías dieciséis años trabajabas en un restaurante, ¿verdad?*
4. *Me gustaba acostarme tarde cuando era más joven.*
5. *Martín y Clara tocaban el piano juntos en las fiestas.*

Regular Preterite

1. *Alberto se levantó a las siete, se bañó y desayunó antes de ir al trabajo.*
2. *Yo vi a Alberto a las nueve y nosotros tomamos un café.*
3. *Alberto y sus colegas hablaron (por) varias horas sobre un problema. Finalmente decidieron votar por una solución.*
4. *¿Por qué llegaste tú tarde ayer? ¿Comiste con Alberto después de la reunión?*
5. *Yo salí con Eliana y ella me llevó a un restaurante salvadoreño muy bueno.*

Track 41: Irregular Preterite

¿Qué hiciste con tus amigos anoche? (What did you do with your friends last night?)
Anoche mis amigos y yo fuimos al cine. (Last night my friends and I went to the movies.)

¿Dónde estuvo Jaime el sábado? (Where was Jaime on Saturday?)
El sábado Jaime estuvo en casa de su novia. (Jaime was at his girlfriend's house on Saturday.)

Alguien llamó por teléfono, ¿quién fue? (Someone called; who was it?)
Fue María quien llamó.

¿Se divirtieron ustedes en la fiesta de Ana? (Did you have a good time at Ana's party?)

Sí, nos divertimos mucho. Fue una fiesta muy animada. (Yes, we had a great time. It was a very lively party.)

¿A qué hora se durmieron los niños? (What time did the children go to sleep?)
Los niños se durmieron a las ocho. (The children went to sleep at eight.)

Imperfect or Preterite?

Era sábado y Alfredo quería dormir tarde. Él estaba muy cansado después de una semana de trabajo. Pero, a las ocho sonó el teléfono y Alfredo se despertó. Era su amigo, Juan, quien llamaba para invitar a Alfredo a jugar al fútbol. Alfredo no quiso decir que no, así que se levantó rápidamente, se bañó y se vistió. En quince minutos, cuando Juan llegó en el coche, Alberto estaba listo. Los chicos jugaron hasta el mediodía y se divirtieron mucho.

Translation: It was (set the scene) Saturday and Alfredo wanted (had the desire) to sleep late. He was very tired (state of being) after a week of work. But, at eight o'clock the phone rang (simple past action) and Alfredo woke up (simple past action). It was (description) his friend, Juan, who was calling (ongoing action in the past) to invite Alfredo to play soccer. Alfredo did not want to say no (chose not to say—simple past action), so he got up quickly, bathed, and got dressed (sequence of actions). In fifteen minutes, when Juan arrived (simple past action) with the car, Alberto was ready (state of being). The young men played (completed action) until noon and they enjoyed themselves (completed action) very much.

Track 42: Present Perfect

¿Qué has hecho esta semana? (What have you done this week?)
Esta semana he trabajado y he salido con mis amigos. (This week I have worked and gone out with friends.)

¿Qué películas buenas has visto recientemente? (What good films have you seen recently?)
No he ido al cine pero he visto algunas películas en DVD. (I haven't gone to the movies but I've seen some movies on DVD.)

¿Te han llamado tus padres hoy? (Have your parents called you today?)
No, mis padres no me han llamado todavía. (No, my parents haven't called yet.)

¿Han leído tus amigos este libro? (Have your friends read this book?)
Sí, mis amigos han recomendado este libro. (Yes, my friends have recommended this book.)

¿Han comido ustedes en un restaurante español? (Have you eaten in a Spanish restaurant?)
No, todavía no hemos comido en un restaurante español, pero hemos comido en muchos restaurantes mexicanos. (No, we haven't yet eaten in a Spanish restaurant but we've eaten in a lot of Mexican restaurants.)

Chapter 10

Polite Requests and Responses

1. *¿Puede usted llamarme mañana, por favor?*
2. *Por supuesto, llamaré mañana con mucho gusto.*
3. *¿Quieres explicarme cómo funciona esto?*
4. *Lo siento. No sé cómo funciona. ¿Puedes preguntar a Melena?*
5. *¿Me hace el favor de mandar este paquete?*
6. *Cómo no; mandaré el paquete con mucho gusto.*
7. *Por favor, ¿me avisas cuando llegue el señor Gallardo?*
8. *No puedo, lo siento. Voy a salir temprano porque tengo cita con el médico.*

Demonstratives in the Garden

1. *¿Puede recortar estos arbustos, por favor?*
2. *¿Quiere cortar el césped y recoger esas hojas?*

3. *¿Me hace el favor de plantar estas flores?*
4. *¿Puede regar aquellas macetas, por favor?*
5. *¿Me quita este árbol muerto, por favor?*

Polite and Indirect Requests

1. *Señora Álvarez, hay que lavar y planchar esta ropa.*
2. *Mi amor, ¿quieres hacerme el favor de arreglar la lavadora?*
3. *¿Pueden ordenar el dormitorio y guardar esos juguetes, por favor?*
4. *Señora Álvarez, ¿puede limpiar los baños, por favor?*
5. *M'hija, hay que fregar el piso de la cocina.*

Chapter 11

Job Ads

Entrepreneur in the area of information technology seeks associates with extensive experience in all aspects of IT. They should be creative and flexible and need to know how to collaborate in a group. All interested persons should send their resume by e-mail to *sramírez@ecuador.net.ec.*

1. *Es una empresa nueva dedicada a la informática.*
2. *Los candidatos deben tener experiencia en todos los aspectos de la informática y necesitan ser creativos, flexibles y saber trabajar en grupo.*

International company seeks bilingual secretary. Must have perfect control of English as well as Spanish. Needs to assume responsibility for correspondence and filing for three departments. Good benefits and competitive salary. Should call in the morning: 203-43-09.

1. *Es una empresa internacional.*
2. *Debe hablar inglés y español y encargarse de la correspondencia y archivos de tres departamentos.*

Chapter 12

The Conditional

1. *¿Adónde te gustaría ir de vacaciones?* (Where would you like to go for vacation?)
   Me gustaría ir a la costa de Chile. (I'd like to go to the coast of Chile.)
2. *¿Por qué preferirías ir allí?* (Why would you prefer to go there?)
   Preferiría ir allí porque tiene parques nacionales muy interesantes. (I would prefer to go there because it has very interesting national parks.)
3. *¿Con quién viajarías?* (Who would you travel with?)
   Viajaría con mi amiga. (I would travel with my friend.)
4. *¿Qué tendrían que hacer en preparación para el viaje?* (What would you have to do in preparation for the trip?)
   Tendríamos que pedir vacaciones, consultar un mapa y hacer algunas reservaciones. (We would have to ask for vacation, consult a map, and make some reservations.)
5. *¿Qué podrían hacer allí que no pueden hacer aquí?* (What would you be able to do there that you can't do here?)
   En el sur de Chile podríamos ver pingüinos. (In the south of Chile we would be able to see penguins.)
6. *¿Cuánto tiempo pasarían allí?* (How much time would you spend there?)
   Pasaríamos tres semanas o más. (We would spend three weeks or more.)
7. *¿Sacarías muchas fotos o no llevarías una cámara?* (Would you take lots of pictures or wouldn't you take a camera?)
   ¡Por supuesto llevaría una cámara y sacaría muchas fotos! (Of course I would take a camera and I would take lots of pictures!)

8. *¿Cúanto costaría el viaje?* (How much would the trip cost?)
   Pues, no sé cuánto costaría; tendría que investigarlo. (Well, I don't know how much it would cost; I would have to look into it.)

Affirmative Commands

1. *Para tener más flexibilidad, alquila un coche.*
2. *Siéntese al lado de la ventanilla para ver el paisaje.*
3. *Si quieren una experiencia inolvidable, hagan un viaje en barco por el río Amazonas.*
4. *Por favor, cambiad de asiento.*
5. *Explique qué pasó, señora.*

Track 52: Negative Commands

Me gustaría visitar Buenos Aires en julio. (I would like to visit Buenos Aires in July.)
No visites Buenos Aires en julio. Visita en diciembre cuando hace calor. (Don't visit Buenos Aires in July. Visit in December when it's hot.)

Pensamos alquilar un coche para una semana. (We are thinking about renting a car for a week.)
No alquilen un coche. Usen el tren. (Don't rent a car. Use the train.)

¿Es mejor quedarnos cerca del aeropuerto? (Is it better to stay near the airport?)
No, no se queden cerca del aeropuerto; quédense en el centro. (No, don't stay near the airport; stay downtown.)

Voy a comprar un boleto para ti también. (I'm going to buy a ticket for you too.)
No compres un boleto para mí. Compra un boleto para Ana. (Don't buy a ticket for me. Buy a ticket for Ana.)

¿Deberíamos viajar en autobús? (Should we travel by bus?)
No, no viajen en autobús. Viajen en avión. (No, don't travel by bus. Travel by plane.)

Chapter 13

Direct Object Pronouns

1. *Debemos hacerlas hoy mismo.*
2. *¿Lo quieres llamar?*
3. *Revísala para saber adónde debemos ir.*
4. *Sí, te hablo.*
5. *Está mirándonos otra vez.*

Track 54: Requesting Changes

Buenas tardes. ¿En qué puedo servirle? (Good afternoon. How can I help you?)
Buenas tardes. Quisiera cambiar de habitación. (Good afternoon. I'd like to change rooms.)

¿En qué habitación está? (What room are you in?)
Estoy en la habitación 209. (I'm in room 209.)

¿Hay un problema con la habitación? (Is there a problem with the room?)
Sí, es muy pequeña. Preferiría una habitación más grande. (Yes, it's very small. I would prefer a larger room.)

Tenemos una habitación doble que da al jardín. (We have a double room that overlooks the garden.)
¿Hay una habitación que dé a la calle? Me gusta la vista. (Is there a room that overlooks the street? I like the view.)

A ver. . . . Sí, hay una habitación doble en el quinto piso. Da a la calle y tiene una vista del parque. (Let's see. . . . Yes, there is a double room on the fifth floor. It overlooks the street and has a view of the park.)
Perfecto. ¿Puedo verla? (Perfect. May I see it?)

Cómo no. Vamos a verla. Sígame, por favor. (Of course. Let's go see it. Follow me, please.)
Gracias. (Thank you.)

De nada. Estamos para servirle. (You're welcome. We're at your service.)

Track 56: Place Your Order

Buenas noches. ¿Qué desea? (Good evening. What would you like?)
Quisiera pedir algo de comer y beber, por favor. (I'd like to order something to eat and drink, please.)

Muy bien. ¿Quiere algún antojito para empezar? (Very good. Would you like an appetizer to start?)
Sí, el gazpacho, por favor. (Yes, the gazpacho, please.)

¿Qué más? (What else?)
El bistec, por favor. (The steak, please)

¿Desea algo de postre? (Would you like any dessert?)
¿Es bueno el flan? (Is the flan any good?)

Sí, el flan es excelente. (Yes, the flan is excellent.)
Bueno, el flan, por favor. Y café. (Okay, flan, please. And coffee.)

¿Crema y azúcar con el café? (Cream and sugar with the coffee?)
Sí, gracias. (Yes, thanks.)

Muy bien, el gazpacho, el bistec, flan y café. ¿En qué habitación está? (Very good, the gazpacho, the steak, flan, and coffee. What room are you in?)
Habitación número 409. (Room 409.)

De acuerdo. Su pedido llegará dentro de media hora. (Okay. Your order will arrive within half an hour.)
Gracias. (Thank you.)

Rent a Vacation Home

Beautiful two-bedroom apartment with kitchen, living-dining room, and utility room. Only two blocks from the beach. Balcony with sea view. Security door with intercom, parking space, all inclusive. Weekly or monthly contract. Contact us by e-mail for more details.

The house of your dreams! Spacious rustic country home with garden and orchard on the outskirts of Alicante. Kitchen, dining room, living room, three bedrooms, and two full baths. Caretaker next door. Good access. Half an hour to the beach or downtown. Rental by the month. Electric, water, and gas not included. Write to us for more information.

1. *El chalet es más grande.*
2. *El piso está más cerca de la playa.*
3. *El piso incluye los gastos.*
4. *El piso está disponible por semana o por mes.*
5. *Me interesa más el chalet porque está más lejos de la ciudad y tiene jardín. Será más tranquilo.*

Managing Minor Inconveniences

1. *Disculpe, no funciona la conexión del Internet.*
2. *Perdone, hay un pequeño problema con el inodoro.*
3. *Disculpe, creo que la bombilla está fundida.*
4. *Perdone, no encuentro el control remoto.*
5. *Disculpe; ¿puede explicarme cómo funciona la calefacción?*
6. *Perdone; creo que el ventilador está roto.*
7. *No hay mucha presión en la ducha.*
8. *Disculpe; creo que el inodoro está tapado.*

Chapter 14

Track 58: Lunch at *El Mesón del Sol*

Buenas tardes. ¿Qué desea tomar? (Good afternoon. What would you like to order?)
¿Qué recomienda usted para empezar? (What do you recommend to start out?)

Bueno, la Crema de calabaza es particularmente buena pero los espárragos y el paté también son excelentes. (Well, the cream of squash is particularly good but the asparagus and paté are also excellent.)
Bueno, tráigame la Crema de calabaza, por favor. (Well, bring me the cream of squash, please.)

Muy bien. Estoy seguro de que le gustará. ¿Qué quiere de segundo? (Very good. I'm sure you'll like it. What would you like as an entreé?)

¿Me puede decir qué es la Suprema de lubina? (Can you tell me what *Suprema de lubina* is?)

La Suprema de lubina es una especialidad regional. Es un pescado blanco con un sabor muy rico. Lo preparamos con una salsa de vino blanco. Se lo recomiendo. (The *Suprema de lubina* is a regional specialty. It's a white fish with a delicious flavor. We prepare it with a white wine sauce. I recommend it to you.)

Pues, no me gusta mucho el pescado. Creo que voy a pedir la ternera. (Well, I don't care much for fish. I think I'll order the veal.)

¿Y para tomar? El vino de la casa es muy bueno. (And to drink? The house wine is quite good.)

Bien, vino tinto y una botella de agua mineral, por favor. (Okay, red wine and a bottle of mineral water, please.)

De acuerdo. Agua mineral y vino tinto. ¿Botella, media o copa? (Right. Mineral water and red wine. A bottle, half bottle or glass?)

Media botella, por favor. (A half bottle, please.)

Muy bien. En seguida le traigo las bebidas. (Very good. I'll bring the drinks to you right away.)

Indirect Object Pronouns

1. *¿Nos da la carta, por favor?*
2. *Pregúntale al mesero cuáles son las especialidades.*
3. *¿Me puede traer más agua, por favor?* or *¿Puede traerme más agua, por favor?*
4. *¿Le dice qué lleva la paella, por favor?*
5. *El chef les puede preparar algo vegetariano.* or *El chef puede prepararles algo vegetariano.*

Chapter 15

Track 62: Direct Object Pronouns

1. *Ese collar es muy bonito. Quisiera verlo.*
2. *Hay una sortija que me gusta en la vitrina. ¿La puedo ver?*
3. *Esos relojes son muy elegantes. Me gustaría verlos.*
4. *La perla en este arete no es muy buena. Si usted la cambia, compraré los aretes.*
5. *Estas pulseras son perfectas para Susana. Voy a comprarlas para ella.*

Track 63: Not That One, This One

Buenas tardes, señora. ¿Puedo mostrarle algo?
Buenas tardes. Hay un pendiente en la vitrina que me gusta.

Muy bien. ¿Cuál le gusta?
Me gusta ése con lapis.

Éste es muy bonito y no cuesta demasiado.
Hmm. Sí éste es muy bonito pero prefiero ése más grande.

¿Éste o aquél?
Aquél, por favor.

Ah, sí. Es el mejor que tengo. Mírelo en la luz.
Sí la piedra es bonita. Me gusta mucho este pendiente. Lo compraré.

Track 66: What a Deal!

Buenas tardes. ¿Qué le gusta?
Me gusta esta cerámica.

Esta cerámica es muy fina. Tengo estos platos aquí y algunos más en esa mesa.
¿Cuánto cuesta el plato grande?

Bueno, el plato grande cuesta 120 pesos pero se lo dejo en 115.

Me gustan estos platos pequeños también. ¿Cuánto cuestan?

Si usted se lleva el plato grande y el pequeño, le puedo rebajarlos un poco más.
Yo le daré 150 por los dos.

No, lo siento, no es posible. El grande cuesta 120 y el pequeño 75. Yo le estoy ofreciendo los dos por 170. Es un descuento de casi diez por ciento.
De acuerdo. Me los llevo.

Muy bien. Usted ha hecho una buena compra.

Chapter 16

The Superlative

The best:

- *las mejores fuentes*
- *la iglesia más bonita*
- *el barrio más histórico*
- *las calles más interesantes*
- *los museos más grandes*

The worst:

- *la plaza más fea*
- *el peor restaurante*
- *los peores lugares*
- *el museo menos interesante*
- *las calles menos bonitas*

Track 67: Vamos a

¿Quieres visitar el museo de arte o la catedral?

¡Vamos a visitar la catedral primero!

¿Prefieres comer ahora o ver el monumento de Colón?

¡Vamos a comer! Tengo mucha hambre.

¿Te gustaría ir de compras o explorar el barrio histórico?

Vamos a hacer las dos cosas: ¡podemos ir de compras en las tiendas del barrio histórico!

¿Quieres ver las plazas más grandes o las más pequeñas?

Vamos a las plazas más pequeñas. Son las más interesantes.

Estoy muy cansado. Quiero dormir la siesta.

Bueno, vamos a regesar al hotel.

Lost and Found

Buenas tardes. Disculpe. Estoy un poco perdida. ¿Me puede decir dónde está el Museo de Picasso? (Good afternoon. Excuse me. I'm a little lost. Can you tell me where the Picasso Museum is?)

Sí, con mucho gusto. No está muy lejos. Siga esta calle derecho por tres manzanas. En la avenida, doble a la derecha y camine dos manzanas más. Cuando llegue a una plazita con una pastelería, cruce la avenida y tome la calle Princesa. Es la ruta más interesante. Verá una entrada al Metro en la esquina. Va a llegar a otra plaza con una iglesia. Camine al lado de la iglesia hasta la calle Montcada. Entonces, doble a la izquierda. El Museo de Picasso está casi al final de la calle. (Certainly, with pleasure. It's not very far. Follow this street straight for three blocks. At the avenue, turn right and walk two blocks more. When you get to a little plaza with a bakery, cross the avenue and take Princesa Street. It's the most interesting route. You'll see an entrance to the Metro on the corner. You're going to get to another plaza with a church. Walk along the side of the church to Montcada Street. Then turn left. The Picasso Museum is almost at the end of the street.)

Impersonal Expressions with *Se*

1. *¿Cómo se entra al museo?* or *¿Por dónde se entra al museo?*
2. *¿Se debe dejar la llave en recepción?*

3. *Se debe ver la fuente de noche.*
4. *Se puede ver la catedral desde la plaza.*
5. *Se toma el autobús número 7 para ir (llegar) al barrio histórico.*

Managing Difficulties

1. *Mirábamos el desfile y nos quitaron las carteras.*
2. *Me siento muy mal. ¿Puede decirme dónde está la clínica más cercana?*
3. *Tiene que ir a la Embajada porque se le perdió el pasaporte.*
4. *Todo está cerrado hoy por la fiesta. ¿Puede recomendarnos algo?*
5. *Se nos ha ido el último tren. ¿Conoce usted un hotel por aquí?*

Chapter 17

One Great Day

Querido diario,

Hoy Alberto y yo descubrimos las maravillas de Sevilla. Nosotros nos sorprendimos de la variedad de los sitios de interés y acabamos el día muy cansados. Pero, déjame contarte, diario, todo lo que ocurrió.

Yo me levanté a las seis de la mañana y me senté a leer un poco nuestra guía. También averigüé los horarios de la catedral y el Alcázar porque me parecieron los sitios más importantes de la ciudad. Después, yo charlé un ratito con el conserje y él me enseñó otra guía turística de la ciudad y me indicó los mejores sitios en el plano. Yo esperé hasta las ocho y entonces desperté a Alberto. A las nueve fuimos a la catedral donde admiramos sus tesoros. Entonces, nosotros subimos la torre de la Giralda desde donde hay una vista panorámica espléndida. Alberto se cansó por la subida y bajada de la torre que es muy alta. Entonces, yo me acordé de una plaza muy tranquila cerca de la catedral. Allí, Alberto me invitó a un café y después de media hora continuamos. Nos acercamos al Alcázar y buscamos la entrada. Yo la encontré sin dificultad mientras Alberto paró un

momento para comprar una guía en la librería. ¡Qué increíble es el Alcázar con su arquitectura extraordinaria y hermosos jardines! Nuestra guía nos informó de muchos detalles interesantes. Después de más de dos horas, nosotros salimos. Teníamos mucha hambre así fuimos al Barrio de Santa Cruz para buscar donde comer.

Track 69: Irregular Preterite 1

1. *¿Quién consiguió los boletos para el tablao? Arturo los consiguió.*

2. *¿Qué museo prefirieron tus amigos? Mis amigos prefirieron el museo arqueológico.*

3. *¿Qué hotel sugirió tu agente de viajes? Mi agente de viajes sugirió el Hotel Condesa.*

4. *¿Qué te pidió ese hombre? Ese hombre me pidió direcciones.*

5. *¿Se divirtieron tus padres en la Feria? Sí, mis padres se divirtieron mucho en la Feria.*

Track 70: Irregular Preterite 2

1. *¿Cuándo supiste que Gabriel fue a Sevilla? Supe que Gabriel fue a Sevilla ayer.*

2. *¿Pudieron ustedes ver algo de las procesiones de Semana Santa? Sí, pudimos ver algunas procesiones de Semana Santa.*

3. *¿No vino tu amiga también? No, mi amiga no vino.*

4. *¿A quién le diste tu guía turística? Le di la guía a Susana porque quiere ir a Sevilla también.*

5. *¿Dónde quisieron hacer reservaciones para comer Ana y Marco? Quisieron hacer reservaciones en un restaurante muy elegante pero no pudieron.*

Irregular Preterite

1. *Juan me pidió las llaves del coche y condujo a Granada.*

2. *Marta y Elena no oyeron la explicación pero leyeron su guía.*
3. *No sé dónde puse mi bolso.*
4. *El conserje sugirió un tablao y los amigos consiguieron entradas para esa noche.*
5. *Yo no traje un vestido pero tú amiga me dio una falda bonita.*

Regular and Irregular Preterite Verbs

1. *Yo busqué el museo de arqueología pero no lo encontré.*
2. *Un niño muy simpático nos guió por el Barrio de Santa Cruz.*
3. *Yo me equivoqué de autobús y nosotros tuvimos que volver al centro y esperar a otro.*
4. *Alberto decidió comprarme un pañuelo de regalo y él mismo lo escogió en una tienda muy cara.*
5. *Otro día Alberto me trajo una olla de cerámica muy bonita.*
6. *Yo quise tocar una escultura en el museo, pero el guardián no me lo permitió.*

Postcards

La Semana Santa empezó ayer y muchas personas llevaban vestidos y trajes flamencos enfrente de la catedral. Mientras esperaban la procesión, algunos cantaban y bailaban. Yo subí la Giralda y saqué fotos. Había mucha gente que miraba desde las ventanas. Fue muy bonito.

Preterite Versus Imperfect

1. *Tuvimos que esperar una hora para subir a la Giralda.*
2. *Mientras esperábamos, yo me fijé en que había mucha gente en la plaza.*
3. *Raúl me decía algo sobre lo que hizo anoche.*
4. *Raúl me dijo que fue a un tablao.*
5. *Queríamos ir al Alcázar por la tarde pero supimos que estaba cerrado.*

Chapter 18

Vacation in the Mountains

1. *Mis amigos y yo esquiamos en la Sierra Nevada en una hermosa estación de esquí.*
2. *Rafael sufrió un accidente y chocó con un árbol en la pista.*
3. *Cargaste una mochila con comida y agua cuando saliste a caminar por el cañón, ¿verdad?*
4. *Juan y Marta prefirieron el teleférico pero María subió a pie.*
5. *Hay muchos senderos para subir al prado en la cima de la montaña.*

Track 72: Basic Prepositions

1. *José caminó por el cañón hasta las tres de la tarde.*
   José walked through (along) the canyon until three in the afternoon.

2. *Esquié desde la cima de la montaña hasta la estación de esquí.*
   I skied from the top of the mountain to the ski lodge.

3. *Bajamos por el sendero entre el arroyo y el precipicio.*
   We went down by way of the path between the river and the cliff.

4. *Dejaste tus botas bajo la mesa y los palos de esquí contra la pared.*
   You left your boots under the table and the ski poles against the wall.

5. *Ramón y Jorge atravesaron el cráter del volcán sin mochilas desde el norte hasta el sur.*
   Ramon and Jorge crossed the crater of the volcano without back packs from the north to the south.

By the Water

1. *Nos relajamos en una hamaca entre dos palmeras.*
2. *María montó un mosquitero sobre su saco de dormir.*
3. *Silvia tomó el sol desde las ocho hasta las diez.*
4. *Encontraste unas conchas bajo el muelle.*
5. *Fui a pescar en el barco de vela.*

More Verb and Preposition Partnerships

Todo comenzó cuando yo aprendí a bucear. Jaime decidió que teníamos que hacer un viaje a la playa para acampar y disfrutar del mar. Yo no me atreví a decir que no aunque no me gusta dormir fuera. Entonces, yo conté con Jaime para traer todo el equipo necesario y yo me preocupé por la comida. Pues, cuando llegamos a la playa y Jaime comenzó a organizar sus cosas, yo me enteré de que Jaime no trajo una tienda de campaña, mosquetero, ollas, o fósforos. Por suerte nosotros pudimos conseguir algunas cosas esenciales de otras personas. Al final nosotros nos reímos de nuestra aventura porque gozamos de todo lo que hicimos ese fin de semana.

Everthing started when I learned to scuba-dive. Jaime decided that we had to take a trip to the beach to camp and enjoy the sea. I didn't dare tell him no although I don't like to sleep outside. Then I counted on Jaime to bring all the necessary equipment and I worried about the food. Well, when we got to the beach and Jaime began to organize his things, I found out that Jaime didn't bring a tent, mosquito net, pans, or matches. Luckily, we were able to get some essential things from other people. In the end, we laughed about our adventure because we enjoyed everything we did that weekend.

Track 75: Weather Prediction 1

Hoy, jueves, va a hacer muy buen tiempo. Hará mucho sol pero no mucho calor. Hará poco viento. Hay pocas posibilidades de lluvia hasta el fin de semana. Así que vayan ustedes a la playa hoy o mañana.

(Today, Thursday, it's going to be very good weather. It's going to be sunny but not very hot. There won't be much wind. There is little chance of rain until the weekend. So, go to the beach today or tomorrow.)

1. *Va a hacer muy buen tiempo.*
2. *Hará mucho sol.*
3. *No va a llover hasta el fin de semana.*

Track 76: Weather Prediction 2

Este fin de semana se esperan tormentas en la costa y nieve en las montañas. Va a hacer frío. En las montañas dejará de nevar el domingo y será un buen día para esquiar aunque puede estar un poco nublado.

(This weekend we're expecting storms on the coast and snow in the mountains. It's going to be cold. In the mountains it's going to stop snowing Sunday and it will be a good day for skiing though it might be a little cloudy.)

1. *No, va a llover.*
2. *Va a nevar.*
3. *El domingo será un buen día para esquiar.*

Index

THE EVERYTHING SERIES!

BUSINESS & PERSONAL FINANCE

Everything® Accounting Book
Everything® Budgeting Book
Everything® Business Planning Book
Everything® Coaching and Mentoring Book
Everything® Fundraising Book
Everything® Get Out of Debt Book
Everything® Grant Writing Book
Everything® Guide to Personal Finance for Single Mothers
Everything® Home-Based Business Book, 2nd Ed.
Everything® Homebuying Book, 2nd Ed.
Everything® Homeselling Book, 2nd Ed.
Everything® Improve Your Credit Book
Everything® Investing Book, 2nd Ed.
Everything® Landlording Book
Everything® Leadership Book
Everything® Managing People Book, 2nd Ed.
Everything® Negotiating Book
Everything® Online Auctions Book
Everything® Online Business Book
Everything® Personal Finance Book
Everything® Personal Finance in Your 20s and 30s Book
Everything® Project Management Book
Everything® Real Estate Investing Book
Everything® Retirement Planning Book
Everything® Robert's Rules Book, $7.95
Everything® Selling Book
Everything® Start Your Own Business Book, 2nd Ed.
Everything® Wills & Estate Planning Book

COOKING

Everything® Barbecue Cookbook
Everything® Bartender's Book, $9.95
Everything® Cheese Book
Everything® Chinese Cookbook
Everything® Classic Recipes Book
Everything® Cocktail Parties and Drinks Book
Everything® College Cookbook
Everything® Cooking for Baby and Toddler Book
Everything® Cooking for Two Cookbook
Everything® Diabetes Cookbook
Everything® Easy Gourmet Cookbook
Everything® Fondue Cookbook
Everything® Fondue Party Book
Everything® Gluten-Free Cookbook
Everything® Glycemic Index Cookbook
Everything® Grilling Cookbook

Everything® Healthy Meals in Minutes Cookbook
Everything® Holiday Cookbook
Everything® Indian Cookbook
Everything® Italian Cookbook
Everything® Low-Carb Cookbook
Everything® Low-Fat High-Flavor Cookbook
Everything® Low-Salt Cookbook
Everything® Meals for a Month Cookbook
Everything® Mediterranean Cookbook
Everything® Mexican Cookbook
Everything® No Trans Fat Cookbook
Everything® One-Pot Cookbook
Everything® Pizza Cookbook
Everything® Quick and Easy 30-Minute, 5-Ingredient Cookbook
Everything® Quick Meals Cookbook
Everything® Slow Cooker Cookbook
Everything® Slow Cooking for a Crowd Cookbook
Everything® Soup Cookbook
Everything® Stir-Fry Cookbook
Everything® Tex-Mex Cookbook
Everything® Thai Cookbook
Everything® Vegetarian Cookbook
Everything® Wild Game Cookbook
Everything® Wine Book, 2nd Ed.

GAMES

Everything® 15-Minute Sudoku Book, $9.95
Everything® 30-Minute Sudoku Book, $9.95
Everything® Blackjack Strategy Book
Everything® Brain Strain Book, $9.95
Everything® Bridge Book
Everything® Card Games Book
Everything® Card Tricks Book, $9.95
Everything® Casino Gambling Book, 2nd Ed.
Everything® Chess Basics Book
Everything® Craps Strategy Book
Everything® Crossword and Puzzle Book
Everything® Crossword Challenge Book
Everything® Crosswords for the Beach Book, $9.95
Everything® Cryptograms Book, $9.95
Everything® Easy Crosswords Book
Everything® Easy Kakuro Book, $9.95
Everything® Easy Large Print Crosswords Book
Everything® Games Book, 2nd Ed.
Everything® Giant Sudoku Book, $9.95
Everything® Kakuro Challenge Book, $9.95
Everything® Large-Print Crossword Challenge Book

Everything® Large-Print Crosswords Book
Everything® Lateral Thinking Puzzles Book, $9.95
Everything® Mazes Book
Everything® Movie Crosswords Book, $9.95
Everything® Online Poker Book, $12.95
Everything® Pencil Puzzles Book, $9.95
Everything® Poker Strategy Book
Everything® Pool & Billiards Book
Everything® Sports Crosswords Book, $9.95
Everything® Test Your IQ Book, $9.95
Everything® Texas Hold 'Em Book, $9.95
Everything® Travel Crosswords Book, $9.95
Everything® Word Games Challenge Book
Everything® Word Scramble Book
Everything® Word Search Book

HEALTH

Everything® Alzheimer's Book
Everything® Diabetes Book
Everything® Health Guide to Adult Bipolar Disorder
Everything® Health Guide to Controlling Anxiety
Everything® Health Guide to Fibromyalgia
Everything® Health Guide to Postpartum Care
Everything® Health Guide to Thyroid Disease
Everything® Hypnosis Book
Everything® Low Cholesterol Book
Everything® Massage Book
Everything® Menopause Book
Everything® Nutrition Book
Everything® Reflexology Book
Everything® Stress Management Book

HISTORY

Everything® American Government Book
Everything® American History Book, 2nd Ed.
Everything® Civil War Book
Everything® Freemasons Book
Everything® Irish History & Heritage Book
Everything® Middle East Book

HOBBIES

Everything® Candlemaking Book
Everything® Cartooning Book
Everything® Coin Collecting Book
Everything® Drawing Book
Everything® Family Tree Book, 2nd Ed.
Everything® Knitting Book
Everything® Knots Book
Everything® Photography Book

Everything® Quilting Book
Everything® Scrapbooking Book
Everything® Sewing Book
Everything® Soapmaking Book, 2nd Ed.
Everything® Woodworking Book

HOME IMPROVEMENT

Everything® Feng Shui Book
Everything® Feng Shui Decluttering Book, $9.95
Everything® Fix-It Book
Everything® Home Decorating Book
Everything® Home Storage Solutions Book
Everything® Homebuilding Book
Everything® Organize Your Home Book

KIDS' BOOKS

All titles are $7.95

Everything® Kids' Animal Puzzle & Activity Book
Everything® Kids' Baseball Book, 4th Ed.
Everything® Kids' Bible Trivia Book
Everything® Kids' Bugs Book
Everything® Kids' Cars and Trucks Puzzle & Activity Book
Everything® Kids' Christmas Puzzle & Activity Book
Everything® Kids' Cookbook
Everything® Kids' Crazy Puzzles Book
Everything® Kids' Dinosaurs Book
Everything® Kids' First Spanish Puzzle and Activity Book
Everything® Kids' Gross Cookbook
Everything® Kids' Gross Hidden Pictures Book
Everything® Kids' Gross Jokes Book
Everything® Kids' Gross Mazes Book
Everything® Kids' Gross Puzzle and Activity Book
Everything® Kids' Halloween Puzzle & Activity Book
Everything® Kids' Hidden Pictures Book
Everything® Kids' Horses Book
Everything® Kids' Joke Book
Everything® Kids' Knock Knock Book
Everything® Kids' Learning Spanish Book
Everything® Kids' Math Puzzles Book
Everything® Kids' Mazes Book
Everything® Kids' Money Book
Everything® Kids' Nature Book
Everything® Kids' Pirates Puzzle and Activity Book
Everything® Kids' Presidents Book
Everything® Kids' Princess Puzzle and Activity Book
Everything® Kids' Puzzle Book
Everything® Kids' Riddles & Brain Teasers Book
Everything® Kids' Science Experiments Book
Everything® Kids' Sharks Book
Everything® Kids' Soccer Book
Everything® Kids' States Book
Everything® Kids' Travel Activity Book

KIDS' STORY BOOKS

Everything® Fairy Tales Book

LANGUAGE

Everything® Conversational Japanese Book with CD, $19.95
Everything® French Grammar Book
Everything® French Phrase Book, $9.95
Everything® French Verb Book, $9.95
Everything® German Practice Book with CD, $19.95
Everything® Inglés Book
Everything® Intermediate Spanish Book with CD, $19.95
Everything® Learning Brazilian Portuguese Book with CD, $19.95
Everything® Learning French Book
Everything® Learning German Book
Everything® Learning Italian Book
Everything® Learning Latin Book
Everything® Learning Spanish Book with CD, 2nd Edition, $19.95
Everything® Russian Practice Book with CD, $19.95
Everything® Sign Language Book
Everything® Spanish Grammar Book
Everything® Spanish Phrase Book, $9.95
Everything® Spanish Practice Book with CD, $19.95
Everything® Spanish Verb Book, $9.95
Everything® Speaking Mandarin Chinese Book with CD, $19.95

MUSIC

Everything® Drums Book with CD, $19.95
Everything® Guitar Book with CD, 2nd Edition, $19.95
Everything® Guitar Chords Book with CD, $19.95
Everything® Home Recording Book
Everything® Music Theory Book with CD, $19.95
Everything® Reading Music Book with CD, $19.95
Everything® Rock & Blues Guitar Book with CD, $19.95
Everything® Rock and Blues Piano Book with CD, $19.95
Everything® Songwriting Book

NEW AGE

Everything® Astrology Book, 2nd Ed.
Everything® Birthday Personology Book
Everything® Dreams Book, 2nd Ed.
Everything® Love Signs Book, $9.95
Everything® Numerology Book
Everything® Paganism Book
Everything® Palmistry Book
Everything® Psychic Book
Everything® Reiki Book

Everything® Sex Signs Book, $9.95
Everything® Tarot Book, 2nd Ed.
Everything® Toltec Wisdom Book
Everything® Wicca and Witchcraft Book

PARENTING

Everything® Baby Names Book, 2nd Ed.
Everything® Baby Shower Book
Everything® Baby's First Year Book
Everything® Birthing Book
Everything® Breastfeeding Book
Everything® Father-to-Be Book
Everything® Father's First Year Book
Everything® Get Ready for Baby Book
Everything® Get Your Baby to Sleep Book, $9.95
Everything® Getting Pregnant Book
Everything® Guide to Raising a One-Year-Old
Everything® Guide to Raising a Two-Year-Old
Everything® Homeschooling Book
Everything® Mother's First Year Book
Everything® Parent's Guide to Childhood Illnesses
Everything® Parent's Guide to Children and Divorce
Everything® Parent's Guide to Children with ADD/ADHD
Everything® Parent's Guide to Children with Asperger's Syndrome
Everything® Parent's Guide to Children with Autism
Everything® Parent's Guide to Children with Bipolar Disorder
Everything® Parent's Guide to Children with Depression
Everything® Parent's Guide to Children with Dyslexia
Everything® Parent's Guide to Children with Juvenile Diabetes
Everything® Parent's Guide to Positive Discipline
Everything® Parent's Guide to Raising a Successful Child
Everything® Parent's Guide to Raising Boys
Everything® Parent's Guide to Raising Girls
Everything® Parent's Guide to Raising Siblings
Everything® Parent's Guide to Sensory Integration Disorder
Everything® Parent's Guide to Tantrums
Everything® Parent's Guide to the Strong-Willed Child
Everything® Parenting a Teenager Book
Everything® Potty Training Book, $9.95
Everything® Pregnancy Book, 3rd Ed.
Everything® Pregnancy Fitness Book
Everything® Pregnancy Nutrition Book
Everything® Pregnancy Organizer, 2nd Ed., $16.95
Everything® Toddler Activities Book
Everything® Toddler Book

Everything® Tween Book
Everything® Twins, Triplets, and More Book

PETS

Everything® Aquarium Book
Everything® Boxer Book
Everything® Cat Book, 2nd Ed.
Everything® Chihuahua Book
Everything® Dachshund Book
Everything® Dog Book
Everything® Dog Health Book
Everything® Dog Obedience Book
Everything® Dog Owner's Organizer, $16.95
Everything® Dog Training and Tricks Book
Everything® German Shepherd Book
Everything® Golden Retriever Book
Everything® Horse Book
Everything® Horse Care Book
Everything® Horseback Riding Book
Everything® Labrador Retriever Book
Everything® Poodle Book
Everything® Pug Book
Everything® Puppy Book
Everything® Rottweiler Book
Everything® Small Dogs Book
Everything® Tropical Fish Book
Everything® Yorkshire Terrier Book

REFERENCE

Everything® American Presidents Book
Everything® Blogging Book
Everything® Build Your Vocabulary Book
Everything® Car Care Book
Everything® Classical Mythology Book
Everything® Da Vinci Book
Everything® Divorce Book
Everything® Einstein Book
Everything® Enneagram Book
Everything® Etiquette Book, 2nd Ed.
Everything® Inventions and Patents Book
Everything® Mafia Book
Everything® Philosophy Book
Everything® Pirates Book
Everything® Psychology Book

RELIGION

Everything® Angels Book
Everything® Bible Book
Everything® Buddhism Book
Everything® Catholicism Book
Everything® Christianity Book
Everything® Gnostic Gospels Book
Everything® History of the Bible Book
Everything® Jesus Book

Everything® Jewish History & Heritage Book
Everything® Judaism Book
Everything® Kabbalah Book
Everything® Koran Book
Everything® Mary Book
Everything® Mary Magdalene Book
Everything® Prayer Book
Everything® Saints Book, 2nd Ed.
Everything® Torah Book
Everything® Understanding Islam Book
Everything® World's Religions Book
Everything® Zen Book

SCHOOL & CAREERS

Everything® Alternative Careers Book
Everything® Career Tests Book
Everything® College Major Test Book
Everything® College Survival Book, 2nd Ed.
Everything® Cover Letter Book, 2nd Ed.
Everything® Filmmaking Book
Everything® Get-a-Job Book, 2nd Ed.
Everything® Guide to Being a Paralegal
Everything® Guide to Being a Personal Trainer
Everything® Guide to Being a Real Estate Agent
Everything® Guide to Being a Sales Rep
Everything® Guide to Careers in Health Care
Everything® Guide to Careers in Law Enforcement
Everything® Guide to Government Jobs
Everything® Guide to Starting and Running a Restaurant
Everything® Job Interview Book
Everything® New Nurse Book
Everything® New Teacher Book
Everything® Paying for College Book
Everything® Practice Interview Book
Everything® Resume Book, 2nd Ed.
Everything® Study Book

SELF-HELP

Everything® Dating Book, 2nd Ed.
Everything® Great Sex Book
Everything® Self-Esteem Book
Everything® Tantric Sex Book

SPORTS & FITNESS

Everything® Easy Fitness Book
Everything® Running Book
Everything® Weight Training Book

TRAVEL

Everything® Family Guide to Cruise Vacations
Everything® Family Guide to Hawaii
Everything® Family Guide to Las Vegas, 2nd Ed.
Everything® Family Guide to Mexico
Everything® Family Guide to New York City, 2nd Ed.
Everything® Family Guide to RV Travel & Campgrounds
Everything® Family Guide to the Caribbean
Everything® Family Guide to the Walt Disney World Resort®, Universal Studios®, and Greater Orlando, 4th Ed.
Everything® Family Guide to Timeshares
Everything® Family Guide to Washington D.C., 2nd Ed.

WEDDINGS

Everything® Bachelorette Party Book, $9.95
Everything® Bridesmaid Book, $9.95
Everything® Destination Wedding Book
Everything® Elopement Book, $9.95
Everything® Father of the Bride Book, $9.95
Everything® Groom Book, $9.95
Everything® Mother of the Bride Book, $9.95
Everything® Outdoor Wedding Book
Everything® Wedding Book, 3rd Ed.
Everything® Wedding Checklist, $9.95
Everything® Wedding Etiquette Book, $9.95
Everything® Wedding Organizer, 2nd Ed., $16.95
Everything® Wedding Shower Book, $9.95
Everything® Wedding Vows Book, $9.95
Everything® Wedding Workout Book
Everything® Weddings on a Budget Book, $9.95

WRITING

Everything® Creative Writing Book
Everything® Get Published Book, 2nd Ed.
Everything® Grammar and Style Book
Everything® Guide to Magazine Writing
Everything® Guide to Writing a Book Proposal
Everything® Guide to Writing a Novel
Everything® Guide to Writing Children's Books
Everything® Guide to Writing Copy
Everything® Guide to Writing Research Papers
Everything® Screenwriting Book
Everything® Writing Poetry Book
Everything® Writing Well Book